STUDIES IN THE ANTIQUITIES OF STOBI

GENERAL EDITORS

DJORDJE MANO-ZISSI   JAMES WISEMAN

STUDIES IN THE ANTIQUITIES OF STOBI

VOLUME II

EDITED BY
JAMES WISEMAN

BEOGRAD 1975

Published by Boston University and the National Museum of Titov Veles with a publication grant from the Smithsonian Institution.

FOR THE PUBLISHER

TIHO NAJDOVSKI

EDITORIAL ASSISTANT

DUŠANKA BOŽOVIĆ

Copyright by James Wiseman, 1975.

PRINTED IN YUGOSLAVIA
,,NAUČNO DELO", BEOGRAD

TABLE OF CONTENTS

СОДРЖИНА

Foreword by Tiho Najdovski	VII
Предговор од Тихо Најдовски	VIII
Preface by James Wiseman	IX
Увод од Џејмс Вајзман	XI
Staff of the Stobi Project, 1970—1975	
Членови на екипата на проектот Стоби	XIII
List of Abbreviations — Список на скратеници	XV
E. Mott Davis and Carolyn S. Snively, *Earth-Moving Equipment at Stobi: The Application of Archaeological Standards in Machine Excavation*	1
E. Мот Дејвис и Каролина Снајвли, *Опрема за остранување на земјата во Стоби: примена на археолошките стандарди при машинско ископување* (Resumé)	12
William B. Dinsmoor, Jr., *The Baptistery: Its Roofing and Related Problems*	15
Вилијам Б. Динсмор, Јр., *Кршталник: неговиот покрив и други сродни проблеми* (Resumé)	26
Robert L. Folk and S. Valastro, Jr., *Radiocarbon Dating of Mortar at Stobi*	29
Роберт Л. Фолк и С. Валастро, Јр., *Радиокарбонско одредување на староста на малтерите во Стоби* (Resumé)	40
Elizabeth R. Gebhard, *Protective Devices in Roman Theaters*	43
Елизабет Р. Гебхард, *Заштитни мерки во римските театри* (Resumé)	64

Ruth Kolarik and Momčilo Petrovski, *Technical Observations on Mosaics at Stobi* 65
Рут Коларик и Момчило Петровски, *Технички набљудувања врз мозаиците во Стоби* (Resumé) 107

Djordje Mano-Zissi, *Observations on the Conservation and Presentation of the Monuments at Stobi* 111
Горге Мано-Зиси, *Опсервација на конзервацијата и презентацијата на објектите во Стоби* (Resumé) 120

Viktorija Sokolovska, *Investigations in the House of Peristerias* 123
Викторија Соколовска, *Истражувањата на куката Перистерија* (Resumé) 138

Al B. Wesolowsky, *The Pathology of Human Remains from Stobi* 143
Ал Б. Везаловски, *Патологија на остатите од човек во Стоби* (Resumé) 161

James Wiseman and Djordje Georgievski, *Wall Decoration at Stobi* . . . 163
Џејмс Вајзман и Ѓорѓи Георгиевски, *Сидна декорација во Стоби* (Resumé) 187

Plan of the Site — План на локалитетот

FOREWORD

The long tradition of cooperation between Yugoslavia and the United States in many scientific fields is exemplified by the completion of the six-year project (1970—1975) of archaeological excavations and research at Stobi in the central part of the Socialist Republic of Macedonia.

During the past six years the Project has achieved significant scientific results. Some of those results are included in this volume and in the first volume of *Studies in the Antiquities of Stobi* (Beograd 1973). The definitive studies of the results of the excavations will be published in a second series of volumes also under the sponsorship of the Yugoslav-American Stobi Project.

The Yugoslav and American staffmembers have had the same goals: to discover and to study the antiquities of this important ancient city. The cooperative efforts have been fruitful and many-sided; many pleasant hours have been spent in work and friendship. The staffmembers not only have discovered new knowledge about ancient Stobi, but have also come to realize that in taking this scientific step together new possibilities have been created for closer friendship, good understanding, and mutual beneficial cooperation among people in a world which from day to day becomes more integral.

To live is to create. And we at Stobi feel that we have lived a truly creative life over the past six summers. The evidence for this kind of living experience is Stobi itself, in the facilities that have been developed there and in its present appearance. The visions of Stobi that we have shared are now nearer a new understanding in which are woven the results of the great efforts of the archaeologists and all the other members of the staff of this Yugoslav-American Project (one of the largest of its kind) for the archaeological investigation of Stobi.

The cooperative experience and work of all the staff of the Project will be a lasting contribution to the life of each participant, and to Stobi as well.

It is a pleasure to acknowledge with gratitude the generous support of all members of the Yugoslav-American team and the numerous collaborating institutions from Yugoslavia and the United States, especially Boston Univerity, whose help was of great significance in accomplishing many of the goals of the Project.

It is also a pleasure to acknowledge the cooperation and kindness of the Project Co-Directors, Djordje Mano-Zissi and James Wiseman, talented men and scholars.

TIHO NAJDOVSKI
Director of the National Museum of Titov Veles
June, 1975

ПРЕДГОВОР

Мошне значајната, традиционална соработка меѓу СФРЈ и САД во повеќе научни области е надополнета со веќе реализираниот 6-годишен Проект (1970—1975) на археолошките ископувања на познатиот локалитет Стоби, сместен во централниот дел на СР Македонија.

Во изминатите 6 години се постигнати значајни научни резултати. Дел од нив се содржани во оваа и во предходната книга, а другите ќе бидат публикувани во наредните книги чиј издавач ќе биде југословенско-американскиот Проект Стоби.

Наоѓајќи се на иста задача: да се открие велот на вековните тајни на овој мошне значаен антички град, остварена е плодна и сестрана соработка — исполнета со пријатни мигови во работата и живеењето. Откриени се не само нови сознанија за античкиот Стоби, туку и нови можности што еден ваков научен потфат ги нуди за зближување, поблиско разбирање и спријателување на луѓето од современиот свет, кој од ден на ден станува сè поблизок и поинтегрален.

Да се живее — значи да се твори. Ние во Стоби во изминатите 6 години навистина творечки живеевме. Тоа живеење најдобро ќе го даде на показ сегашниот Стоби, визиите што денес ги имаме за него, поблиски за едно поново сознание во кое е вткаен резултатот на големиот труд на археолозите и на сите други стручни работници — учесници во екипата на југословенско-американскиот Проект, еден од најголемите, во археолошките истражувања на Стоби и во општо.

Заемните искуства, корисни за сите учесници во Проектот, ќе бидат трајна придобивка за секој учесник, а посебно за Стоби.

Искрена благодарност кон сите членови на југословенско-американската екипа, кон многубројните соработнички институции од Југославија и САД, а посебно кон Бостонскиот универзитет, кон сите помагачи на Проектот — со чија поддршка и помош тој успеа да ја реализира својата цел.

Особена благодарност кон ко-директорите Ѓорѓе Мано Зиси и Џејмс Вајзман, извонредни луѓе и стручњаци.

ТИХО НАЈДОВСКИ
Директор на Народниот музеј
Титов Велес
Јуни, 1975 г.

PREFACE

The concept of the series of volumes entitled *Studies in the Antiquities of Stobi* is set out in the "Preface" to the first volume.

"The series will include articles of the following types: 1) reports of special, limited excavations; 2) technical studies and reports on methodology; 3) special studies on archaeological, historical, or art historical topics."

The articles published in this second volume of the series include studies in each of those three broad categories and emphasize, perhaps even moreso than the first volume, the interdisciplinary nature of the Stobi Project. And I do mean here inter-, not multi-disciplinary; the distinction is an important one, as discussed recently by William A. McDonald in a volume dealing with some of the results of the Minnesota Messenia Expedition in the Greek Peloponnesus. An interdisciplinary archaeological project involves an integration of studies concerned with ancient people and their environment, as well as an integration of the results of those studies. It is more usual for separate studies (when they exist) to remain separate in every sense.

The approach to research at Stobi is unusual and in some ways unique, since some of the methods employed and tasks undertaken (as a result of the questions asked) seem to represent their first occurrence at a large historical site in the Old World. But there is no need to list here those methods and tasks; hopefully they are manifest in the preliminary reports and in the two volumes of *Studies* that have appeared.

The earlier history of the excavations has been detailed in the preliminary reports and in *Studies* I. An analytical bibliography also appears in *Studies* I; publications on Stobi since 1973 are noted in the preliminary reports that have appeared in the *Journal of Field Archaeology* 1 (1974) and 2 (1975).

Boston University replaced the University of Texas at Austin as the sponsoring American institution in fall, 1973; the National Museum of Titov Veles remains the Yugoslavian sponsor. The Project has continued to be funded chiefly through the U.S. Foreign Currency Program administered by the Smithsonian Institution and, since 1974, by the Yugoslav-American Joint Board for Scientific and Technological Cooperation. Other funds, equipment, supplies, and services were contributed by the institutions named above, and by the Socialist Republic of Macedonia, the City of Titov Veles, the Archaeoloical Museum of Skopje, the National Museum of Štip, the National Museum of Prilep, the Conservation Institute of Macedonia, and a number of private donors in the United States. Travel funds for Charles Ehrhorn (1973) and Frederick P. Hemans III (1974) were provided by Cornell University. It is a pleasure to acknowledge with gratitude the generous support of all these institutions and individuals.

The articles by Djordje Mano-Zissi and Viktorija Sokolovska were translated into English from Serbian by Branko Radošević with the assistance of the Editor and, in the case of the former, Ruth Kolarik. The Macedonian resumés were translated from English or Serbian by various teams; Kolarik and Momčilo Petrovski translated their own resumé with the assistance of Vojislav Sanev; Kolarik and Sanev (resumés of Davis-Snively, Dinsmoor, Folk-Valastro, Gebhard, Wesolowsky); Kolarik, Sanev, and Wiseman (Mano-Zissi); Blaga Aleksova and Wiseman (Wiseman-Georgievski). The "Foreword" was translated into English by the Editor with the help of Tiho Najdovski and the "Preface" was translated by Aleksova, Najdovski, and Wiseman. The Editor gratefully acknowledges the conscientious attention to accuracy of those who were involved in the translations, especially Ruth Kolarik and Tiho Najdovski who were helpful in many ways in preparing the manuscripts for publication. E. Mott Davis, Carolyn S. Snively, Judy Sullivan, and especially Lucy Wiseman also provided valuable assistance, as did Duca Božović, our proofreader and assistant in Beograd.

It is a pleasure to acknowledge also the counsel, cooperation, and kindnesses of the Project Co-Director, Djordje Mano-Zissi; his Deputy at Stobi, Blaga Aleksova, and our Administrative Director, Tiho Najdovski. Finally, the Staff of the Stobi Project, 1970—1975, deserves recognition here for their constant concern for the archaeological integrity of the Project, for their diligence, industry, and general good will. It has been a rewarding experience to work with such a talented group of people.

Stobi, Macedonia
June, 1975

JAMES WISEMAN
Boston University

УВОД

Концепцијата за серијата на книги под наслов Студии за старините на Стоби е започната во уводот кон првата книга.

"Во серијата ќе бидат вклучени следните видови статии: 1. Извештаи за специјални, ограничени ископувања; 2. Технички студии и извештаи за методологијата; 3. Специјални студии од археолошка, историска или уметничко-историска област."

Во статиите објавени во оваа втора книга на серијата се вклучени и проучавањата на секоја од тие три опширни категории, каде што е истакната, може би дури и многу повеќе отколку во првата книга, интердисциплинарната природа на Проектот Стоби. Имам желба да кажам дека овде на интер- а не на мултидисциплинарната природа постои битна разлика која што е дискутирана неодамна од страна на Вилијам А. Мекдоналд во една книга за неколику резултати од Минесота Месенија експедицијата на Пелопонез во Грција.

Интердисциплинарниот археолошки проект вовлекува интеграција од кои имаат интерес за античкиот човек и неговата околина и, исто така, интеграција од резултатите на овие студии. Повеќе е вообичаено посебните студии, (кога тие постојат) да останат одвоени во секоја смисла.

Приодот кон испитувањата во Стоби е необичен и на некој начин единствен, бидејќи некои од методите што се употребени и работите што се преземени (како резултат на поставените прашања) од страна на Проектот Стоби изгледа претставувает единствен настан на големиот историски локалитет на Стариот Свет. Но, овде нема потреба да ги споменуваме овие методи и работи, се надевам дека ти се јасни во уводните прикази и во двете книги на Студии што досега излегоа од печат.

Пораната историја на ископувањата беше дадена подетално во уводните прикази и во Студијата I. Аналитичката библиографија исто така се појави во Студијата I; Публикациите за Стоби после 1973 години се одбележени во прелиминарниот извештај што излезе од печат во Journal of Archaeology 1 (1974) и во 2(1975). Неодамна Универзитетот во Бостон се прифати да ја преземе работата од Универзитетот на Тексас во Остин како гарантна американска институција (есента 1973 година); Народниот музеј на Титов Велес останува и понатаму Југословенски гарант. Проектот продолжи да биде финансиран главно преку Американската програма со пари за странство раководена од Смитсониан институтот и, уште од 1974 година, од страна на Југословенско-Американскиот совет за заедничка техничка и научна соработка. Другите фондови, опрема, набавки и услуги беа обезбедувани од институците споменати горе, од Социјалистичка Република Македонија, градот Титов Велес, Археолошкиот музеј од Скопје, Народниот музеј од Штип, Народниот музеј од Прилеп, Републичкиот завод за заштита и од приватни добротвори од Америка. Пари за патни трошоци за Чарлс Ерхорн (1973 год.) и Фредерик П. Хименс (1974 год.) беа обезбедени од Универзитетот во Корнел. Ми причинува особено задоволство да им изразам искрена благодарност за сестраната подршка на сите овие институции и поединци.

Статиите од Горѓе Мано-Зиси и Викторија Соколовска се преведени на англиски од српскохрватски од Бранко Радошевиќ со помош на редакторот, а во првиот случај заедно со Рут Коларик. Македонските резимеа се преведени од англиски и српскохрватски од повеќе групи: Р. Коларик и М. Петровски го преведоа своето резиме со помош на В. Санев; Р. Коларик и В. Санев (резимеа на Дејвис-Снивели, Динсмор, Фолк-Валастро, Гебхард, Везаловски); Коларик, Санев и Вајзман (Мано-Зиси); Б. Алексова и Вајзман (Вајсман--Георгиевски). Уводот е напишан од Редакторот со помош на Тихо Најдовски а преведен од Алексова, Најдовски и Вајзман. Редакторот со благодарност признава на совесното внимание и точноста на сите што беа вовлечени во преведувањето, посебно на Рут Коларик и Тихо Најдовски кои беа на помош во повеќе случаеви во припремањето на ракописите за публикација. Е. Мот Дејвис, Џуди Суливан и Луси Вајзман беа од особена помош, а исто така и Д. Божовиќ, коректор и од помош во Белград.

Особена благодарност исто така изразувам и кон советот, соработката и љубезноста на ко-директорот на проектот Горѓе Мано-Зиси; на неговиот заменик Блага Алексова и нашиот директор за администрација Тихо Најдовски. На крајот му се заблагодарувам на персоналот на Проектот Стоби, кој работеше овде во периодот од 1970—1975 година и заслужува признание за неговата постојана грижа за археолошкиот интегритет на Проектот, за неговата работливост, трудољубивост и нивната добра желба за соработка. Ми причинува особено задоволство да работам со една таква надарена група стручњаци.

Стоби, Македонија
Јуни, 1975

ЏЕЈМС ВАЈЗМАН
Универзитет во Бостон

STAFF OF THE STOBI PROJECT
ЧЛАНОВИ ЕКИПЕ ПРОЈЕКТА СТОБИ

Blaga Aleksova, Archaeological Museum, Skopje, 1970, 1973—74
Virginia Anderson, University of Texas at Austin, 1971—74
Stevo Andov, National Museum, Titov Veles, 1970—74
Angel Arnaudovski, National Museum, Štip, 1974
Vera Bitrakova, Archaeological Museum, Skopje, 1974
Robert Black, Grand Rapids, Michigan, 1974
Harriett Blitzer, Indiana University, 1971
Duca Božović, University of Belgrade, 1972—74
Marko Camaj, University of Skopje, 1972
Elena Čipan, Archaeological Museum, Ohrid, 1973
John Cherry, University of Texas at Austin, 1971—72
Dimče Černakovski, Archaeological Museum, Skopje, 1973—74
Milorad Ćorluka, Conservation Institute of Macedonia, 1970
Dorothy Crawford, Cambridge University, 1972
Michael H. Crawford, Christ's College, Cambridge University, 1972, 1974
Božidar Damjanovski, Belgrade Academy of Arts, 1972—73
Djordje Dapčev, Conservation Institute of Macedonia, 1974
Beth O. Davis, Austin, Texas, 1972—74
E. Mott Davis, University of Texas at Austin, 1970—74
Phyllis Della Croce, University of Texas at Austin, 1970
Nina Dimčeva, Archaeological Museum, Skopje, 1970—71
Mirjana Dimovska, Conservation Institute of Macedonia, 1974
William B. Dinsmoor, Jr., Athenian Agora Excavations, Greece, 1970—71, 1973
Charles Ehrhorn, Cornell University, 1973
Tom Eals, University of Missouri, 1972—73
Ranko Findrih, Serbian Conservation Institute, 1972
Robert L. Folk, University of Texas at Austin, 1971, 1973
Elizabeth Gebhard, University of Illinois at Chicago Circle, 1970—71, 1973—74
Djordje Georgievski, Conservation Institute of Macedonia, 1970—74
Geraldine Gilligan, Tufts University, 1970—71
Todor Gruev, National Museum, Titov Veles, 1970—72
A. G. Grulich, University of Oregon, 1970
Margie Grulich, Eugene, Oregon, 1970
Frederick P. Hemans, III, Cornell University, 1974
Marilyn Huffman, Denver, Colorado, 1971
Paul Huffman, Denver, Colorado, 1971
Radmila Ivanišević, National Museum, Prilep, 1971—73
Apostol Keramidčiev, Archaeological Museum, Skopje, 1970—71
Blagoje Kitanovski, National Museum, Prilep, 1971—72
Ruth Kolarik, Harvard University, 1972—74

Kostadin Kepeski, National Museum, Prilep, 1973
Pane Kocevski, Skopje Akademija Likovne Umetnosti, 1974
Kiro Krstevski, Archaeological Museum, Skopje, 1970—74
Blaže Kuzmanovski, Academy of Arts, Zagreb, 1974
Clive Luke, University of Texas at Austin, 1972
Djordje Mano-Zissi, National Museum, Belgrade, and University of Belgrade, 1970—74
Tošo Maksimov, National Theater, Štip, 1974
Ivan Mikulčić, University of Skopje, 1970—74
Ankica Milošević, University of Belgrade, 1972—74
Dean L. Moe, Harvard University, 1974
Tihomir Najdovski, National Museum, Titov Veles, 1972—74
James Parkey, University of Texas at Austin, 1971
Sharon Parkey, Austin, Texas, 1971
Radmila Pašić, Archaeological Museum, Skopje, 1973—74
David B. Peck, Yale University, 1972
Diane G. Peck, New Haven, Connecticut, 1972
Djordje Petački, National Museum, Titov Veles, 1974
Eleonora Petrova, University of Skopje, 1972
Momčilo Petrovski, Conservation Institute of Macedonia, 1972—74
Thomas Poyner, University of Texas at Austin, 1970
Mitko Prendžov, Conservation Institute of Macedonia, 1973—74
Nada Proeva, University of Belgrade, 1971—72
Žika Radošević, University of Belgrade, 1970—74
G. Kenneth Sams, University of North Carolina at Chapel Hill, 1972
Vojislav Sanev, National Museum, Štip, 1973—74
Saržo Saržovski, Conservation Institute of Macedonia, 1971, 1973—74
Susan Schaffner, Bryn Mawr College, 1971
Ellen C. Schwartz, Institute of Fine Arts, New York University, 1972
Elizabeth Shropshire, University of Texas at Austin, 1970
Timothy Shropshire, University of Texas at Austin, 1970
Carolyn S. Snively, University of Texas at Austin, 1971—74
Viktorija Sokolovska, Archaeological Museum, Skopje, 1970—71
Veljo Tašovski, Academy of Arts, Ljubljana, 1972—74
Richard Trimble, University of Texas at Austin, 1971
Dragan Vergovski Alpi, Skopje Academy of Arts, 1972—74
Marija Vinčić, Skopje Academy of Arts, 1970
Živojin Vinčić, Conservation Institute of Macedonia, 1970
Wendy Webb, State University of New York at Buffalo, 1970
Al B. Wesolowsky, Christ's College, Cambridge University, 1970—74
Wendy White, Harvard University, 1974
Eunice Whittlesey, Wilton, Connecticut, 1973—74
Julian Whittlesey, Wilton, Connecticut, 1973—74
James A. Wiseman, Boston University, 1971—72
James R. Wiseman, Boston University, 1970—74
Lucy Wiseman, Sudbury, Massachusetts, 1970—74
Paul Worman, Hampshire College, 1972
Marija Zojeva, University of Skopje, 1971

LIST OF ABBREVIATIONS
СПИСАК СКРАЋЕНИЦА

AA	Jahrbuch des deutschen archäologischen Instituts. Archäologischer Anzeiger
AJA	American Journal of Archaeology
AJP	American Journal of Philology
AM	Mitteilungen des deutschen archäologischen Instituts. Athenische Abteilung
AnatSt	Anatolian Studies
ArchJug	Archaeologia Jugoslavica
ArchPreg	Arheološki Pregled
BCH	Bulettin de correspondance hellénique
BIABulg	Bulgarska akademia na naukite Sofia. Arkhelogicheski institut. Izvestiia Bulletin
BRGK	Berichte der römisch-germanischen Kommission
CIG	Corpus Inscriptionum Graecarum
CIL	Corpus Inscriptionum Latinarum
CISB	Atti del V Congresse Internazionale di Studi Bizantini
CSHB	Corpus Scriptorum Historiae Byzantinae
DenkschrWien (phil-hist Kl.)	K. Akademie der Wissenschaften, Wien. Philosophische-historische Klasse. Denkschriften
Der 6. Kongress	Bericht über den 6. Internationalen Kongress für Archäologie, Berlin 21—26 August, 1939
DOPapers	Dumbarton Oaks Papers
Glasnik	Glasnik Skopskog naučnog društva
Glasnik Sarajevo	Glasnik zemaljskih muzeja u Sarajevu
Godišnjak	Godišnjak Srpske Akademije Nauka
IG	Inscriptiones Graecae
IGRR	Inscriptiones Graecae ad Res Romanas Pertinentes
JFA	Journal of Field Archaeology
JÖAI	Jahreshefte des österreichischen archäologischen Instituts

Kitzinger, Survey	E. Kitzinger, "A Survey of the Early Christian Town of Stobi," *Dumbarton Oaks Papers* 3 (1946) 83—161
MGRD	Fanula Papazoglu, *Makedonski Gradovi u Rimsko Doba* (Skopje 1957)
MP	Demetrios Konstantinos Kanatsoulis, Μακεδονική Προσοπογραφία (Thessalonica 1955)
MusN	American Numismatic Society Museum Notes
NC	Numismatic Chronicle
NE	Narodna enciklopedija srpsko-hrvatsko-slovenačka
PIR	Prosopographia Imperii Romani
RA	Revue archéologique
RBN	Revue belge de numismatique
RE	Pauly-Wissowa-Kroll, Real-Encyclopädie der Klassischen Altertumswissenschaft
REG	Revue des études grecques
RM	Mitteilungen des deutschen archäologischen Instituts. Römische Abteilung
SEG	Supplementum Epigraphicum Graecum
SIG[3]	Wilhelm Dittenberger, *Sylloge Inscriptionum Graecarum* (1898)
Spomenik	Spomenik Srpske Akademije nauka
Starinar	Starinar. Organ Srpskog arheološkog društva
Studies I, II	Djordje Mano-Zissi and James Wiseman (General Editors), *Studies in the Antiquities of Stobi* I (Beograd 1973), II (Beograd 1975)
TAPA	Transactions of the American Philological Society
Wiseman, *Guide*	James Wiseman, *Stobi. A Guide to the Excavations* (Beograd 1973)
W-MZ (1971)	James Wiseman and Dj. Mano-Zissi, "Excavations at Stobi, 1970," *American Journal of Archaeology* 75 (1971) 395—411
W-MZ (1972)	James Wiseman and Dj. Mano-Zissi, "Excavations at Stobi, 1971," *American Journal of Archaeology* 76 (1972) 407—424
W-MZ (1973)	James Wiseman and Dj. Mano-Zissi, "Excavations at Stobi, 1972," *American Journal of Archaeology* 77 (1973) 391—403
W-MZ (1974)	"Excavations at Stobi, 1973—1974", *Journal of Field Archaeology* 1 (1974) 117—148
WJh	Wiener Jahreshefte
Zbornik	Zbornik Narodnog Muzeja u Beogradu
Zbornik Skopje	Godišen Zbornik na filozofskiot fakultet na univerzitetot vo Skopje
ZNW	Zeitschrift für die neutestamentliche Wissenschaft
ŽA	Živa Antika

EARTH-MOVING EQUIPMENT AT STOBI: THE APPLICATION OF ARCHAEOLOGICAL STANDARDS IN MACHINE EXCAVATION

by

E. MOTT DAVIS and CAROLYN S. SNIVELY

Earth-moving machinery has been used at Stobi by the joint Yugoslav-American project for two purposes: to remove overburden above deeply buried cultural evidences, and to carry away spoil dirt from our own and previous excavations. This article is to serve as a report of the machine excavations of 1972, 1973, and 1974 and as a discussion of the principles and techniques involved in the proper use of earth-moving machinery in archaeological excavation. The authors were responsible for supervision of the earth-moving equipment at Stobi.[1] The senior author has been using heavy machinery in archaeology since 1949.

MACHINE EXCAVATION AT STOBI

The most important machine work at Stobi was performed in 1972 and 1973 in the area of the East City Wall, and in 1973 and 1974 at the Inner City Wall (See Plan of Site). The work was done by a hydraulic excavator with a bucket capacity of about 0.67 cubic meter.

At the East City Wall, very deep exploratory trenches dug by hand in the winter of 1970—71, and work nearby at the Turkish Bridge in the summer of 1971, had revealed that Roman structures were buried more than 4 m. beneath the Crna River floodplain.[2] With those sondages as guides, and with an archaeologist in close supervision, a hydraulic excavator was employed to remove all but about 1 m. of the riverine sands and silts that covered the structures. Two dump trucks were used to carry the dirt away.

---

[1] In 1972 the supervision of the machinery was shared by John F. Cherry.
[2] W—MZ (1972) 412.

In the course of this work, several poorly preserved stone features were encountered 1—1.5 m. below the surface in 1972. Machine work was discontinued in the vicinity of these features so that they could be uncovered by hand, completely documented, and eventually removed. These tasks were not completed until early in the 1973 season. An excavator was then able to remove another 2—2.5 m. of earth, stopping a short distance above the deeply buried walls, which could thereafter be investigated by hand.

By the time the machine work at the East City Wall was completed, an area of somewhat more than 500 sq. m. had been excavated to an averge depth of 4 m. The whole job of excavation took about 42 hours of machine time.

In 1973 and 1974 a hydraulic excavator removed deposits from both sides of the Inner City Wall, which is partly buried in floodplain silts. Previous excavations by hand[3] served as guides for the work. In the two seasons an area slightly over 500 sq. m. was excavated to an average depth of approximately 2 m. Total machine time was about 27 hours. As at the East City Wall, this work underwent one major interruption to permit documentation and removal of structural features that were found.

In 1974 the machine also dug a trench connecting the excavations at the East City Wall with those at the Inner City Wall. The trench was 39 m. long and 5 m. wide, with an average depth of 1.8 m. The work took 8 hours. In the course of the work a wall and several clusters of rocks were found and documented, and were left in place for future investigation.

In addition to performing this work of overburden removal, machinery was used in 1972—1974 to remove spoil dirt, including large accumulations resulting from several decades of early archaeological investigations in the areas of the Episcopal Basilica and the Theater, as well as our own dump piles in these and other parts of the site—the House of the Fuller, Inner City Wall, and East City Wall. The hydraulic excavator proved in most places to be inefficient for this purpose and where possible was replaced by a team of bulldozer, front-end loader, and several dump trucks (Fig. 5), all supervised by an archaeologist or an assistant.

The earth removed in these operations was carried by dump truck to several locations at the edge of the site: two down the scarp of the floodplain terrace at the edge of the Crna River and one down the western scarp of the site.

In all of this work, strict rules of archaeological procedure were observed; and the principal purpose of this article is to review these rules as they apply to the use of heavy machinery. As will be seen, the machine work at Stobi exemplifies many of the advantages and problems involved in such use.

GENERAL CONSIDERATIONS AFFECTING THE USE OF MACHINERY ON ARCHAEOLOGICAL SITES

Our basic thesis in discussing the use of heavy equipment in archaeology is that the same principles must be followed in employing machinery as in the use of hand tools. These principles are based directly on the initial purpose of excavation—the discovery and recording of contexts. By contexts here we mean the

---

[3] W—MZ (1973) 393—394.

relationships of objects and features to one another and to the layers of earth that enclose them. Since excavation destroys contexts by removing the earth and the moveable objects in it, the archaeologist has a responsibility to recognize the pertinent contextual information as it is revealed and to record it completely and accurately.

All tools for archaeological excavation, no matter what the size, are destructive of contexts. Vital information can be lost as easily through the improper use of a camel's-hair brush as through the careless operation of a bulldozer. The bulldozer, of course, can do far more spectacular damage than the brush, but the difference is in degree, not in kind. Still, it is understandable that field workers are cautious about employing heavy excavation equipment, and it is true that the disadvantages of such use often outweigh the advantages. But there are also times when the reverse is true, and the archaeologist should be prepared to make judgments accordingly.

Let us review the advantages and disadvantages of earth-moving machinery in archaeology. The advantages are that large amounts of earth can be moved rapidly and efficiently, and with considerable precision if the operator is skilled and can work effectively with the archaeologist.

The disadvantages of heavy equipment have to do with its cost, its power, and its weight. Looking first at the matter of cost, the price per hour of a machine and its operator—often with supplementary dump trucks—is quite high compared to that of hand labor, and if the work is interrupted because something of archaeological significance comes to light, the cost continues while the machine and its operator wait. Machine excavation must be planned in advance in order that the maximum amount of work may be done without adversely affecting the budget of the project. If there is any likelihood that the work may be interrupted (and such a possibility is almost always present), alternative places for the machine to work should be prepared. Furthermore, the cost of interruption may tempt the archaeologist to keep the machine moving when a small feature of uncertain significance has been encountered. This is a natural impulse, but it is important not to let it affect decisions.

The disadvantages of power are obvious. A minor miscalculation on the part of the operator or the supervisor, or the sudden striking of an unexpected feature, can result in a surprising amount of damage. A slowly moving bucket or blade looks gentle enough, but without straining the machine it can smash a masonry wall, destroy a house floor, or kill an archaeologist.

The third problem is that of weight. A heavy machine moving on an archaeological site presents special problems that must be anticipated by the archaeologist. Materials below the surface are less vulnerable to crushing than one might expect, but in soft earth the pressure caused by the weight of a heavy machine can be appreciable. The most common damage, however, results from the churning of earth when the machine turns, especially if the machine has caterpillar treads rather than wheels. At Stobi, in the removal of old spoil dirt from the area of the Episcopal Basilica in 1973, a bulldozer in the hands of a skilled operator removed the dirt to a level within 10 cm. of the desired elevation, but his subsequent turning of the machine in the same area churned and dug the soft spoil dirt to a further depth of more than 60 cm. Fortunately, we had left a large margin for error and no damage was done. A few days later in the Theater area, where the earth was hard, the same machine disturbed the earth to a depth of less than 5 cm. It is evident that where the movement of a machine on a site may do damage, trial runs should be made to determine the effect of the particular machine on the particular type of earth.

RULES FOR THE USE OF MACHINERY

We suggest five rules to be followed when heavy machinery is used on an archaeological site.
1. Test before the machine work begins.
2. Always stay with the machine.
3. Train and form a team with the operator.
4. Maintain horizontal and vertical controls and keep complete records.
5. Be prepared for rapid investigation by hand tools if anything of significance is encountered during the machine work.

1. *Test before the machine work begins.* No machine should be allowed to move earth on a site unless systematic testing by traditional methods—the digging of pits or trenches by hand—has been performed in the area to be excavated. The purpose of the testing is to determine whether the proposed machine excavation is justifiable archaeologically. Testing gives a preview of the deposits and of the nature and quantity of archaeological information that may be extracted from them.

The archaeologist must keep in mind, however, that tests, although they permit planning, provide only an incomplete sample of the existing deposits, and subsequent machine work must be carried on with as much care as if no tests had been made. Any number of unexpected features may still be encountered by the machine. Some years ago the senior author, working in Nebraska, prepared for the machine excavation of a deep geologic section trench by carrying out extensive testing that indicated the area was archaeologically sterile. Nevertheless, by the time the trench was completed we had found a stratigraphic sequence of more than seven cultural zones, none of which had been encountered in the testing. An example at Stobi is the work at the East City Wall, where two very long and deep exploratory trenches were dug by hand in anticipation of machine work (Fig. 1). We used the detailed record of the trenches as a guide in machine excavation in 1972, expecting to remove approximately 3.5 m. of overburden and thereby to stop a short distance above the walls of the deeply buried building (the Casa Romana) that the test trenches had revealed. The tests had shown little evidence of cultural remains above those walls. Contrary to our expectations, we were obliged to discontinue the machine work only 1 m. below the surface because a number of small masonry walls appeared at that depth.

Since, as these examples illustrate, unexpected finds can be made even though advance testing has been carried out, it is evident that using machinery without having tested at all is, from the archaeological point of view, irresponsible.

Figure 1. An archaeologist supervises the removal of overburden by a hydraulic excavator in the East City Wall area, 1972. At the lower right is a deep test trench dug earlier by hand, the evidence from which is being used as a guide in the machine excavation.

2. *Always stay with the machine.* The results of machine excavation are the responsibility of the archaeologist, not of the machine operator, and, as we have just seen, one cannot predict what the machine may encounter. Only by staying close to the machine whenever it is in operation, walking next to the blade or standing beside the bucket, can the archaeologist be in a position to react immediately, and to direct the machine appropriately, if a significant feature comes to light.

Examples of the need for this close attention are multitudinous, and a few have just been related. Another impressive instance occurred at Stobi in 1973 during the removal of spoil dirt from old excavations—some of which dated from as long ago as World War I—in the area of the Episcopal Basilica. The rule that the archaeologist must stay with the machine is often relaxed in the moving of spoil dirt, particularly if the dirt results from well-controlled and well-documented excavations; still, one must pay attention lest the machine move out of spoil dirt into unexcavated deposits. At the Episcopal Basilica we were concerned with this latter possibility, and besides maintaining a constant check on the depth of machine excavation with a dumpy level and rod, we stayed close to the machine to watch for possible changes in the fill. We were not particularly concerned with what might be in the earth itself, since it had presumably been excavated under the supervision of earlier archaeologists. It was a surprise, therefore, when the bulldozer pushed out from the spoil dirt a fragment of a marble column, over a half meter in length, presumably from the World War I operations. Another fragment soon followed, and then others. Eventually eight fragments and two nearly complete columns appeared in this spoil dirt.

When the first fragment appeared, we suspected that, despite our caution, the machine had begun digging undisturbed deposits that lay higher than our previous hand excavations had shown. However, careful and repeated checking showed unequivocally that all the marble pieces were in spoil dirt. It was fortunate that we were close to the machine throughout this operation.

3. *Train and form a team with the operator.* Operators of heavy machinery are, as a rule, skilled technicians, able to operate their massive equipment with impressive precision. But by training and inclination they are dedicated to one end, the movement of large quantities of earth quickly and efficiently; and this end may conflict with the archaeological necessity that caution be exercised concerning possible materials and features in the earth that is being moved. The first job of the archaeologist is, then, to train the operator, preferably during preliminary work in a non-sensitive area. The task is to create an effective working relationship, making the following matters clear: (a) the objectives of the work; (b) what sorts of things are to be watched for; (c) what is to be done if anything is encountered; (d) why the operator must always watch the archaeologist for hand signals (the noise of the machine precludes communication by voice); (e) what hand signals will be used when the archaeologist wants the blade or bucket to be placed or moved precisely (Fig. 2).

Large amounts of careful work can be accomplished by an archaeologist and a machine operator when they work as a team. Each respects and utilizes the knowledge and abilities of the other to get the job done properly. The archaeologist is, of course, in charge, since it is he who ultimately stands responsible for the results of machine excavation.

4. *Maintain horizontal and vertical controls and keep complete records.* Because any interruption of machine operation is costly, the archaeologist must be prepared for rapid documentation of discoveries, in particular those that can be removed immediately so that the machine work need not stop. (This situation occurs most often during salvage operations, where the site is soon to be destroyed by engineering activity such as the construction of a highway, building, or pipeline.) Reference points should be established in advance near the excavation so that locations can be measured with tapes. A leveling instrument should be set up, always ready for elevation measurements. The leveling instrument is normally in frequent use during machine work, maintaining a check on the depth to which the machine is excavating.

The record of the work should be like that of any other archaeological activity: a running account of procedures and discoveries; a discussion of stratification; locations and descriptions of anything found; photographs; sketches; and interpretations. It is not justifiable to take only minimal records as if machine work were a non-archaeological precursor to serious investigation.

5. *Be prepared for rapid investigation by hand tools if anything of significance is encountered during the machine work.* The archaeologist should have at least one assistant at hand, with excavation tools, so that any feature encountered can be investigated and documented immediately without seriously interrupting the machine work (Fig. 4). It is even better to have a crew working nearby, ready to move in and dig to determine rapidly whether the find is worthy of detailed in-

Figure 2. Machine excavation by a hydraulic excavator in the East City Wall area, 1973. Using earlier hand excavations at the nearby Turkish Bridge as a guide, the archaeologist is directing the operator of the machine, by hand signals, as to the precise placement of the bucket.

vestigation or is not of archaeological significance. If the find appears to be significant it must be investigated as quickly as possible so that a decision may be made about the continuation of machine excavation in that location. At Stobi, during the 1972 and 1973 excavations in the East City Wall area, we were able to record and remove a number of small clusters of rocks in this way.

TYPES OF MACHINERY

The type of machine used on a site will depend, of course, on need, availability, and cost. The brief review that follows is based on experience in many parts of the United States and at Stobi.[4]

The back-hoe or "back-acter" (and less comonly its larger version, the hydraulic excavator) is probably the most widely used machine on archaeological sites today. With a bucket on a long jointed arm, it can reach outward and downward, pick up large or small quantities of earth, swing around, and dump (Figs. 1—3). The quantity of earth moved is small compared to the capacity of other machines such as the bulldozer or front-end loader, but the flexibility of the back-hoe—its ability to reach out and down and to swing around—and its precision of operation are considerably greater. While the machine is working, its base remains stationary, so that the ground beneath is not disturbed. The back-hoe and excavator can dig ditches, sondages, or large excavations. They can cut into hard earth as well as soft. Most of the work at Stobi has been done with an excavator.

Figure 3. Close supervision of machine excavation at the Inner City Wall, 1974.

The front-end loader or "front shovel" (Fig. 5) is probably second to the back-hoe in usefulness and popularity; in fact, the two are often combined in

---

[4] A detailed discussion of types of earth-moving machines and how they may be used in archaeology has been presented by D. F. Petch, "Earthmoving Machines and Their Employment in Archaeological Excavations," *Journal of the Chester Archaeological Society* 55 (1968) 15—28.

Figure 4. Working close to the Inner City Wall in 1974, two archaeologists and a laborer remained at hand: one archaeologist to supervise the machine, and the other two persons constituting a crew for rapid investigation and documentation of any discoveries that might be made.

a single machine, a tractor with a loader on front and a back-hoe on the back. The front-end loader scoops earth with a bucket on the front of the machine, lifts the bucket, moves to another place, and dumps. The whole machine must move in order to work. It is the principal type of equipment used to move spoil dirt and it can be used to remove overburden from large areas, but it cannot dig into very hard earth.

The bulldozer, a machine on caterpillar treads with a large blade on the front that can be lifted and lowered, is designed for one task, to push earth. It is very powerful, very heavy, can dig into hard earth, can excavate a ditch as wide as the blade is long, and can leave a smooth surface accurate in elevation to about 10 cm. It is used to scrape overburden from large areas and to push spoil dirt into piles for removal by a front-end loader (Fig. 5). Being on tracks rather than wheels, it may churn the earth when it turns.

These three — back-hoe, front-end loader, and bulldozer — are the most common machines used on archaeological sites, but a number of others are also employed. Light farm tractors with small buckets, scoops, or blades are often useful. Special ditch-diggers with buckets on chains, used to excavate trenches for underground pipes and cables, have been used in excavating exploratory trenches on archaeological sites. Scrapers, which are large machines that scoop up, haul away, and

Figure 5. Spoil dirt removal at the Episcopal Basilica, 1973; looking east. At the left, a bulldozer is pushing dirt into a pile. In the center the front-end loader has scooped up a load of spoil dirt from the pile made by the bulldozer, and has backed up, allowing a dump truck to move into position; the load is being dumped into the truck. In the distance another truck is dumping its load off the terrace scarp above the Crna River at the eastern edge of the site.

dump great quantities of earth while moving at 20—50 km. per hour, have been used to remove overburden from large areas. Despite their awe-inspiring size, capacity, and power, they can take slices of earth as small as 10 cm. at a time. The road grader or highway maintainer, with an adjustable blade suspended beneath the frame, has been used to scrape earth carefully from sites. Like the scraper and bulldozer it leaves a clean surface that can be inspected by the archaeologist who walks directly behind it.

Although earth-moving machinery has been employed extensively in scientific archaeology for more than two decades, it is still viewed with apprehension by many archaeologists, to whom its use is uncomfortably reminiscent of the careless mass-excavation techniques of yesteryear. We have even found, in the course of conversations attendant upon the writing of this paper, that there are archaeologists who have used heavy machinery but prefer not to discuss it for fear that knowledge of such use might damage their reputations. This attitude, now outmoded, was general in the profession until the late 1940s when salvage archaeology began on a large scale in the United States in connection with the post-World War II reservoir-building program, especially in the Missouri River Basin. In that scientific emergency field workers found themselves obliged, for the first time, to make regular, disciplined use of machinery in order to gain information quickly about sites that were soon to be destroyed.[5] Since that time

---

[5] W. R. Wedel, "The Use of Earth-moving Machinery in Archaeological Excavations," in J. B. Griffin (ed.), *Essays on Archaeological Methods*, Anthropological Papers No. 8, Museum of Anthropology, University of Michigan (Ann Arbor 1951) 17—33.

an increasing number of field projects have utilized heavy earth-moving equipment as an additional item in the archaeological tool kit. Indeed, in 1965 the Council on British Archaeology sponsored a conference on the use of mechanical aids in excavation.[6] Today it is widely recognized that earth-moving machinery, used as one form of regular archaeological equipment, is a valuable and legitimate means toward the attainment of scientific archaeological objectives.

---

[6] Petch, op. cit. (in note 4).

ОПРЕМА ЗА ОСТРАНУВАЊЕ НА ЗЕМЈАТА ВО СТОБИ: ПРИМЕНА НА АРХЕОЛОШКИТЕ СТАНДАРДИ ПРИ МАШИНСКО ИСКОПУВАЊЕ

Е. МОТ ДЕЈВИС И КАРОЛИНА С. СНАЈВЛИ

Од страна на здружениот југословенско — американски Проект во Стоби се употребуваше опрема за остранување на стерилните слоеви од земја и наноси наталожени врз културните слоеви кои се наоѓаат подлабоко, како и за остранување на исфрлената земја од нашите и поранешните ископувања.

Во текот на трите сезони 1972—1974, еден хидроуличен копач со црпалка, со капацитет од околу 0,67 кубни метри извлече околу 3350 кубни метри земја од просторот покрај источниот градски ѕид, потоа од двете страни на внатрешниот ѕид, и од ровот кој ги поврзува овие две места. Вложен е труд од околу 77 часови машинско време. Во 1972 и во 1973 год. машинската работа беше прекинувана со откривањето на значајни археолошки наоди за кои беше потребно натамошно рачно истражување.

Како додаток на ова, една група од булдужери и утоварувач остранија големи количества од натрупана земја, исфрлена особено од поранешните ископувања на Епископската Базилика и Театарот, но исто така и од нашата сопствена работа на многу места на теренот. Повремено за таа цел беше користен и хидроуличен копач кој се покажа помалку ефикасен од утоварувачот.

За време на ископувањето, еден археолог беше во постојан надзор на работите кој исто така често вршеше надзор над исфрлувањето на порано исфрлената земја. За време на изведувањето на работите беше применета истата археолошка процедура каква се употребува во ископувањата со рачни алатки.

Овие правила се темелат врз најосновите цели на ископувањата — откривање и нотирање на контексите — а факт е дека секое ископување, било тоа да се работи со рачни алатки или со тешки машини, со остранувањето на земјата ги уништува контексите и подвижните предмети во неа. Археологот, било тоа какви алатки или машини да употребува мора да ги препознае сите битни врски на информациите онака како што се откриени и да ги забележи комплетно и точно.

Проблемите поврзани со употребата на тешките машини за ископувања се разликуваат само по степен, но не по вид, од оние кои настануваат кога се употребуваат рачни алатки. Тешките машини ја имаат предноста што тие можат да остранат големи количества земја брзо и ефикасно, со голема прецизност и внимание. Незгодите од машините лежат во високото чинење на работата и потенцијалното оштетување од нивната сила и тежина.

Ние предлагаме пет правила кои треба да се проследат кога се употребуваат тешки машини на земјиште кое археолошки се испитува:

1. *Тест пред да започне машинската работа*

Сондажите мора да се копаат рачно и тоа однапред за да се одреди дали работата на машината е оправдана од археолошка гледна точка.

2. *Секогаш бидете покрај машината*

Резултатите од машинското ископување преставуваат одговорност на археологот и само наоѓајќи се во близина на машината може да се реагира во право време и да се насочи кон саканото место, ако некој важен наод не го попречи тоа.

3. *Обучете го управувачот и здружете се со него*

Лицето што управува со машината мора да ги разбира објективностите на работата, видовите на облиците на наоди што веројатно би се појавиле, да се знаат процедурите ако нешто се појави, да се внимава на сигналите на археологот (шумот на машината ја спречува гласната комуникација) и да го разбира секој сигнал.

4. *Одржување на хоризонталните и вертикалните контроли и запишување на комплетните забелешки*

Кога сте во допир со било каква машинска работа треба да имате ознаки за хоризонтални мерења и иснтрумент за висински мерења. Запишувањето на извршената работа треба да биде исто така комплетно како и секој друг вид на археолошки ископувања. Не постои оправдување ако се остави машинската работа да не се забележи адекватно, тоа тогаш би значело како воопшто да немало археолошка активност.

5. *Бидете подготвени за брзо истражување со рачни алатки ако нешто значајно се појави при машинската работа*

Рачната работа е потребна за да се одреди дали еден наод е вреден за подетално истражување или не е од археолошко значење. Ако пронајдокот се покаже како значаен треба да се продолжи и понатаму со рачната работа за да може да се донесе одлука дали машината треба да продолжи да работи на тоа место. Било каква дополнителна рачна работа од овој вид мора да се изврши брзо, бидејќи чинењето на час на опремата за работа продолжува дури и тогаш кога машината не работи.

Најпознатите типови на машини кои денеска се употребуваат за вршење на вакви врсти на работи на археолошки локалитет се багери, мали и големи, утоварувач и булдужер. Многу други видови на опрема, од доста голема до релативно мала, исто така успешно се употребува. Дали тие ќе бидат големи или мали, мора да се употребуваат според истите принципи за научно истражување што археологот ги употребува со неговиот комплет од алатки.

THE BAPTISTERY:
ITS ROOFING AND RELATED PROBLEMS

by

WILLIAM B. DINSMOOR, JR.

During the 1971 season at Stobi, a Baptistery was excavated to the S of and abutting the Episcopal Basilica at approximately its center.[1] The plan of the baptismal chamber is a circle with a diameter of 7.80—7.90 m. inscribed in a somewhat lopsided square, the sides of which vary in length from 8.80 to 9.70 m. (Fig. 1). Around the periphery of the room there are four semi-circular niches which create a semblance of a quatrefoil plan.[2] Each niche contains an arched doorway. On the S side there is a fifth, and somewhat wider, doorway. In the center of the room lies a sunken and roughly circular basin surrounded by a parapet wall, ca. 0.96 m. wide, which once rose some 0.64 m. above the floor of the room proper. This parapet contains two semi-circular niches facing out into the room and originally had, as well, four sets of steps which led down into the marble-floored pool (Fig. 2). The floor of the pool lies 0.69 m. below the mosaic floor. To enter it from any of its sets of stairs, one had to step up 0.45 m. to the first tread and then descend steep risers of 0.35 m., 0.38 m., and 0.41 m. In the center of the basin is a spirally-fluted, hollow, marble cylinder through which water was introduced for baptism by a lead pressure pipe which traces a course from the S and entered the building under the eastern side of the main doorway. The walls of the parapet are faced on both sides with alternating black and white, and, occasionally, rose-colored

---

[1] Preliminary reports on the baptistery have appeared in W—MZ (1971) 400—401, W—MZ (1972) 408, 421—424; W—MZ (1973) 392, 398—399; and W—MZ (1974) 144—146. See also Wiseman, *Guide*, pp. 62—66, Dj. Mano-Zissi, "Stratigraphic Problems and the Urban Development of Stobi," *Studies* I, pp. 220—223. Reference herein to A. Khatchatrian, *Les Baptistères Paléochrétiens* (Paris 1962) and to R. Krautheimer, *Early Christian and Byzantine Architecture* (The Pelican History of Art, Penguin Books 1965) will be given only as Khatchatrian and Krautheimer.

[2] For some examples of baptisteries of similar plan see Khatchatrian: St. John the Baptist, Gerasa, 529—531 A. C., pl. 63a; Mar Gabriel, Qartamin, ca. 500 A. C., pl. 112; Circular building Miletus, 7th century A. C., pl. 113; Church of the Virgin, Ephesus, middle 4th century A. C., pl. 117; Capama, Cos, 5th-6th centuries A. C., pl. 185.

vertical strips of marble and slate. The Baptistery floor between the basin and the outer walls of the chamber is covered with figured mosaics, in four quadrants, separated and surrounded by borders with a double-braided guilloche pattern. Each of the four quadrants of the mosaic floor depicts an overflowing kantharos about which are clustered deer and birds in two panels and peacocks and other birds in the remaining two. The floors within the doorways and within the niches of the parapet wall contain geometric patterns in mosaic.

Numerous marble fragments from two series of Ionic columns (bases, shafts, and capitals) were uncovered within the area of the Baptistery during the 1971 season (Fig. 3). Their positions were meticulously recorded. As excavations continued deeper, more building members were found and recorded. In addition to the architectural members, a marble kantharos was discovered, broken away from its base and lying within the confines of the pool.

This article is primarily concerned with a brief consideration of the roofing and roofing supports of the Baptistery in its different stages.

The Baptistery was built in the latter part of the 4th century or early 5th century A. C.[3] It was separate from the church proper, as this adjunct to a Christian basilica normally was in the early period of Christianity. Its floor lies more than 4 m. lower than that of the church and the baptismal chamber was reached through a series of rooms after one had descended a stairway at the SW corner of the basilica.

Architecturally the Baptistery was self-contained. Its outer quadrangular walls were independent of, but built against, the terrace wall of the basilica. As mentioned earlier, the plan of the room is circular and it is certain that it supported a dome, made of brick and concrete. The walls of the Baptistery are preserved to their greatest height, 3.767 m., at the N side of the room where the top, which is protected by the still higher wall of the basilica, forms a fairly uniform ledge (Fig. 4). Since at this level there does not yet exist any vertical curvature of the wall, the assumption is made herein that the curved dome began at the level of this ledge. With a semi-hemispherical dome starting at this point, the overall height from the floor to the apex of the dome would have been ca. 7.72 m. (Fig. 5). The thickness of the dome at its springline is limited by the width of the walls to 0.70 m. or less, and it would have narrowed in thickness as it ascended.

The mosaic floor, the basin, and the parapet walls (but not necessarily their encrusted faces) around it are obviously original, but it is impossible to determine now whether there existed a baldacchino at that time. It could be that some form of covering, aside from the dome over the entire room, was placed over the pool. Such a covering might possibly have been supported by one of the two series of Ionic columns found during the excavations. They would have been placed on the parapet wall since the mosaic floor was intended to be viewed in its entirety.[4] It

---

[3] W—MZ (1973) 398—399; Wiseman, *Guide*, p. 66.

[4] For some examples of baptisteries with columns placed on the parapet wall of the pool see Khatchatrian: Sbeitla, Tunisia, 5th—6th centuries, pl. 280; Announa, Algeria, 5th—6th centuries, pl. 282; Cathedral of Aquilea, Italy, baptistery rebuilt end of 5th century, pl. 308d; Cuma, Italy, 5th—6th centuries, pl. 312; the Lateran, Rome, baptistery rebuilt in 5th century, pl. 326; Baptistery of S. Maria Maggiore, Nocera, 6th century, pl. 350.

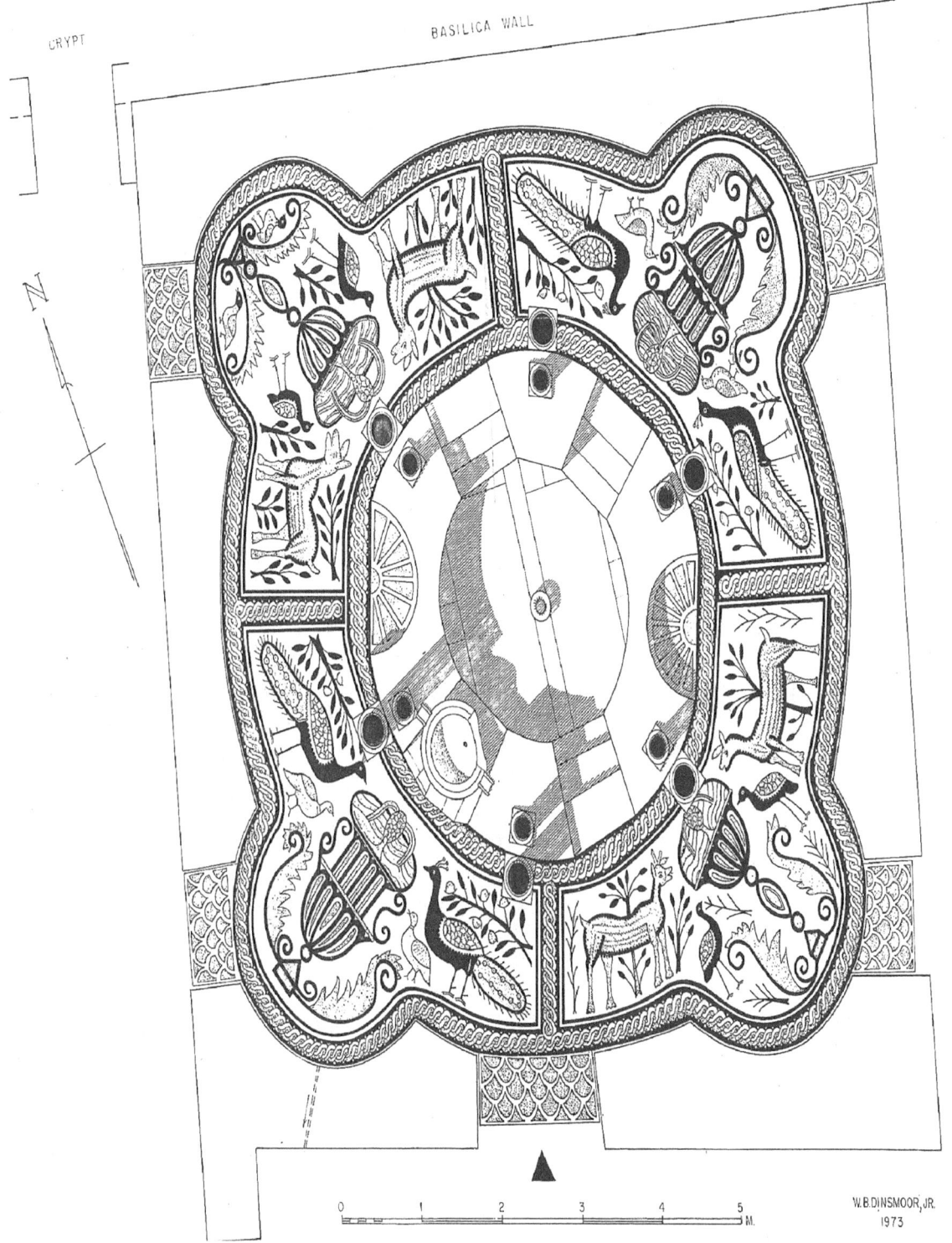

Figure 1. Restored plan of the Baptistery in its final phase.

Figure 2. The Baptistery after final clearing. View from NE.

Figure 3. The Baptistery during excavation. View from N.

Figure 4. Ledge at top of N Wall.

is more likely, however, that any original columns would have been broken during the collapse of the dome and would have been discarded.

The masonry dome may have been destroyed during the invasion of Theodoric in 479 A. C. Parts of the mosaic floor are mutilated and undoubtedly some of the mutilation was caused by the collapse of the dome. Certain areas of the mosaic were patched in expert fashion while others were merely filled in with cement. Different periods of repair are certainly indicated. One need hardly say that the debris from the collapsed dome was completely carted away before the Baptistery was rebuilt.

The floor patches and a later wall fresco with simple geometric motifs, which covered an earlier figured one, constitute some of the archaeological evidence that remodelling, probably starting in the 5th century, continued on into the 6th.[5] On the evidence of the architectural remains that were found in the excavations, the appearance of the Baptistery during its latter phase, before the final destruction of the city sometime after 570 A. C., can be reconstructed more readily than can the original scheme.

---

[5] Wiseman, *Guide*, p. 66.

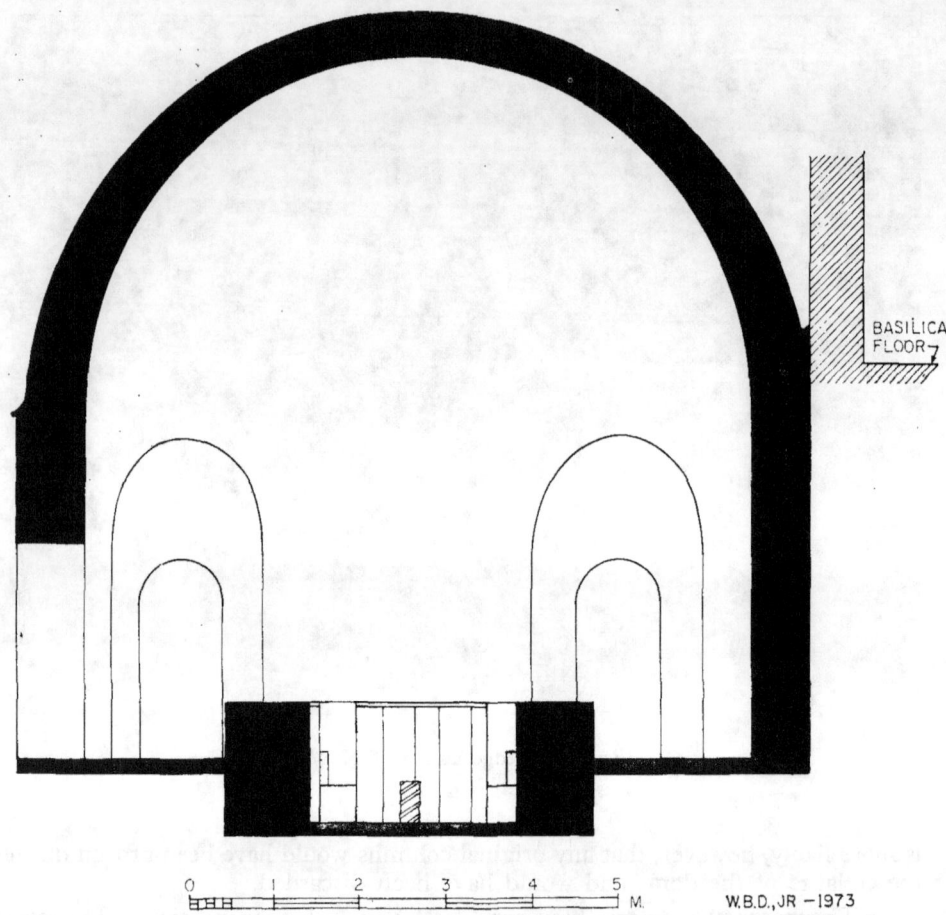

Figure 5. Section through the Baptistery in its initial phase, with dome.

Almost all of two series of Ionic columns, six columns to each series, were found within the baptismal chamber during the excavations. They lay, at somewhat different levels, on earth which had infiltrated the room and covered the mosaic floor. Since there was no disturbance at this level after the final collapse of the building, the original position of the majority of the columns can be ascertained from the places in which they fell. The exact location of the larger series is evident from square lime-mortar beddings which were employed to level the column bases on the somewhat irregularly set mosaic floor around the outer periphery of the parapet wall: two of the bases were even found *in situ*.

The bases, shafts, and capitals of this larger series are by no means consistent with each other in dimensions. The bases have attached square plinths of different widths, varying from 0.345 m. to 0.392 m., and they also vary from each other more than 0.025 m. in height. The scotia and torus mouldings of these bases also differ considerably. Although none of the monolithic shafts is preserved intact, two of them, the fragments of which have been fitted together, yield differing heights of 1.818 m. and 1.840 m. The lower diameters are ca. 0.251 m. and the upper ca. 0.222 m. A comparative uniformity is maintained in the overall design of the Ionic capitals with their integrally carved impost blocks. Here too, however, differences arise in their horizontal and vertical dimensions with the heights varying as much as 0.038 m. A variety of carved ornament is also employed. The complete height of the columns averages ca. 2.235 m.[6]

The component parts of the smaller series of Ionic columns vary more than do those of the larger ones. Individual bases measure from 0.283 m. to 0.305 m. along the sides of the attached square plinths, and they differ from each other more than 0.022 m. in height. Shaft heights, where measurable, yield dimensions of 1.216 m. and 1.248 m. There is a considerable discrepancy in the diameters, both lower and upper, the lower ones averaging ca. 0.182 m. and the upper ca. 0.155 m. Here again the capitals with integrally carved impost blocks vary in size, the heights ranging from 0.188 m. to 0.290 m. The imposts have steeper slopes on the sides than do those of the larger series and they are, comparatively, much heavier. One capital has no attached impost block and either a separate one was placed on top of it or none was used. In spite of these differences, the small columns can be so assembled that their average heights are approximately constant, ca. 1.610 m.

The problem now arises as to where this smaller order was placed in the remodelling of the Baptistery. The thought of a superimposed order might come to mind; however, there was no trace of an epistyle course found and upper columns placed directly upon lower ones without such an intervening course would be unique. When utilized contiguously with a baptismal pool, columns normally were placed on top of the parapet wall to hold a baldacchino.[7] If we examine more closely the various elements with which we are presented, it becomes apparent that the combined height of the parapet wall and of the smaller order of columns is very close to that of the larger order by itself, and that the two series of columns must have been used in pairs to support a covering structure for the pool.[8] There is no other location available for the smaller columns.

Where the smaller columns were placed on the parapet wall is slightly more problematic. They must have been on the same radial lines of the pool circle as were the larger ones, to work in tandem. To learn the answer to the exact placing of the smaller columns we must turn to the kantharos that was found within the pool.

This most unusual kantharos, beautifully carved out of a single block of marble, is more than a meter high, is 0.84 m. in diameter across the upper rim,

---

[6] The various columns probably were of slightly different heights, but this is no more disturbing than the fact that the spacings of the columns varied considerably. These inconsistencies would not have caused serious problems in erecting brick arches over the colonnade (see below).

[7] See note 4 above.

[8] Although the combination of short and tall columns in pairs is most unusual, columns of the same height were sometimes employed together in this manner. See Krautheimer: Haghia Sophia, narthex gallery, 532—537 A. C., pl. 78(B); Baptistery of S. Maria Maggiore, Nocera, 6th century, pl. 67(B); The Great Church at Tigzirt, Algeria, in the nave, pl. 65(A); S. Agnese in Rome, the Mausoleum of Constantina, 350 A. C., pl. 9.

and is 1.09 m. wide across the handles. It is almost Classical in its concept and workmanship, but probably dates from the 2nd century A. C. The opening into which the kantharos was set was one of the original four stairways leading into the pool. The steps were removed, the base and lower part of the vessel were set below the mosaic floor level at a point where the upper volutes of the marble handles would just clear the parapet coping, and a marble floor, at the level of the mosaic floor, was then installed around the vessel. This new flooring completely buried the lower part of the kantharos and transformed the visible shape of the container into that of a gigantic cup (Fig. 6). There is no clue as to the original provenience of the kantharos prior to its reuse in the Baptistery, but when it was installed as a container for holy water, presumably after the central spiral-fluted cylinder ceased to function as a fountain, a triangular section, 0.54 m. wide at the top, was chiselled out from one quadrant of the kantharos to a depth of 0.21 m. below the rim in order to make it easier for a priest, standing within the pool area, to reach into it. A hole, 0.05 m. in diameter was drilled through the bottom of the vessel and was connected to a lead pipe drain which was installed on an angle below the marble floor of the niche where the kantharos was located. This drain pipe emerged through the marble revetment 0.36 m. above the floor of the pool (Fig. 7).

At the time of final destruction of the building, the vessel was broken at its narrowest point, just above its base. The late marble floor which had been installed around it at the same time was also mostly broken away. The base, the highest point of which lies ca. 0.18 m. below the floor, is still *in situ*. It is from the break-lines on top of the base, corresponding to those on the broken bottom of the upper section, and from the location of the drain, that we can determine exactly how the kantharos sat in its position within the recess. The installers could have placed the vase snugly in the opening with a clearance between it and the revetted walls if it had been centered in the space and if the handles had been turned on an angle. This was not the case, however. The base was placed north of center and the handles were placed parallel to the parapet wall. As a result both handles had to be set partially into the walls, with the northern handle being the more greatly buried of the two. Because of this poor planning the northern handle, which is intact, came into conflict with the placing of the nearby smaller column which rested on the parapet wall just to the north of the kantharos (Fig.6). That the smaller columns and the marble vessel both stood at the same time is assured because they were lying together in the destruction debris. Since we know the exact position of the handle, and since we must assume that the parapet column was placed somewhere along an axial line back of the larger column, we can now determine where in the width of the parapet this particular smaller column (and therefore the rest of the series of smaller columns as well) was located, i.e. whether it was placed a) near the outer edge of the wall, b) at the center, or c) near the inner edge of the wall. A position at the center of the parapet can logically be ruled out because the handle of the kantharos would have bitten deeply into the column base. A position near the inner face of the wall is also to be eliminated logically because either the column base would have extended out beyond the revetted face of the opening in the parapet or, at best, it would still have partly rested over the mortar back-up for the revetment, transmitting the weight of the column and of the superimposed load onto the weakest part of the wall. This elimination leaves

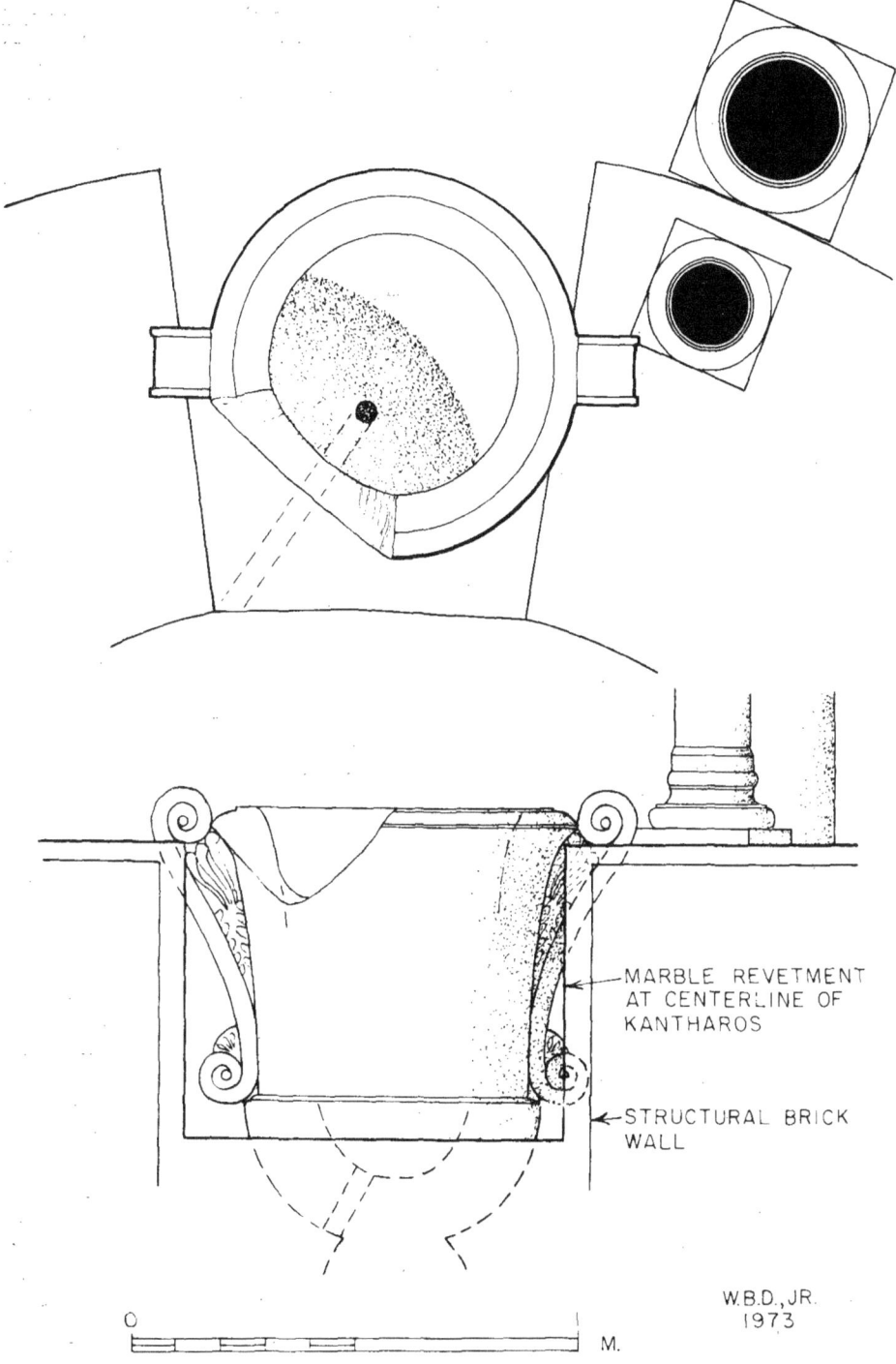

Figure 6. Plan and elevation of the kantharos in its final setting place.

Figure 7. Broken base of the kantharos and traces of the drain.

only a position near the outer face of the wall, near the second series of columns, and gives us a closely associated tandem arrangement of columns for which we have parallels.[9]

If we turn for a moment to the capitals of the columns, it may be noted that the impost segments are rectangular. The narrower sides of these, which bear carved decorations in the form either of plain crosses or crosses designed in conjunction with floral or wild-life designs, fall over the voluted faces of the Ionic capitals. The plain, longer sides fall over the balusters of the capitals. Invariably in Greek, Roman, and early Christian architecture the volute faces of Ionic capitals, and the decorated faces of impost blocks, are turned to face the observer. There can hardly be an exception in our structure. The decorated, narrower faces of the capitals must have faced outwards. If we abut the narrow faces of the impost blocks of the larger and smaller series of columns, we arrive at a center-to-center dimension for the pairs of columns of ca. 0.425 m. If we add to this half of the width of the base of the smaller columns, we find that even then, for the smaller column just

---

[9] See note 8 above. The pairs of columns supporting the arches and dome both of the Baptistery of S. Maria Maggiore and of the Mausoleum of Constantina have two Corinthian capitals back to back. At Tigzirt the pairs of columns have two Ionic capitals back to back.

north of the kantharos, the plinth of the base must have been nicked into slightly by the marble handle of that vessel (Fig. 6). The column could not have been moved further inwards on the wall or the situation would have been worsened. Therefore the impost blocks of the capitals must have been contiguous.[10] Because of the sloping faces of the imposts, the decoration on the abutting ends would have been visible, but it is not a happy situation and it certainly precludes the columns having been designed for their location. They were re-used as was the kantharos (Fig. 8).

The columns were obviously erected as supports for some sort of superstructure. One would have expected a baldacchino, built in the form of a masonry dome, but the lack of fallen masonry in the destruction debris would preclude this idea.[11] Also, if we attempt to roof the repaired Baptistery in the manner suggested below, there would not be enough height for clearance of a dome below the roof (Fig. 9). Arches, however, must certainly have been employed over the columns in canonical Roman fashion. The interaxial column spacings vary considerably, from ca. 2.34 m. to 2.72 m. on center. These irregularities would have prevented the arches from being uniform, but such a problem would have been of minor consideration in the overall design where none of the elements bore any but the roughest semblance of regularity to each other. To the casual observer the asymmetry of the curvilinear and richly decorated chamber would not have been readily apparent (Fig. 8).

The roofing of the Baptistery in its later period is purely conjectural A dome, as was certainly used in the original period, must be ruled out. Such a plethora of brickwork would have left its traces in the destruction debris, much more so than would the brickwork from a hypothetical smaller baldacchino dome, which we have already ruled out. A simple wooden frame construction would seem more fitting for the late remodeling.

There was a great lack of roof tiles in the fill within the baptismal room. This lack could have been caused by the later vandalism or by the fact that the roof was sloping and the tiles slid off the roof into the rooms to the east and west, where tiles were found. If we limit ourselves again, as we did for the original dome, to using the ledge on top of the north wall of the Baptistery as the starting point for the roof, a pitched roof, with gabled front, works quite well (Fig. 9). The timbers did not need to be large for they could be supported to a great degree by the arches which were presumably carried by the columns around the pool. There would have been enough height below the ceiling for these arches to have fitted very pleasantly (Fig. 8).

---

[10] In the instances cited in note 9 a single impost block was placed over the pairs of capitals. Our materials were all used second hand, but by abutting our pairs of impost blocks, the effect of the design comes closer to that of the other examples than if our blocks were separated.

[11] It had been thought before the excavation of the Baptistery was finished that the ruins were undisturbed: W—MZ (1972) 423—424. However, not all of the architectural members were found in the debris. Furthermore, in the campaign of 1973, one of the capitals of the smaller series of columns was discovered just above the destruction level of the room to the E of the Baptistery. It is evident now that there was some post-destruction looting which could account for the disconcertingly small amount of brick that was found in the debris. Since the looting was not extremely thorough, however, it is doubtful that there were ever great masses of fallen brick, as would have existed if there had been a brick dome over the columns. Some of this masonry would certainly have escaped the plunderers and would have been found in the excavations.

Figure 8. Perspective of the Baptistery in its final phase. View from NE.

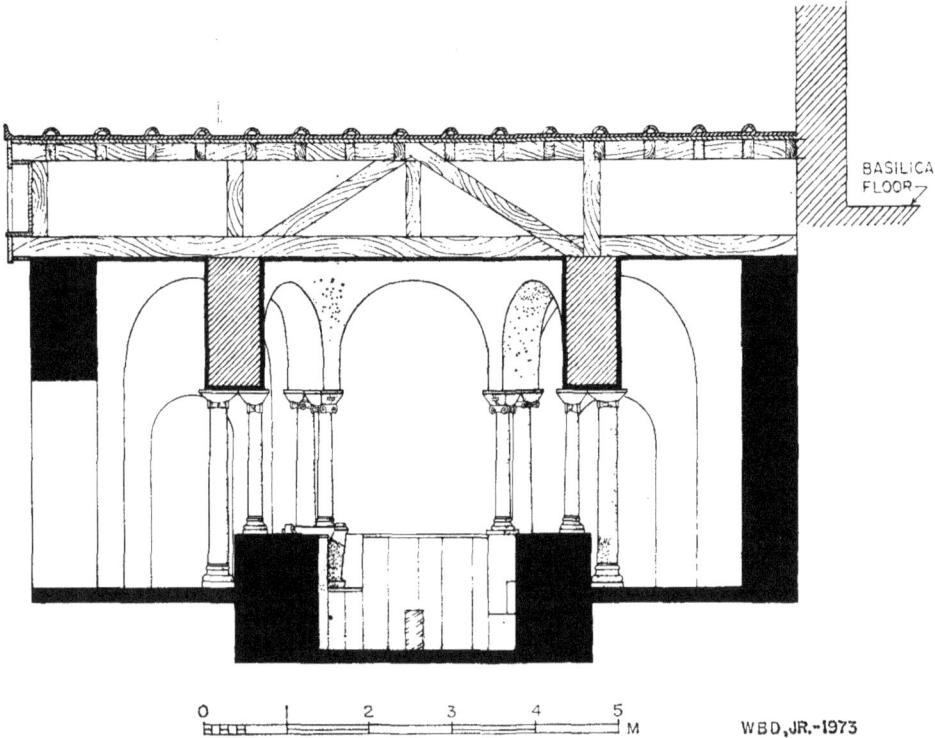

Figure 9. Section through the Baptistery in its final phase, with pitched roof.

The alternatives to a pitched roof would be a flat roof, which was not used in this part of the world because of climatic conditions, or a shed roof, which, because of its one-way pitch, would have swept so low at the south front that it would have obviated the possibility of an arched construction over the interior columns and would have given headroom of only ca 1.68 m. at the front door (a pitch of about 1 : 4 for tiled roofs was used in the Greek and Roman periods, as it is today, so that rain could not lash back up under the tiles and damage the interior of the building).

The final destruction of the Baptistery occured either from the collapse of this wooden roof or during the general holocaust ca. 570 A. C. In either case it is clear that the building had been adandoned for some time before its destruction, at least long enough for an accumulation of earth, mostly wind-blown dust, to cover the mosaic floor after certain depredations to the floor of the chamber had occurred.[12] This earth fill fortunately created a protective cushion for the mosaic floor from the falling architectural members and it underlay all of the fallen members within the room. The plundering of the Baptistery must have been done in the early years of the Dark Ages, when the upper part of the fallen debris—brickwork, tiles, and some parts of the columns—was carted off by squatters. Then the whole area was sealed off by earth fill until the year 1971 A. C.

---

[12] W—MZ (1973) 398, note 25.

КРШТАЛНИК:
НЕГОВИОТ ПОКРИВ И ДРУГИ СРОДНИ ПРОБЛЕМИ

ВИЛИЈАМ Б. ДИНСМОР, JP.

Кршталницата на Епископската Базилика се наоѓа на понизок терен, јужно од Базиликата. Претходните прикази за ископините на кршталникот и соседните места се објавени и се цитирани во фуснотата 1. Извесни описни и технички проучувања за мозаикот на подот и ѕидните фрески се објавени во спомнатите прикази и во статиите од Студиите I и II. Оваа студија, главно, дава краток опис за покривот и подпирачите на покривот и неговата конструкција во текот на неговите фази.

За да се разбере обликот и суштината на покривот потребно е да се даде краток преглед на главните архитектонски елементи на зградата. Според планот кој е кружен (д. 7,80—7,90 м.) впишан во нешто неправилен квадрат чијшто страни се разликуваат по должина (8,80 — 9,70) (Сл. 1). Постојат четири полукружни вдлабнатини кои прават сличен облик на четворолистен план; секоја вдлабнатина има по еден влез згора лачно засведен, а на јужната страна постои уште еден поширок влез. Во средината на просторијата има еден вдлабнат прилично кружен базен којшто служел како кршталник. Базенот е заграден со ограден ѕид (0,96 м. широк) со височина од 0,64 м. над мозаичниот под на просторијата; мермерниот под на базенот се наоѓа на 0,69 м. под мозаичниот под и таму можело да се дојде, уште во неговата прва фаза со помошта на четири кратки скалила (Сл. 2). Мермерните фрагменти од двете серии на јонски столбови (бази — стебла капители) се пронајдени внатре во кршталникот во 1971 г. (Сл. 3) а други архитектонски фрагменти се пронајдени во близина со подоцнежните работи. Исто така беше откриен и мермерен кантарос, откршен од базата и поставен внатре во просторот на базенот.

Архитектонски кршталникот бил самостоен. Неговите надворешни четвороаголни ѕидови биле независни, поставени до потпорниот ѕид на базиликата и неговиот под со мозаик лежи околу 4 м. под подот на јужниот брод на базиликата.

I фаза (кон крајот на IV или почетокот на V век н.е.) Покривот бил направен во вид на полухемисферна купола од продолжен малтер тули и се претпоставува дека врвот на куполата изнесува околу 7,72 м. над подот (Сл. 5). Мозаичниот под, базенот и оградните ѕидови околу него припаѓаат на оригиналната конструкција (не е сигурно за оплатите од плочи на ѕидовите) но сега не е можно да се одреди дали постоел или непостоел балдахин во тоа време.

II фаза (кон крајот на V или почетокот на VI век). Кога ѕидната купола паднала (или биле срушена), големата маса од цемент без сомнение предизвикала извесни оштетувања на мозаичниот под. Потоа следуваат серии на поправки што можат да се видат на мозаикот (види ја статијата во оваа книга од Р. Коларик и М. Петровски). Изгледот на крсталникот во оваа подоцнежна фаза може многу поуспешно да биде реконструиран отколку првобитниот модел, бидејќи повеќе од архитектонските делови и од нивната крајна структура (уништена некада после 570 години од н.е.) беа откриени во текот на ископувањата. Група од помали столбови стоеја на страничната ограда и беа поставени едни спроти други со повисоките столбови, поставени на мозаичниот под около оградата; нивната точна локација е утврдена. Тоа е демонстрирано и во статијата во која се вели дека столбовите (сигурно биле сполии) потпирале лакови изградени од тули но немало купола; дали имало или не посебен покрив или некоја друга форма на балдахин ќе се дознае наскоро.

Податоците за поставувањето на мермерниот кантарос се презентирани подетално, бидејќи само тие можат да дадат одговор на прашањето за распоредот на столбовите. Вешто обработениот кантарос бил направен порано, на неодредена локација. Во оваа последна фаза на крсталникот тој бил поставен во отвор на оградата каде предходно имало и скали (Сл. 6 и 7). Една проекција од реставрацијата на ентериерот на крсталникот е презентирана во сл. 8.

Финалниот покрив на крсталникот е хипотетичен, но нашите податоци повеќе зборуваат дека покривот бил на две води отколку со купола, рамен, или покрив на една вода. Покривот од тој вид може да се види во цртежот на сл. 9.

RADIOCARBON DATING OF MORTARS AT STOBI

by

ROBERT L. FOLK and S. VALASTRO, JR.

INTRODUCTION

We describe here a modified technique that offers hope of detailed dating of the construction of buildings, including resolution of the different times of construction of different parts of the structure.[1] Much radiocarbon dating relies upon analysis of pieces of charred wood. However, this technique, when applied to archaeological dates where extreme sensitivity is required, is subject to a serious drawback. The date obtained from the charcoal gives the time when that fragment of wood was still a living tree, not the time when it was built into the building. For example, let us say that a 150-year-old tree was cut down in 300 A.C.and used in the construction of a building that burned down around 400 A.C. Wood from the center of the tree is naturally older than that near the bark; when wood burns, the outside of the log disappears first and the central core--the oldest wood--is most likely to be preserved as charcoal. Thus the dates obtained on charcoal from this tree that was cut in 300 A.C. could well give a date of 150—200 A.C., the date when the tree was young, long before the structure was built and even longer before it burned down. Mortar dating, by contrast, gives the date of construction with much better precision.

MORTAR DATING

The idea of dating mortar was first conceived by G. Delibrias and J. Labeyrie[2] who obtained excellent results with the technique in France. Dating has also been

---

[1] We acknowledge the assistance of Prof. E. Mott Davis in the task of integrating the results of our work with the archaeological evidence at Stobi.

[2] "The Dating of Mortars by the Carbon-14 Method," *Proc. 6th Internat.Conference on Radiocarbon and Tritium Dating* (Clearing House for Federal Scientific and Technical Information, U. S. Department of Commerce, 1965) 344—347.

attempted in England, but without success.[3] We have now refined the technique to make it workable by (1) removing the aggregate and dating only the "live" mortar fraction, (2) using only the first fraction of CO_2 gas, which is evolved from the most reactive mortar, and (3) applying corrections with dendrochronology and $\delta^{13}C$.

Mortar and lime plaster have been used since prehistoric times and are made by the following process. Limestone ($CaCO_3$) is crushed to small fragments and burned, often in a kiln, over a very hot wood fire at over 1000°C. The heat calcines the limestone, driving off the CO_2 and converting the limestone to CaO, quicklime, a white powder.[4] When the material is ready to be used in construction, a variable amount of "aggregate" is added. This consists of sand or gravel, often obtained from a local river, and is used to add bulk. Sometimes left-over broken bits of brick or marble are thrown in. Water is added, the lime mixed with aggregate, and the material is then used to affix building stones or to plaster walls. As mortar hardens or "sets," it re-absorbs CO_2 from the atmosphere, converting back into cryptocrystalline calcite, $CaCO_3$ with a crystal size of 1 micron or less. Thus, on crystallization during the setting process, mortar absorbs the correct proportion of ^{14}C from the atmosphere, and consequently can be used for dating the time of construction.

To use this technique, one must be sure that the mortar does indeed have lime ($CaCO_3$) as its base. Some plaster utilized in buildings is really Plaster of Paris (gypsum), $CaSO_4.2H_2O$. Obviously this is useless for radiocarbon dating, since it contains no carbon. The two may be told apart by the fact that vinegar or weak acid will cause true lime mortar to effervesce violently, whereas gypsum mortar will not have a visible reaction. True cement, calcium aluminosilicate, also lacks carbon and cannot be used for dating.

Three complicating effects deserve mention. If the lime is improperly burned (too low a temperature, too coarse pieces of limestone), not all of the limestone will be converted to CaO, and the residual pieces would yield dead carbon and give too old a date.[5] Secondly, if the mortar is far inside a joint between two building stones, so that it is difficult for atmospheric CO_2 to get in and make the mortar harden, it may not set until some years after the time of construction. This is probably a very small effect, however, far less than the resolution error of ^{14}C dating. Most mortar has apparently set by the first 5 or 10 years.[6]

A far more serious effect, which has made attempts to date mortar in England fail, is the aggregate problem.[7] If the aggregate used as filler in the mortar consists of quartz, chert, or feldspar sand, there is no problem; all the carbon will come from the crystallization of mortar and a correct date will be obtained. Luckily this was the situation in mortars successfully dated by Delibrias and Labeyrie.[8]

---

[3] M. S. Baxter and A. Walton, "Glasgow University Radiocarbon Measurements III," *Radiocarbon* 12 (1970) 496—502; idem, "Radiocarbon Dating of Mortars," *Nature* 225 (1970) 937—938.

[4] G. L. Clark, W. F. Bradley, and V. J. Azbe, "Problems in Lime Burning: a New X-Ray Approach," *Industrial and Engineering Chemistry* 32 (1940) 972—976.

[5] M. Stuiver and C. S. Smith, "Radiocarbon Dating of Ancient Mortar and Plaster," *Proc. 6th Internat. Conference on Radiocarbon and Tritium Dating* (Clearing House for Scientific and Technical Information, U. S. Department of Commerce, 1965) 338—343.

[6] Baxter and Walton, op. cit. first ref. (in note 3) p. 501.

[7] Stuiver and Smith, op. cit. (in note 5).

[8] Op. cit. (in note 2).

However, if the aggregate contains sand or gravel-sized bits of reworked limestone —which do occur in some rivers draining terranes of carbonate rocks—or if the aggregate is made of left-over scraps of marble or limestone used in construction then there is a serious problem, and unless special steps are taken, a large amount of dead carbon (that is, carbon so old that none of the radioactive istotope ^{14}C remains) from the aggregate will be present along with the live carbon (containing ^{14}C) from the mortar itself, and a date obtained on this mixture will be uselessly old. Previous workers have not attempted to separate the mortar from the aggregate and have simply crushed the bulk material.

SAMPLE PREPARATION AND PRE-TREATMENT

We have developed a simple technique for eliminating the dead carbon contributed by rock chips in the aggregate. The mortar sample, as received from the archaeologist, is gently rinsed with distilled water to remove extraneous dust, and then is dried in an oven at approximately 100°C. For full study, a piece of mortar about 2 kg. in weight should be collected.

The dried mortar lumps are gently broken with a rubber pestle to approximately 1 cm. in size in order to separate the binding mortar powder, which is soft and friable, from the aggregate. Care should be taken not to crush sand grains or pebbles used as aggregate, but to make as clean a separation as possible between aggregate and live mortar (that is, mortar in which the carbon includes ^{14}C) by rubbing with a soft rubber pestle. Aggregate grains are usually much harder than the mortar itself, so that separation is not a difficult problem but only takes a little care and time. Next, the fine mortar powder is separated from the coarser aggregate by sieving through a series of 10, 30, 100, 200, and 230 mesh U. S. Standard sieves (respectively 2.0, 0.59, 0.149, 0.074, and 0.0625 mm.). Any size screen can be used if, on inspection with a binocular microscope, it is evident that aggregate sand grains are not going down into the "fines." At any rate, the material that passes the screens should be inspected for presence of carbonate sand grains. The sieved fractions are retained and kept in separate containers. This procedure is continued with freshly broken mortar lumps until approximately 300 gm. or more of the powder that passes through the 230 mesh screen (0.0625 mm.) is accumulated.

A quicker method of separating 300 gm. of mortar powder is as follows: place approximately 400 gm. of broken mortar fragments into a two-liter Erlenmeyer flask. To the broken mortar is added enough water to have a supernatant liquid. The liquid and the mortar fragments are continuously agitated until a thick suspension of the mortar is formed. The suspension is then passed through a 230 mesh screen and collected into a three-liter beaker. The shaking is repeated in water until very little suspension is formed. The depleted sample is replaced with a new batch of fresh sample and the operation is continued until it is estimated that 300 gm. of the fine mortar powder has been accumulated. When collection is completed, the supernatant liquid is decanted from the beaker and the sample is dried in an oven at approximately 100°C. The cohesive cake formed by the powder when drying is gently broken by pestle. The collected sample is weighed, and then is stored and kept dry in an aluminum foil container until the sample is ready for the chemical precration.

If the bulk mortar lumps contain pieces of pure white mortar (representing solid masses of lime powder that were not blended properly), the lumps are very gently broken and the pure white mortar separation is carried out by picking them with tweezers and storing them separately. At least 35 gm. of the pure white mortar is necessary to prepare a full ^{14}C sample for liquid scintillation spectrometry (the method of ^{14}C counting used in our laboratory). This particular sample is then prepared by completely leaching it with 1:3 HCl—H_2O acid solution until all the CO_2 is recovered. After the CO_2 has been prepared the normal ^{14}C preparation techniques are then applied.

Out of the sieved fractions set aside, the less than 10 and 230 mesh fractions (those that had the most amount of mortar) were utilized for the ^{14}C assay in our work.

CHEMICAL PREPARATION

It is desirable to have three full-sized samples for ^{14}C determination, that is, to have an amount of mortar that will generate three six-liter volumes of CO_2 gas, which can eventually be converted into three 3-ml. samples of benzene (C_6H_6) for counting. To determine the amount of mortar required, a 2-gm. portion of each piece of mortar is chemically analyzed to determine the amount of C present, and from this one can calculate the weight of mortar required to produce the three sufficient samples.

To determine the ^{14}C content, the proper amount of bulk mortar is weighed out and put into a 3-liter round-bottomed flask. To the contents is added enough water to cover the solids. Vacuum is applied by means of a mechanical pump until the chemical train is evacuated of all the air present and the pump is usually quiet.

From a separatory funnel, altered to suit vacuum techniques and connected to the 3-liter round-bottomed flask by means of a 24—40 vacuum joint, a 1:3 HCl—H_2O acid solution is slowly added in a steady drop-wise flow while the contents of the flask are continuously agitated. Usually 155 ml. of the acid solution are adequate to liberate enough CO_2 to form 3 ml. of benzene which is then utilized in the liquid scintillation technique.

Despite efforts at complete separation of mortar from aggregate, some pieces of dead limestone (from the aggregate or from unburned limestone pieces) may still be present in the sample. If one were to collect all the CO_2 gas evolved from complete acidification of all the $CaCO_3$ present, one could get contamination from the dead limestone pieces. Fortunately, the live mortar is very fine-grained, porous, and powdery, and reacts very quickly in acid, while the dead limestone is much harder and non-porous and reacts more slowly. Thus, by taking the first gas evolved by the acidification, one gets CO_2 evolved from the most reactive live mortar, while most of the dead carbon comes off in the later stages of effervescence. Thus in our technique, the total amout of CO_2 evolved from each sample was divided arbitrarily into three portions. The first six liters of CO_2 to be evolved (designated as the "first fraction") is the all-important one because it consists of the effervescence from the live mortar and gives the proper date. The second and third six-liter quantities of gas are more contaminated with dead carbon, and in our samples have given spurious dates ranging from 200 to over 2000 years older than the first fraction.

Once the CO_2 preparation is carried out, the normal procedure for liquid scintillation techniques as practiced by the Radiocarbon Laboratory at the University of Texas at Austin is carried out. The procedure very simply stated is as follows: the CO_2 prepared is combined stoichiometrically with Li metal to form lithium carbide (Li_2C_2). The carbide form in turn is hydrolized to form acetylene (C_2H_2). The acetylene is then trimerized by means of a silicon vanadium catalyst to form benzene (C_6H_6). Benzene, the final product, is then counted for residual radioactivity over a period of 24 to 48 hours and the age of the sample is then calculated. Dates were corrected for dendrochronology according to the calibration curve by Damon, et al.[9] The samples were also tentatively corrected for $\delta^{13}C$ fractionation (Damon, et al.)[10] using the atmospheric value of CO_2, -7 $^0/^{00}$. All ^{14}C dates here have been calculated on the basis of reference year 1950.

RESULTS

We have dated six samples from Stobi (Table 1). The first trial sample, №. Tx—1431, was collected in 1971 by the senior author from the floor of the narthex of the Central Basilica. The estimated date based on archaeological edivence (imported pottery) is late 4th or 5th century A.C.[11] The sample turned out to be small in terms of the needs of the technique, so that the date, 260 ± 180 A.C.[12] had a very large experimental error. Nevertheless, statistically there was no disagreement with the archaeological evidence, and therefore we continued to work on mortar dating.

Another sample (Tx—1944) was taken from the same body of mortar in the Central Basilica by E. M. Davis in 1973. The sample was split into two parts in the laboratory and the two parts were prepared and counted independently. The average of the two ages is 372 ± 60 A.C., a date that is in agreement with the archaeological age.

Two large samples were collected in 1973 from the Theater by E. M. Davis, one (Tx—1941) from the foundation of the analemma in the east parodos, and the other (Tx—1942) from the south wall of the first radial corridor of the cavea, next to the west parodos. Archaeological evidence based on imported pottery points to an initial construction phase of the Theater in the late first and early second centuries A.C., but it is not yet clear whether one building episode is represented, with modification of the plan as the work proceeded, or whether there was more than one separate stage of construction.[13]

---

[9] Paul Damon, Austin Long, and Donald C. Gray, "Revised Carbon-14 Dates for the Reign of Pharoah Sesostris III," *Jour. Geophys. Res.* 71 (1966) 1055—1063.
[10] Paul E. Damon, Austin Long and E. I. Wallich, "Dendrochronologic Calibration of the Carbon-14 Time Scale," *Proc. 8th Internat. Conference on Radiocarbon Dating* (Wellington, New Zealand 1972) pp. A28—A43.
[11] James Wiseman, personal communication, 1974; Context Storage Lots 123 and 124.
[12] All dates in this paper are based on ^{14}C half-life of 5730 years, and are corrected for dendrochronological value.
[13] Elizabeth Gebhard, personal communication, 1974.

TABLE 1.

AGE DETERMINATIONS ON

University of Texas Radiocarbon Laboratory Cat. No.	Stobi Project Cat. No.	Location	Assay No. Sample Mesh No. and mm. size*	Age Before Present (Half Life 5568) Age Ref. 1950 Uncorrected Dates
Tx—1431	Stobi—Folk	Synagogue Basilica Narthex—Floor	(1)<200 0.074	
Tx—1944	Mortar № 11	Synagogue Basilica Floor 1	(1)<230 0.0625 (2) Mortar Pieces	$1{,}628 \pm 50$ $1{,}560 \pm 90$ Average $1{,}594 \pm 60$
Tx—1941	Mortar № 4	Theater — E. Parodos Analemma Foundation	(1)<230 0.0625 (2)<230 0.0615 (3)<230 0.0625	$1{,}740 \pm 60$ $1{,}720 \pm 60$ $1{,}730 \pm 60$ Average $1{,}730 \pm 34$
Tx—1942	Mortar № 9	Theater — S. Wall Ist Radial Corridor	(1)<230 0.0625 (2)<230 0.0625 (3)<230 0.0625	$1{,}738 \pm 80$ $1{,}690 \pm 70$ $1{,}715 \pm 70$ Average $1{,}713 \pm 43$
Tx—1943	Mortar № 10	Episcopal Basilica S. Aisle Foundation of Principal Structure	(1) Mortar Pieces (2)<230 0.0625 (3)<230 0.0625 (4)<230 0.0625	$1{,}680 \pm 130$ $1{,}627 \pm 70$ $1{,}670 \pm 60$ $1{,}640 \pm 70$ Average $1{,}654 \pm 43$
Tx—1940	Mortar № 1	East City Wall Area — next to E. Wall of Casa Romana	(1)<230 (2)<230 0.0625	$2{,}015 \pm 80$ $2{,}051 \pm 60$ Average $2{,}033 \pm 50$

* Each date is based on the first evolution of CO_2 gas; most samples were split into 2

** Analysis on very small sample.

We split each of the two mortar samples from the Theater into three parts, and prepared and dated each part separately. The three dates from Tx—1941 have an average of 223 ± 40 A.C., and those from Tx—1942 have an average of 243 ± 50 A.C. These dates, being in excellent statistical agreement with each other,

MORTAR SAMPLES FROM STOBI

Age Before Present (Half Life 5730) Age Ref. 1950 Corrected for Dendrochronologic Value—Arizona Method	Date B.C.—A.C. Corrected	Age Before Present (Half Life 5730) Age Ref. 1950 Average Date Corrected for Dendrochronological Value & Corrected for $^{13}C/^{12}C$	Archeological Estimate of Date
1,690±180**	260±180		Late 4th or 5th Century A.C.
1,615± 60	335± 60 A.C.		
1,542±100	408±110 A.C.	$\delta^{13}C = -15.823$	Late 4th or 5th Century A.C.
1,578± 60	Average 372± 60 A.C.	1510±60—440±60 A.C.	
1,740± 70	210± 70 A.C.		
1,716± 70	234± 70 A.C.		Early 2nd
1,726± 70	224± 70 A.C.	$\delta^{13}C = -9.320$	Century A.C.
Average 1,727± 40	Average 223± 40 A.C.	1690±40—260±40 A.C.	
1,730± 90	220± 90 A.C.		
1,680± 80	270± 80 A.C.		Early 2nd
1,710± 80	240± 80 A.C.	$\delta^{13}C = -8.180$	Century A.C.
Average 1,707± 50	Average 243± 50 A.C.	1700±50—250±50 A.C.	
1,670±140	278±130 A.C.		
1,614± 80	336± 70 A.C.		
1,660± 70	290± 60 A.C.		385—410 A.C.
1,629± 80	321± 80 A.C.	$\delta^{13}C = -19.207$	
Average 1,643± 49	Average 306± 49 A.C.	1550±50—400±50 A.C.	
2,040± 90	90± 90 B.C.		
2,090± 70	140± 70 B.C.	$\delta^{13}C = -16.220$	4th Century A.C.
Average 2,065± 60	Average 115± 60 B.C.	1880±60—70±60 A.C.	

or 3 subsamples for replicate analysis.

represent contemporaneity in radiocarbon dating terms. Since the archaeological evidence also is for contemporaneity, all six dates from the two samples can be averaged, giving a mean age of 233±32 A.C. Acknowledging that mortar dating is still under development, the implication of this average is that the construction time of the Theater may be later than the archaeological evidence suggests.

From the Episcopal Basilica, sample Tx—1943 was obtained by Davis in 1973 from the socle foundation of the south wall of the principal construction stage. Architectural style, documentary evidence, and pottery date this stage of construction very close to 400 A.C.[14] As with the samples from the Theater, Tx—1943 was split into four parts which were prepared and counted independently of one another. The resulting average is 306 ± 49 A.C. Charcoal dates on this same structure give ^{14}C dates of 340 and 290 A.C., agreeing with the mortar dates and offering support for the validity of the mortar-dating method.[15] The average date, corrected both for dendrochronological value and for $^{13}C/^{12}C$, corresponds closely with the archaeological estimate of the date.

Finally, we have dated sample no. Tx—1940, which was collected by J. F. Cherry in 1972 from the area of the East City Wall. The sample came from a horizontal layer of mortar one edge of which abutted on the east wall of the Casa Romana. The field evidence is that this thin layer of mortar was laid on an earth surface later than the Casa Romana, well above the base of the wall of that building, and no association with the original construction of the building is indicated (the construction date of the Casa Romana is as yet uncertain; the evidence suggests a time in the 1st or 2nd century A.C.[16]). Pottery in the fill above and below the mortar was of 4th century types, and thus the evidence is strong that the mortar is fourth century A.C. in date.[17]

The sample was split into two parts for preparation and counting. The average of the two resulting dates is 15 ± 60 B. C., far earlier than the archaeological evidence indicates. In this case, four possible explanations for the discrepancy between the ^{14}C and archaeological dates suggest themselves. First, an error may have occurred in sample collection or shipment, as the chunk of mortar actually analyzed was a fist-sized piece — not a thin layer as the field notes would imply. Second, the location is next to the Crna River and has been subject to annual flooding, which may have affected the sample by exchanging old river-borne carbon for true mortar carbon. This possibility, though very unlikely, points up the necessity for careful geologic observations and control in the collection of mortar for dating. Third, the mortar may have been redeposited; that is, it may come from an earlier structure. The Roman builders may have re-used old plaster from part of a flood-damaged, earlier building and spread it out as a slurry to make this rude floor overlying old flood-laid sediment. Fourth, the early date may simply be a manifestation of the uncertainties inherent in radiocarbon dating, which can produce occasional unexpected anomalies and are the reason that series of dates, rather than single dates, are needed for reliable time measurement. However, this last suggestion contributes little to our understanding of the problem at hand. As of now the other three explanations are more likely, but a good deal more research into the field circumstances affecting mortar used for dating must be carried on for clarification of the matter. For more certainty a mortar sample must be collected from the actual structural walls of the Casa Romana.

---

[14] James Wiseman and Ž. Radošević, personal communication, 1974; Lot 995 in Stobi records.
[15] E. Mott Davis, D. Srdoč, and S. Valastro, Jr., "Radiocarbon Dates from Stobi: 1971 Season," *Studies* I, pp. 23—36.
[16] James Wiseman and C. S. Snively, personal communication, 1974.
[17] Lots 724—726.

TABLE 2.

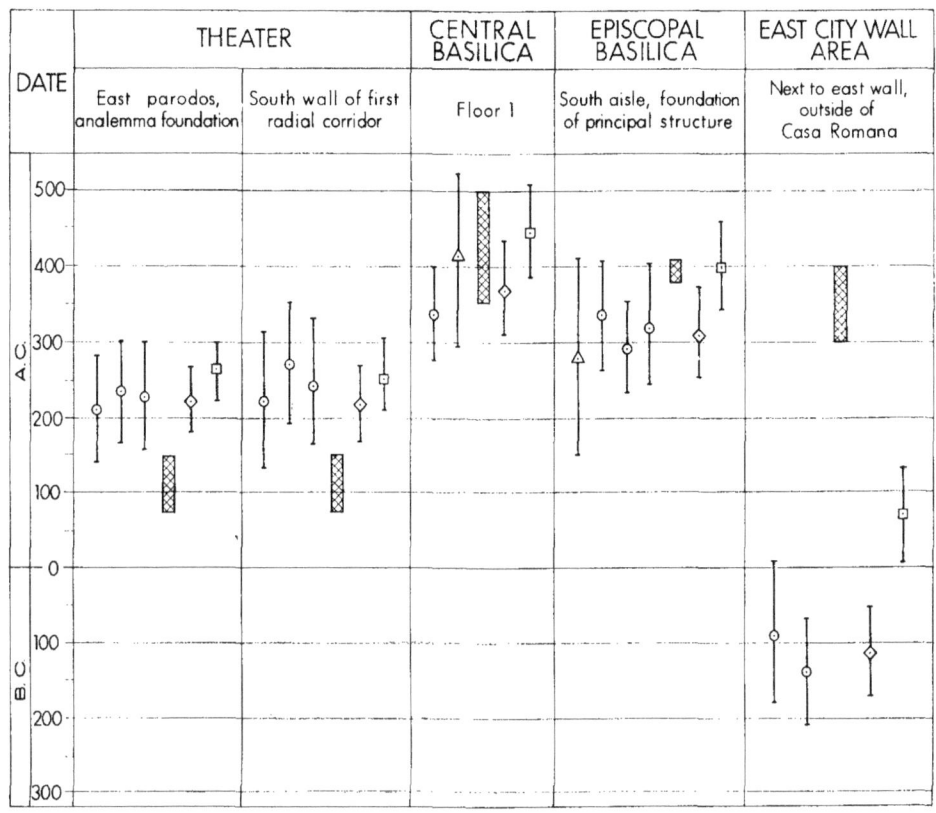

EXPLANATION

- ⌀ ^{14}C ages on mortar powder <230 mesh (H.L.=5730) corrected for dendrochronology
- △ ^{14}C ages on small mortar lumps (H.L.=5730) corrected for dendrochronology
- ◇ Average ^{14}C age
- ▨ Archeological age estimate
- ☐ ^{14}C average age corrected for δ^{13}C

TABLE 3.

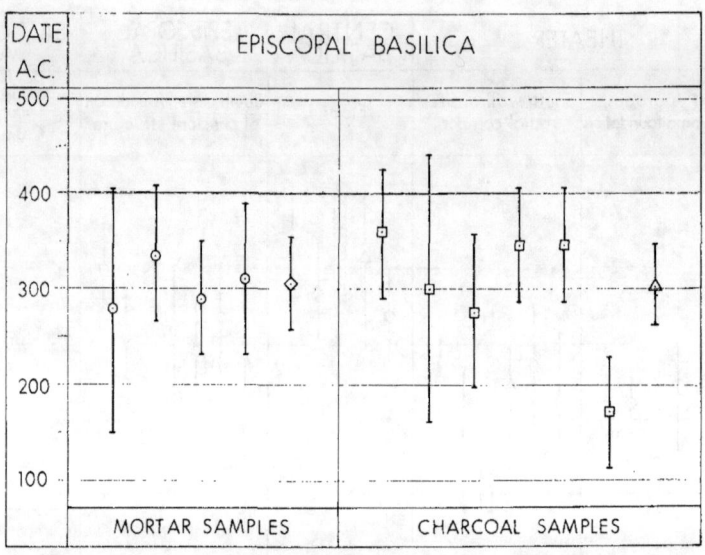

CONCLUSIONS

Radiocarbon dating of mortar is a relatively new technique, the full development of which has been retarded by problems of contamination by dead carbon. In this paper we have shown that if care is taken to remove aggregate containing dead carbon, and to use only the first evolution of CO_2 gas from the live mortar, promising results are obtained.

It is indicative of the value of radiocarbon dating of mortar that the dates from split samples (and in the case of the Theater, from multi-samples) are clustered (Tables 2 and 3). Mortar dates also agree with charcoal dates in the one structure where a cross-check was obtained. Furthermore, the mortar dates fall close to the archaeological dates, even though these latter are subject to some fluctuation as new cultural discoveries are made. In the further development of the method many more samples from well-dated structures, of course, will be required. The patterns of date clusters may then be used to calibrate the radiocarbon dates against the known dates. At that time one may expect the radiocarbon dating of mortars to provide reliable dates for mortar construction in buildings of unknown date.

And, if absolute dates through mortar dating should prove especially difficult to obtain, the technique may well provide relative ages for differentiating building episodes not distinguishable through other lines of evidence. Our experience with the two mortar samples from the Theater, in which contemporaneity is attested to both by archeological evidence and by radiocarbon dating, suggests this likelihood. Mortar dating may also add confirmation to stylistic dating.

Furthermore, dating of mortar and plaster offers much in the way of detailed study of the history of the construction of ancient buildings. Successive construction stages or alterations in a building are not always datable on stylistic or contextual grounds alone, and the application of mortar dating may well provide a valuable line of evidence for discerning such episodes. For instance, mortar dating might help clarify whether the main construction phase of the Theater at Stobi proceeded as a continuous series of modifications of the original plan, or separate building stages were involved. Such information should enhance considerably archaeological research at historical sites.

РУДИОКАРБОНСКО ОДРЕДУВАЊЕ НА СТАРОСТА НА МАЛТЕРИТЕ ВО СТОБИ

РОБЕРТ Л. ФОЛК И С. ВАЛАСТРО, ЈР.

Овде ние даваме опис на поусовршената техника која дава надеж за детално опеределување на староста на зградите вклучувајќи го разрешувањето на времето на градење и различните фази од нејзината структура. Радиокарбонското определување воглавно се докажува со анлизите на парчиња од јагленисано дрво; сепак овие податоци ни даваат можност да го дознаеме времето кога дрвото живеело, пред да било пресечено, меѓутоа, поради овие причини датирањето не може точно да одговара на времето на градењето на зградата. Наспроти тоа, при одредувањето на староста на малтерот бројката што се добива претставува време кога малтерот се втврднува со апсорбирање на CO_2 од атмосверата и така оваа дата се сложува со времето кога се градела зградата во која била малтерот употребен.

Главната тешкотија во поранешните обиди, да се одреди датирањето на малтерот, била контаминацијата на мртвиот јаглен (стар јаглен што не содржи радиоактивни изотопи, 14С потребан за одредување на датата) од варов камен или мермер кои биле додадени во малтерот. Во овој труд ние даваме опис на еден метод со кој се издвојува скоро целиот додатен метеријал во малтерот. Потоа овој материјал е обработуван во киселина при што е собрана првата CO_2 која се ослободува. Јагленот во овој CO_2 беше сиот апсорбиран од атмосверата за време на стврднувањето и со мерење на радиокарбонските состојки може да се добие датата на втврднувањето.

Пет примероци од малтер од Стоби беа плениминарно испитувани во оваа техника. Еден мал примерок од подот во нартексот од Централната Базилика, со археолошки податоци од крајот на IV или V век од н.е., даде радиокарбонски датум од 260—180 н.е. (примерок бр. Тх—1431). На два примероци од Театарот се појавија шест дати во просек 233±32 н.е. (Тх. 1941, Тх—1942); се верува дека театарот археолошки датира на крајот од II век од н.е. Од главната градежна фаза на Епископската Базилика која што археолошки датира на околу 400 год. од н.е. добиени се три дати за одредување на староста на малтерот во просек од 302±60 н.е. (Тх—1943). Еден примерок на малтер од слој кој се наоѓал помеѓу два слоја со керамика од IV век од н.е., сектор према источниот бедем, даде датум 115 ± 60 пред н.е., (Tx. 1940) секако тоа место било изложено на годишни поплави кои можеле да делуваат врз составните елементи на малтерот, а исто така постои можност малтерот да бил донесен од друго место. Геолошките прилики кои очевидно влијаеле врз малтерот треба да се истражуваат.

Овие резултати се охрабрувачки а методот на работа бара натамошно усовршување. Датирањето на малтерот може да послужи како прилог кон другите начини на датирање на зградите а исто така може да овозможи издвојување на различните фази во градењето кои неможат да се разликуваат по друг начин.

PROTECTIVE DEVICES IN ROMAN THEATERS

by

ELIZABETH R. GEBHARD

The auditorium of the Greek and Roman theater was arranged so that the seats came down to the level of the orchestra, and those in the first row(s) were assigned to priests and magistrates. In the Greek world athletic contests took place in a stadium, hippodrome, or palaestra, and they do not seem ever to have been held in the theater. There was thus no need to separate the audience from performances in the orchestra. However, when gladiatorial combats and wild animal shows *(venationes)* were added to the festival program and produced in the same area as theatrical and other events, the problem arose of containing the violent part of the spectacle without obstructing the spectators' view of the rest.

We will first look at the growth of the various festivals, their programs, and how and where they were produced at Rome and throughout the empire. Then we will examine the types of structures that were created or adapted to accommodate the scenic and arena events of a festival program. The arrangement in the theater at Stobi will be described in some detail as an example of a temporary protective device for the audience when beasts were loosed in the orchestra.

When scenic productions *(ludi scenici)* were introduced at Rome in 364 B.C., probably as part of the *Ludi Romani*, they were very likely produced in the Circus Maximus where the rest of the Festival took place.[1] Later, when scenic events were added to other existing *ludi* and new *ludi* with plays begun, the site seems to vary. In the case of the *Ludi Apollinares* and *Ludi Megalenses* they were probably given in front of the appropriate temple.[2] After the festival was over, the stands and stage were dismantled. Wooden theaters were also built. The first permanent theater was begun in 154 B.C., but it was torn down three years later by order of the Senate (to prevent the Roman people from spending too much time in the theater). It was not until Pompey undertook to disguise his theater with the

---

[1] C. Saunders, "The Site of Dramatic Performances at Rome in the Times of Plautus and Terence," *TAPA* 44 (1913) 89.
[2] A. Hanson, *Roman Theater-Temples* (Princeton 1959) 9ff.

transparent fiction of being the monumental approach to a temple of Venus that Rome finally had a permanent theater (55 B.C.). Plays oftens hared the program with athletic contests, acrobats, animal shows, and gladiators, some of which were perhaps performing at the same time in another part of the circus or Forum. Terence records that the audience's preoccupation with other, more exciting events caused his play to be cancelled on two different occasions.[3]

When scenic plays were given with funeral games *(ludi funebres)*, in which gladiatorial games usually played a major role, they were probably held in the *Forum Romanum*, which was the traditional site for these games.[4] An early recollection of viewing places for spectacles in the Forum is preserved in Festus, the 4th century grammarian, under *Maeniana*, which is the standard term for galleries of an auditorium. He says that they take their name from Maenius, the censor for 318 B.C., who first erected timbers beyond the shops in the Forum so that the seating area could be enlarged. His constructions appear to have been balconies on the upper floors of the shops, which were used as viewing places for gladiatorial and other events in the Forum.[5] The second floor of the Basilica Aemilia served a similar purpose.

During the last centuries of the Republic the *venatio* or hunt of wild animals was included in the program of public and private *ludi*.[6] The first performance in 186 B.C. celebrated a victory of M. Fulvius Nobilior, and was given in conjunction with the first Greek athletic contests at Rome (Livy XXXIX. 22.2). Livy further tells us that lions and panthers were hunted in the *venatio*. A few years later in 169 B.C. the curule aediles produced 63 "African beasts", 40 bears, and some elephants (Livy XLIV. 18.8) for a show in the Circus Maximus.[7] According to Seneca *(De Brev. Vitae* 13.5) the first combat of men against 100 unchained lions was produced by Sulla to celebrate his quaestorship in 93 B.C. No mention is made of the location of this *venatio*, but the Circus Maximus is the most likely place. Some type of protection for the spectators and restraint for the beasts would have been necessary whenever wild animals were unrestrained, and it would have had to be a barrier higher and more substantial than any used for horse races and gladiatorial combats.

---

[3] Terence *Hecyra* 1.4—5, 2.40—41. See M. Bieber, *The History of the Greek and Roman Theater* (2nd ed., Princeton 1961) 167ff. for a survey of early theaters at Rome; see also M. Garton, *Personal Aspects of the Roman Theatre* (Toronto 1974) 56ff.

[4] The first *munus gladiatorium* was given in the Forum Boarium in 264 B. C. (Livy *Per.* 16) by the sons of Junius Brutus in honor of their father, but after that they were held in the Forum Romanum (Livy XXIII. 30; Cicero *Pro Sestio* 124). The second abortive production of Terence's *Hecyra* was part of the funeral games of L. Aemilius Paulus and was thus given in the Forum. Gladiatorial combats were not admitted to the public games until 105 B. C., but by the time of Augustus such *munera* were given also in the circus and in other areas of the city (Suetonius *Vita Aug.* 43).

[5] A. Boëthius and J. B. Ward—Perkins, *Etruscan and Roman Architecture* (Harmondsworth 1970) 112—113. Temporary stands to watch gladiatorial combats in the Forum are recorded by Vitruvius X. Praef. 3 and Dio Cassius XXXVII. 58.

[6] A good description of the animals used in *venationes* and of the practices for handling and presenting them is found in G. Jennison, *Animals for Show and Pleasure in Ancient Rome* (Manchester 1937). L. Robert *(Les Gladiateurs dans l'orient grec* [Paris 1940] 309—331) devotes his final chapter to a detailed description of animal hunts.

[7] Jennison, op. cit. (in note 6), 47ff. and 154ff. for early *venaticnes* at Rome.

With the increase of wealth and power which made such displays possible, a separate, permanent structure, the amphitheater, was created to accommodate them. The amphitheater takes its name from its shape, that of two theater auditoria facing each other, and in its canonical oval plan it did not have a scene-building or stage, since it was meant solely for gladiatorial combats, *venationes*, and similar spectacles. This characteristically Roman building, however, did not first appear at Rome, but in Campania, where gladiatorial fights were especially popular.[8] The first amphitheater that is preserved was built at Pompeii by the *duumviri*, G. Q. Valgus and M. Porcius, ca. 80 B.C.[9] The seats enclosed a permanent arena floor surrounded by a wall, whose top provided a walk in front of the first row of seats. This wall with the walk on top separating the seats from the arena is called a podium, and it is the essential feature of an arena arrangement. Along the outer edge of the podium was a parapet rising 0.70 m. above the walk. The arena was thus surrounded by a solid barrier 2.18 m. high.[10] Girosi states specifically that there are no cuttings for an iron grill on top, as had been previously reported.[11] The parapet as it stands would not be sufficiently high to guard against jungle cats, suggesting that non-jumping animals may have been used. For example, one of the paintings that had originally decorated the walls of the arena portrayed a bull and a Molossian hound fighting while chained together by one leg. Such confined combats are attested elsewhere and would have been one way of presenting an animal combat without danger to the spectators. Another way was to set up a cage in the arena, within which a few beasts could fight.[12]

An incident in the circus at Rome during the great shows of Pompey in 55 B.C. throws some light on the problem of containing wild animals. On the last day when 20 African elephants were hunted down by fighters, some of the beasts tried to escape through the iron bars at the foot of the auditorium and frightened the spectators.[13] Nothing is said about the 600 lions and 410 assorted beasts which were also hunted in the same games, so either the iron bars mentioned by Pliny were sufficient to contain them or a temporary protective device was added. A few years later in 49 B.C. Julius Caesar took the precaution to surround the circus arena with a moat of water when he staged a hunt with elephants.[14]

---

[8] See C. Daremberg and E. Saglio, *Dictionnaire des Antiquitées greques et romaines*, s. v. Gladiator (G. Lafaye) Vol. II, Sec. 2 (Paris 1892) 1563—1599; M. Grant, *Gladiators* (London 1967).

[9] See M. Girosi, *L'anfiteatro di Pompeii* (Naples 1933) 32 and bibliography; Bieber, op. cit. (in note 3) 177ff. At Rome a stone amphitheater was built by Statilius Taurus in 29 B.C. (Dio Cassius LI. 23.1)

[10] Girosi, op. cit. (in note 9) Tav. II (section of the amphitheater), and pp. 38ff.

[11] By A. Mau, *Pompeii, Its Life and Art*, trans. by F. Kelsey (London 1902) 214. However, Girosi's statement that such a protection was unnecessary because *venationes* were primarily post- Augustan does not agree with reports of large hunts at Rome in the first century B. C.

[12] Part of a cage appears in the background of a *venatio* scene painted on the arena wall of the theater at Corinth; R. Stillwell, *The Theatre*. Vol. II of *Corinth, Results of the Excavations Conducted by the American School of Classical Studies at Athens* (Princeton 1952) 89ff., Fig. 78. In Apuleius *Metamorphoses* X. 34. a cage is to be used for the execution of a criminal by a wild beast.

[13] It was a famous incident described by Seneca *De Brev. Vitae* 13.6; Pliny *N. H.* VIII. 7, 215; Dio, XXXIX. 38.2—4; Cicero *Ad Fam.* VII. 1.3. See Jennison, op. cit. (in note 6) 52.

[14] Pliny *N. H.* VIII. 7. 21. Jennison, op. cit. (in note 6) 156 notes that an inner barrier would have been necessary to keep thirsty animals out of the water.

Jungle cats, however, presented a different problem. A leopard can jump as high as 4 m. and Jennison notes that "a roughly boarded fence 20 feet (6.14 m.) high would not contain them long." For a hunting arena he suggests that, from his practical experience as a naturalist, "a strong, solid wooden fence 6 feet high (1.85 m.), with nets fastened to the top of it and overhanging the arena to a maximum height of 11 or 12 feet (3.70 m.) would be ample... to contain any of the carnivora and other animals..."[15] Such a barrier could have been set up inside the podium at Pompeii or around the arena in the circus at Rome. After the Colosseum was built, a barrier of this type was apparently set inside the podium which, although about 3.60 m. high, was used as an elaborate seating and walking area by the emperor, and did not have a parapet along its inner edge.

Calpurnius Siculus *(Eclogues* 7.47 ff.*)* describes a protective arrangement in some amphitheater in the city during the first century A.C. Rollers covered with ivory were attached in some way to the podium, and were designed to prevent animals from getting a foothold. "Also twisted nets of gold glistened, nets which projected into the arena on all of the teeth equally spaced. And each tooth, believe me, Lycotas, was longer than our plow." The means of attachment and location of the rolling cylinders to keep off the leaps of wild beasts is not too clear.[16]

Let us now turn to the arrangements made for the Roman games outside of Rome. They had become a popular entertainment wherever Romans settled, and the favor they brought to the magistrate who gave them was so great that from the time of Nero they could not be offered by a local official without permission of the emperor. Many amphitheaters were built in Gaul and North Africa, but only one is known in Greece (in the Roman colony at Corinth), and they were not plentiful in the eastern empire.[17] In many cities, since the only permanent auditorium was in the theater, that structure was adapted in various ways to accommodate the games. When new theaters were built the dual function of theater and arena often influenced their design.[18]

An interesting example of a theater originally built for a mixed program of spectacles and games is found at Stobi, in what is now Yugoslavian Macedonia. It was constructed in the first decades of the 2nd century A.C. and served the needs of this small provincial city until the end of the 4th century.[19] The

---

[15] Ibid.

[16] G. Lugli reconstructs a metal grating ending in revolving wooden cylinders, which was supported on posts fitting into the corbels and post holes beneath the Colosseum floor, *Roma Antica* (Rome 1946) 328ff. Jennison assigns the corbels and post holes to the masts used to support the *velum* and suggests that a wooden barrier was fastened to the masts closing the space between them. On top of this fence he puts the elephant tusks and nets described by Calpurnius. Jennison, op. cit. (in note 6) 157ff., fig. between pp. 156 and 157. The major difference is that Lugli omits the nets and puts the rolling cylinders around the entire arena instead of just at the ends.

[17] Robert, op. cit. (note 6) 33ff. discusses theaters used for *venationes* in the eastern Empire and notes that it was their special needs that necessitated most of the alterations to earlier theater structures.

[18] Bieber, op. cit. (in note 3) 197—201 and note 8.

[19] The theater was partially excavated by B. Saria, and the results of his work appear in a monograph, *Pozorište u Stobima, Godišnjak muzeja Južne Srbije* 1 (1937) 1—68, and in a German version "Das Theater von Stobi," *AA* 53 (1938) 81—148. He includes a section at the end (pp. 47—52) on the place of the theater at Stobi in the history of the architecture of the ancient theater (see also *AA* 53 [1938] 139—48). E. Dyggve, Saria's architect, also studied the theater and especially its use in "Le Théâtre Mixte du Bas-Empire d'Après le Théâtre de Stobi, et les Diptyques

plan of the auditorium follows Greek models with slanting, open parodoi, and a large orchestra without a permanent stage. (Fig. 1). For the *scaenae frons* the design is Roman with a columnar facade and five doorways leading down flights of five steps directly into the orchestra. The absence of any stage (Hellenistic or Roman) is almost unparalled in a theater at this time; the theater at Sparta was a special exception due to the needs of a local festival. At Stobi the absence of a stage probably indicates that dramatic performances did not hold a primary place in the theater program.[20]

On the cavea side the seats rest on a podium 1.60 m. high and 0.80 m. wide effectively separating them from the orchestra (Fig. 2). A small room or refuge behind the podium in the center was entered from the central corridor through the cavea, and it had a door opening into the orchestra.[21] Both podium and refuge were taken from the design of the amphitheater and assure us that the theater was used for gladiatorial combats as well as for theatrical spectacles. But what provision was there for the animal hunts which usually comprised an important adjunct of a gladiatorial display? The podium itself would not have been high enough to protect the spectators in the first rows of seats.

The top of the podium provides us with a clues in the form of three series of cuttings. The smallest of the holes occur singly or in pairs about 0.07 m. from the arena side of the podium (Figs. 2, 3). Some are round and others square in section, 0.02—0.03 m. in width and depth, and they are 1.00—1.50 m. apart. I suspect that they were made to hold a light metal grill which served as a railing at the outer edge of the podium. Its usefulness as a protection from a leaping animal would have been limited, and the total height of the podium and grill could not have exceeded 2.60 (if the grill was about 1 m. high). Not only the small diameter but also the shallowness of the holes would have prevented them from receiving an upright of greater height.

The second series of cuttings consists of rectangular post holes 0.115—0.145 m. wide by 0.15—0.24 m. long by about 0.12 m. deep. They are set back 0.13—0.16 m.

Consulaires," *RA* (1958) Pt. 1, pp. 137ff.; Pt. 2, pp. 20ff; and in "Den senantike Faellescene," *Studier fra Sprog-og Oldtidsforskning* 179 (1938) 3ff, which is substantially the same. The remainder of the cavea and orchestra were cleared under the direction of the Zavod za Zaštita na Spomenicite na Kulturata, Skopje, in 1965 to 1969, and test trenches were dug on the periphery. Since 1970 further excavation by the author under the auspices of the Stobi Excavation Project directed by James Wiseman and Djordje Mano-Zissi has produced evidence for the chronology of the theater and new information concerning its several phases. The theater will be the subject of a longer study by the author; for preliminary reports see W—MZ (1971) 402; W—MZ (1972) 417—419; W—MZ (1973) 400—401; W—MZ (1974) 129—133. See also the earlier bibliography in Ž. Radošević, "The Stobi Bibliography," *Studies* I, 264—265.

[20] Dyggve, *RA* (1958) pt. 2 and J. Formigé, "Les representations dans les théâtres romains," *Bulletin de la Société nationale des Antiquaires de France* (1921) 88—93, discuss the different types of events which were presented in a Roman theater.

[21] In the 3rd century after a severe earthquake the theater was repaired and remodeled so that the orchestra was completely enclosed as an arena, and two smaller refuges were added at the sides. In place of the post and net system a heavy wall of masonry was built on top of the podium, which increased its height to over 3.60 m. (fig. 2). The parodoi were closed by heavy gates and a long curtain wall blocked the front of the scene-building to the height of the porches (fig. 1). The wall had three small doors, opposite although not in line with the stairways behind (fig. 1). These would have functioned much the same as the refuges on the cavea side of the arena.

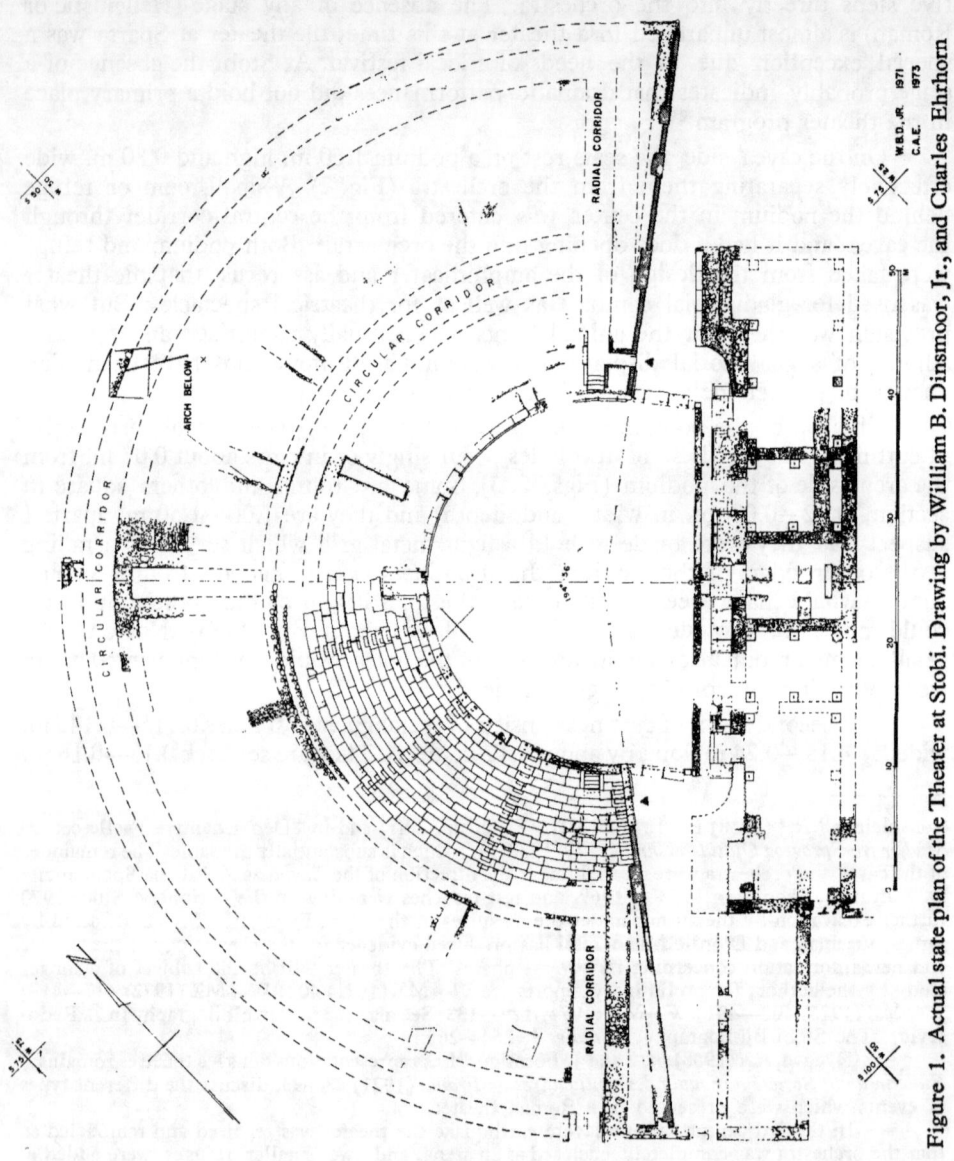

Figure 1. Actual state plan of the Theater at Stobi. Drawing by William B. Dinsmoor, Jr., and Charles Ehrhorn

Figure 2. Podium in the Theater at Stobi, with post holes and later wall in background.

from the edge of the podium and do not correspond in location to the first series. The clear space between them beginning from the west is 1.35, 1.60, 1.63, 1.45, 0.95, 0.95, 0.95, 1.60, 1.70 m. The bottom of the cuttings comes to within 0.11 m. or less of the undercut surface of the podium capping course (Figs. 2, 3). It is evident that the depth of the hole was limited by the angle of the molding. Wooden posts of the thickness indicated by the cuttings could not have stood firmly upright

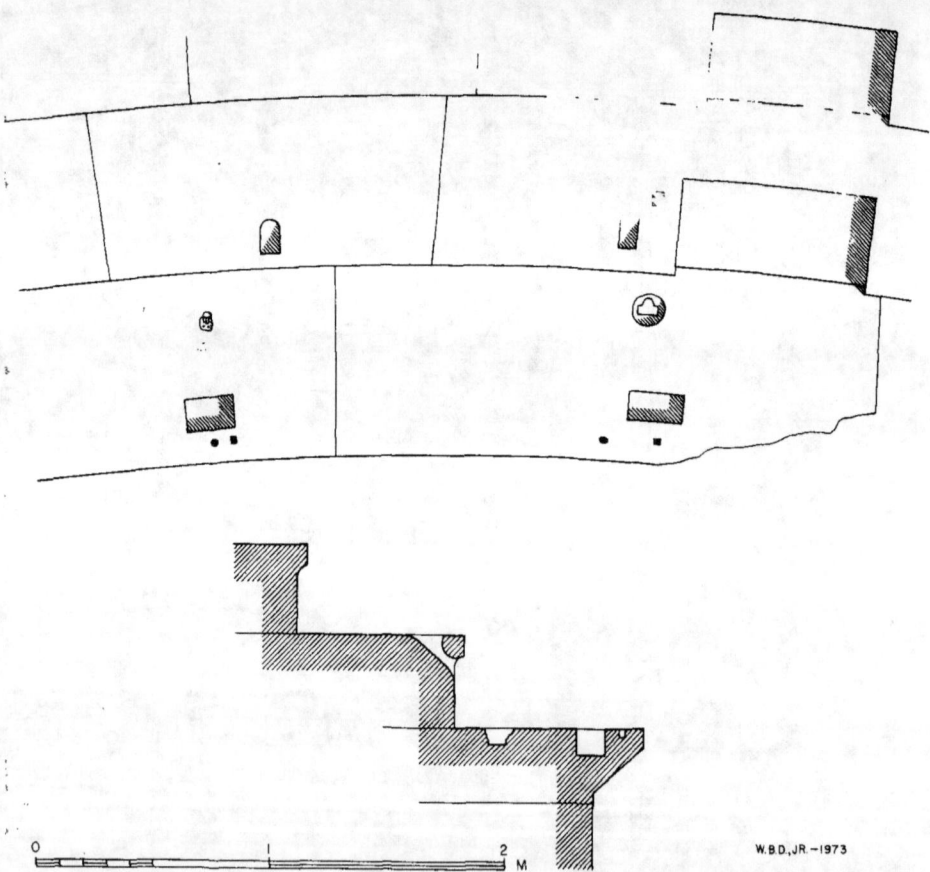

Figure 3. Plan and section of a detail of the podium at the E end of the preserved portion. Drawing by William B. Dinsmoor, Jr.

in such shallow beddings. They were very probably held in place by wedges and may also have been set at an angle slanting toward the orchestra. Iron rings embedded in lead were placed 0.31—0.33 m. behind each post, very likely to hold guy lines which were attached to the top of the post and fastened through the ring (Figs. 4, 5). The shallowness of the holes would have made this extra support necessary; it is not found in other theaters where the post holes are deeper. In three cases at Stobi two lead beddings are found behind a single post hole, and in two others two iron pins protrude from one lead bedding. In each case the eye on top of the pin is broken. Fortunately one complete iron ring is preserved *in situ*. The ring is 0.009 m. thick with an opening 0.040 m. × 0.020 m.; it passes through an iron eye with a pin that was embedded in lead. The guy lines would have been

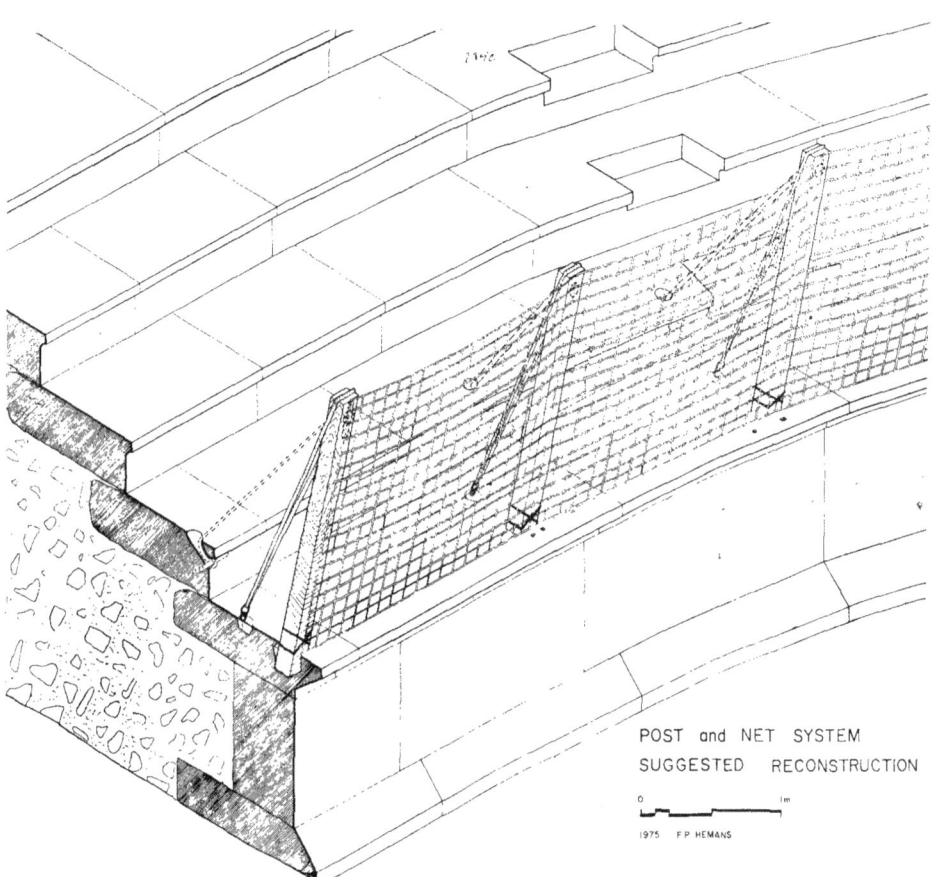

Figure 4. Suggested restoration of post and net system at Stobi. Drawing by Frederick P. Hemans, III.

attached to the top of the posts and tied through the ring. The fact that in some places more than one bedding was made behind a post and that in others more than one ring had been set in a single bedding suggests that the rings were subject to a strain great enough in some instances to pull them from their beds. When that happened another was set into the same bedding or a new bedding provided.

On the first row of seats still another series of cuttings corresponds with the post holes on the podium. They are holes cut diagonally through the front of the seats, from the top surface of the seat to just under the fillet along the front edge (Figs. 3—6). The top opening is about 0.13 m. wide, narrowing to about

Figure 5. Detail of post hole, preserved iron ring, and rope hole, from above.

0.035 m. inside and then opening to about 0.08 m. on the front face. Some wear from a rope occurs inside on the top front surface where the channel is narrowest, from which it may be concluded that the channels were cut to secure ropes. They interrupt and therefore are later than some of the inscriptions which designated

Figure 6. Three sets of post holes, ring beddings, and rope holes, from above.

the occupants of the first row; that the row continued to be used when the ropes were not in place is certain because in one place a name is carefully cut around a hole. Apparently after the iron rings proved unable to hold the guy lines, either the same or additional guys were secured through the channels in the first row (Figs. 4, 6).[22]

Another barrier may have been added across the front of the scene-building in order to enclose the orchestra completely. A series of large post holes were reserved in the concrete foundation of the facade. Five of them have been uncovered, ca. 0.40 m. × 0.33 m. and 0.23 m. × 0.29 m. and 0.36 m. deep. They were made in the outer edge of the foundation (now partially under the later barrier wall), 0.77 m. in front of the façade (Fig. 7). Originally they may have held the large posts for the scaffolding for construction of the façade, but that would not have prevented them from later receiving posts for a temporary barrier of wood or nets.

It seems almost certain that the cuttings on the podium represent a temporary protective barrier which was made by fastening heavy nets to wooden posts. The system resembles that described by Calpurnius, but it is of a simpler, homemade variety. Such nets were used to trap animals for use in the arena, a vivid scene of which is portrayed on a floor mosaic from a villa at Bône (Hippo

---

[22] Saria, *Pozorište*, pp. 8—9, fig. 7. He believed that the post holes held a marble parapet and that the rope holes were to allow for drainage through the late wall on the podium. The holes, however, were filled with mortar at that time, as seen at the west end where the late wall is preserved.

Regius) in Algeria.[23] A heavy net attached to wooden posts is arranged in a horseshoe fashion with three enclosures at the sides, each containing bait. The inside has been camouflaged with bushes so that the lions and leopards do not see the net until they are driven into the trap.

Figure 7. Post hole in scene building foundation platform; barrier wall at top.

---

[23] A large color reproduction is included in R. Wood and M. Wheeler, *Roman Africa in Colour* (London 1966) Pl. 51 See also Jennison, op. cit. (in note 6) 145. The date of the mosaic is late 3rd or 4th century A. C.

Besides visibility a barrier made with a net had the added advantage of being easily set up and removed when there were other events on the festival program. Perhaps the best description of a varied program is found in Apuleius *Metamorphoses* X. 29 ff. The first morning of the shows began with a Pyrrhic dance performed by two choruses, followed by a mime depicting the Judgement of Paris, which also included dancing choruses. The next event was to be a scene between a female criminal and Lucius in the form of an ass, after which she was to be eaten by a wild animal. Gladiatorial combats and perhaps an animal hunt would have completed the three-day festival program in the theater at Corinth, but Lucius ran away before he could tell us about them.

The theater at Stobi would have been well suited to such a variety of events. The choruses and mime personnel would have made grand entrances through the five monumental doors of the scene-building, and the large orchestra would have been a fine place for dancing. When an arena was necessary for the more savage shows, the posts and nets could have been easily set into place.

A post and net protective system on top of the podium is not unique with the theater at Stobi. The closest parallels are found at Philippi, Thasos, and Heraclea Lyncestis. At both Philippi and Thasos there are large notches for upright timbers in the arena side of the podium. At Philippi[24] the notches are ca. 0.105 m. × 0.23 × 0.37 m. deep. The posts were held in place at the front by a stone parapet resting on a small ledge and clamped to the front of the podium. The podium itself was about 1.20 m. high, and the total height of podium and parapet was about 1.75 m. The posts and nets would have added 2 to 3 m., thereby attaining 3.70 m., optimum height for protection against large cats (Figs. 8—10). The arrangement at Thasos is less clear from the published photographs and descriptions, but from the 1st. century A.C. there is evidence that gladiatorial combats and *venationes* were held in the theater, and the heavy gates closing the parodoi were constructed at that period.[25] At the end of the second century a certain Heragoras put up a marble parapet in front of the podium. The slabs are 1.71. m. high and are said to have been surmounted by an iron grill although cuttings for it are not visible in the photographs. On the backs of the slabs are traces of metal brackets to hold upright posts. The parapet slabs stood on a low plinth around the orchestra, and behind this are notches for posts 1.15 m. apart.[26] The total height of the podium faced with slabs would have been something over 1.71 m., and the post and net barrier would have risen above that. At Heraclea

---

[24] See P. Collart, "Le théâtre de Philippes," *BCH* 52 (1928) 114—123; *Philippes* (Paris 1937) 371—388, figs. LVII, LX, 1. Collart assigns the holes to a grill or net (*Philippes*, p. 381). He discusses the need for theaters in smaller cities to be able to accommodate all types of events, and he gives examples of theaters adapted to arena events.

Professor Wiseman kindly furnished the photographs and dimensions for the post holes. Collart dates the post and net system to the second century when the cavea was enlarged. D. Lazaridis, who supervised restoration of the cavea in 1957—1959, places the arena phase in the 3rd century A. C., at the time of the final alterations to the theater, "Chronique des Fouilles," *BCH* 83 (1959) 714, fig. 10.

[25] École Française d'Athènes, *Guide de Thasos* (Paris 1968) 50ff., fig. 17 and bibliography, p. 195.

[26] G. Daux, "Chronique des Fouilles en Thasos," *BCH* 47 (1923) 26ff., pls. 7, 8; Collart, *BCH* 52 (1928) 118. Daux assigned the post holes to a *velum;* Collart identified a protective device.

Figure 8. Top of the podium in the theater at Philippi, orchestra to right.

Lyncestis the podium of the cavea is similar to the one at Stobi with post holes at regular intervals, but there are no iron rings or rope holes behind them. The theater is currently being excavated by the Conservation Institute of Macedonia, and no measurements or photographs are available.

Another type of protective barrier which could not alone have served for animal shows is a parapet about 1 m. high, made of thin, upright slabs placed around the orchestra, as at Delphi, Argos, and the Theater of Dionysos at

Figure 9. Detail of podium at Philippi, note clamp cutting on each side of nothc for post.

Figure 10. Post hole seen from the front, at Philippi.

Athens.[27] This was often used when converting a Greek theater for gladiatorial combats without removing the first rows of seats. It is also found in purely Roman theaters to separate the areas of seating, e.g. at Timgad, Sabratha, Dugga, Leptis Magna, Aspendos, the large theater at Lyons, etc. In some cases we find both a parapet and a podium or post and net barrier which would have supplied additional protection for the auditorium.

In the theater at Delphi, in addition to the low parapet, the first rows of seats were removed to make a podium 1.04 m. high. However there are no post holes for a temporary barrier which would have been needed for the production of *venationes*. At Eretria no parapet or podium was added, but a series of large post holes (0.30 m. square by 0.10 m. deep) cut into the walk in front of the seats probably held the posts, spaced 1.10—1.50 m. apart, for some kind of barrier.[28] There are several series of post holes in the large theater at Argos, the lowest one of which, immediately in front of the proedria, may well have held a temporary barrier system behind the parapet. (Figs. 11, 12).[29] The average size of the holes

---

[27] Low parapet in the theater at Delphi is 0.83 m. high, 0.22 m. thick; at Argos it is about 1.10 m. high, 0.45 m. thick; in the Theater of Dionysos at Athens it is 1.10 m. high, 0.10 m. thick. See W. Dörpfeld and E. Reisch, *Das griechische Theater* (Athens 1896) 387ff. for a description of the ways in which orchestras were transformed into arenas, with examples.

[28] E. Fiechter, *Das Theater in Eretria*, Vol. 8 of *Antike griechische Theaterbauten* (Stuttgart 1937) p. 27, fig. 22, pl. 1.

[29] For a detailed plan see G. Roux, "Chronique des Fouilles en Argos," *BCH* 80 (1956) fig. 41. Measurements and photograph of the theaters at Argos, Delphi, and Athens were taken by the author.

Figure 11. Post holes in front of the proedria in he large Theater at Argos.

Figure 12. Post hole with corresponding rope hole at S end, at Argos.

s 0.14 m. ×0.18 m. ×0.20 m. deep, and they have a clear spacing of about 2.35 m. A space of only 0.18 m. separates them from the seats so that the proedria would not have been used when the barrier was in place, as at Stobi. Three small rope iholes, 0.02—0.03 m. in diameter, are cut through the back of the proedria bench 'opposite the post holes in the first kerkis at the south. In each of the other kerkides only one rope hole occurs. Perhaps the greater depth of the post holes at Argos rendered guys for each post unnecessary. Of course, what type of barrier the posts supported is impossible to say, but in each case where the post holes are located immediately in front of the seats a solid wooden barrier would have blocked the view from the first four to 10 rows of the cavea so that a heavy net would have been the most suitable material.

A comparable combination of parapet and post holes is found in the Theater of Dionysos in Athens. As in other theaters, there is no clear evidence of the date at which the low parapet and post holes were added. The parapet has been associated with the remodeling at the time of Nero, at the time of the Bema of Phaidros, and as late as the Byzantine church.[30] Considering the

---

[30] Dörpfeld-Reisch, op. cit (in note 27) 82ff; E. Fiechter, *Das Dionysos-Theater in Athen*. Vol. 7 of *Antike griechische Theaterbauten* (Stuttgart 1936) pl. 22, fig. 43; *Ant. Theaterbauten* Vol. 8 pl. 5; J. Travlos, *Pictorial Dictionary of Ancient Athens* (London 1971) s. v. "Theater of

popularity of arena events and the fact that Athens did not have an amphitheater, it is likely that the Theater of Dionysos was fitted with some kind of protective device for these shows as early as Nero's visit in 67 A.C. Besides the parapet, which would have been inadequate for *venationes*, one series of post holes occurs at the foot of the proedria thrones, and there are two series of holes behind them. The first set of holes is found ca. 1.07 m. in front of the thrones; they vary between 0.17 m. × 0.175 m. and 0.14 m. × 0.13 m. in length and width. It was impossible to clear them out to measure the depth, but the thickness of the paving slabs would have allowed for at least 0.20 m. The clear space between them is from 1.52 m. to 2.00 m. with a gap in the sixth kerkis (from the west) and in the center where the walk narrows to 1.10 m. behind the parapet. The holes behind the thrones are slightly larger and were probably used for posts to support a sunshade, as has been suggested. The ones in front of the thrones could also have been part of the awning support system, but at the same time nets could have been attached for temporary protection. Inside the gutter another series of smaller holes, about 0.11 m. in diameter, occurs at wider intervals and possibly also received supports for a barrier.[31] When Hadrian visited Athens in 125 or 128 he is reported to have given a *venatio* of 1,000 wild beasts[32], which would have required substantial protection for the spectators. Both Philostratos and Dio Chrysostomos describe gladiatorial combats in the Theater of Dionysos, the latter adding that often one of the gladiators was killed among the thrones of the priests.[33] The mention of frequent gladiatorial games in the theater is suggestive, though not certain evidence that *venationes* were also held there regularly.

In other cities where arena events apparently played a greater role in the festivals, the theaters, Greek or early Roman, were more permanently transformed into amphitheaters. The stage was removed and a wall continuing the line of the podium was added at each side of the scene-building, or across the front of it. Heavy gates closed the parodoi. The orchestra was then a completely enclosed space and became a permanent arena. Examples of this type of arena-theater are found at Tyndaris, Cyrene, Dodona, Corinth, Stobi in the final phase, and many other places.[34] At Corinth the seats were cut back to an average height of 1.60

Dionysos," pp. 537—552. See A. Pickard-Cambridge, *The Theatre of Dionysos in Athens* (Oxford 1946) 254ff. for a summary of the arguments. In regard to the necessity of having a Roman stage at the time of Nero, it should be noted that when Nero himself competed at the Isthmian Games in musical events, there was no pulpitum in the theater. The old Greek proskenion was rebuilt as a high, shallow stage.

[31] E. Fiechter, *Das Dionysos-Theater in Athen: Die Ruine*. Vol. 5 of *Antike griechische Theaterbauten* (Stuttgart 1934) p. 60f.

[32] Jennison, op. cit. (in note 6) 83 ff.

[33] *Vita Apoll.* iv. 22 and *Oratio* xxxi. 121 respectively. This has been taken to mean that the barrier wall is very late, after the time of Dio Chrysostomos (Pickard-Cambridge, op. cit. (in note 30) 58ff.), but it does not necessarily follow. The barrier is only 0.82 m. above the walk in front of the seats and 1.10 m. above the orchestra, so that it would not have been too difficult for a large gladiator to have been pushed over it in the heat of combat, and he might well have died at the feet of the priests.

[34] For Tyndaris, see H. Bulle, *Untersuchungen an griechischen Theatern*. Vol. 33 of the *Abhandlungen der bayerischen Akademie der Wissenschaften, Phil.-hist. Klasse* (Munich 1928) 131ff.; pls. 33, 34. For Cyrene, see G. Caputo, "Note sugli edifici theatrali della Cirenaica," *Anthemon* (Florence 1955) 82; for Dodona, see S. Dakaris, "τὸ ἱερὸν τῆς Δωδώνης," Ἀρχ. Δελτίον 16 (1960) 4ff., figs. 8, 11, and G. Daux "Chronique des Fouilles,"*BCH* 84 (1960) 735. It was converted

m., and the podium was continued upward by squared blocks of masonry which formed a parapet at the outer edge. The top of the parapet was finished in a deep cavetto molding, curving toward the arena. The total height may have been about 3.50 m. (Fig. 13). The same arrangement is found at Tyndaris and Dodona; at Tyndaris the total height of the podium was 3.52 m. including the parapet.

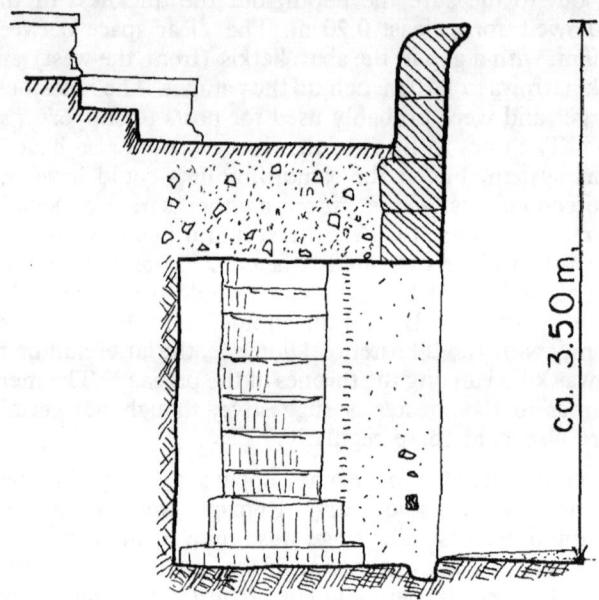

Figure 13. Restored section of podium and parapet in the Theater at Corinth. Drawing from Stillwell, op. cit. in note 12.

In Asia Minor less modification was necessary because the high front of the Hellenistic proskenion, retained in the Roman remodeling, was walled up to form one side of the arena. At Ephesos this was done in 140—144 A.C.; the podium was 2.40 m. high, equal in height to the stage which was rebuilt to the same height as the proskenion.[35] The arena-theater arrangement seems to be early Roman at

---

into an arena in the time of Augustus. For Corinth, see R. Stillwell, op. cit. (in note 12) 84ff., pls. I, VII b, fig. 73 (reproduced as our fig 13). He dates the arena to the time of an anticipated visit of Caracalla in 214—217 A. C. The Odeum at Corinth was also made into a full arena in the 3rd century; O. Broneer, *Corinth* X: *The Odeum* (Cambridge, Mass. 1932) pp. 54ff., pl. I. See also the theater at Kourion on Cyprus, R. Stillwell, "Kourion: the Theatre," *Proceeedings of the American Philosophical Society* 105 (1961) 37ff.

[35] See Bieber, op. cit. (in note 3) 218, figs. 733, 734, and note 57 for bibliography. The theaters at Miletus and Magnesia-on-the-Meander are other examples of this type of arena conversion, see F. Krauss, *Das Theater von Milet* (Berlin 1973) Vol. I, pl. 21, fig. 12 and Dörpfeld--Reisch, op. cit. (in note 27) 156.

Sagalassos and Termessos; the stage front was 2.77 m. high at the former and 2.36 m. at the latter, with a podium height of 1.75 m.[36]

In Gaul and Britain many of the structures, new or remodeled, were even more like amphitheaters, in that the scene building was very small and incidental in relation to the large area of the arena, for example at Autun, Lillebonne, and Augusta Raurica, converted in 38 A.C.[37]

CONCLUSIONS

Gladiatorial combats and wild animal hunts, together with scenic plays, originally were given in the Roman Forum as part of funeral games for wealthy citizens. Temporary protective barriers were probably set up for the occasion. These events also took place in the circuses as part of other festivals, and there, too, temporary barriers would have been erected when wild animals were set loose. The growing popularity of this part of the program led to the creation of a special structure for it, the amphitheater, first built of masonry at Pompeii and of wood at Rome in the 1st century B.C. In towns where the theater contained the only auditorium it was used for all types of shows, musical, theatrical, gladiatorial, and hunting, and temporary protective barriers for the wild animal events were often added. Beddings and attachments for a post and net barrier on top of the podium have been found in the theaters at Stobi, Philippi, Thasos, and Heraclea Lyncestis. In other theaters without a podium, as in the Theater of Dionysos at Athens, at Argos, and also at Dugga and Timgad, a temporary barrier supported by posts provided the only protection for the spectators in addition to a low parapet surrounding the orchestra.

Where arena events took precedence over theatrical spectacles, the orchestra was completely enclosed by a permanent barrier, as at Tyndaris, Cyrene, Dodona, Corinth, and Stobi in the last phase; in Asia Minor at Ephesos, Miletos, Termessos, and Sagalossos; and in Gaul and Britian where the amphitheater element was increased even more and the scene-building greatly reduced. The enclosure of the orchestra to form an arena did not occur only in the 2nd and 3rd centuries, as some have suggested on the basis of an increase in violent games at that time. Rather, temporary protective barriers, which probably go back to the very beginning of wild animal hunts as part of a festival program, were preceded the permanent enclosures of the arena. In two cases, the theaters at Corinth and at Augusta Raurica, the arena phase was in turn succeeded by a conversion back to a predominantly scenic theater.

---

[36] Bieber, op. cit. (in note 3) 219—220, figs 740, 742; Bulle, op. cit. (in note 34) p. 269; Daria de Bernardi, *Teatri Classici in Asia Minore* II (Rome 1973) pp. 11—34 (Termessos); 41—58 (Sagalassos).

[37] They are described in A. Grenier, *Manuel d'Archeologie gallo-romaine*, pr. 3 *Ludi et Circences* (Paris 1958) 801ff., 901ff., and for Augusta Raurica see R. Laur-Belart, *Führer durch Augusta Raurica: Das Theater* (4th ed., Basel 1966) 49ff., plan II, fig. 36. The demi-amphitheaters at Drévant, Sanxay, Valognes, etc. had such a reduced scene building that they constitute a type of building even closer to the amphitheater than the others listed. The same is true of the theater at Verulameum, England, see K. Kenyon "The Theatre at Verulameum," *Archaeologia* 84 (1934) 213—216, pl. LXX.

ЗАШТИТНИ МЕРКИ ВО РИМСКИТЕ ТЕАТРИ

ЕЛИЗАБЕТ Р. ГЕБХАРД

Битките на гладијаторите и ловот на диви животни, заедно со сценските игри, за првпат беа прикажани во Римскиот Форум како дел од погребните свечаности на богатите граѓани. По тој повод биле поставувани привремени трибини и веројатно заштитни огради. Овие игри се изведувале и во циркусите како дел од другите свечености, но и таму исто така биле поставувани заштитни огради кога ги одврзувале дивите животни. Зголемената популарност на овој дел од програмата довело до создавање на посебна врста објект за таа цел — амфитеатар, кој за првпат бил изграден во I век пред новата ера и тоа во Помпеја од ѕидови, а во Рим од дрво. Во градовите каде што театарот се користел за сите видови престави, односно за музички, театарски, гладијаторски и ловечки, често биле употребувани привремени заштитни огради за време на игрите со дивите животни. Лежиштата и потпирачите на оградата од мрежа и столбови се пронајдени на површината од подиумот во театрите во Стоби, Филипи, Тасос и Хераклеја Линкестис. Во другите театри немало подиум, како што се театрите на Дионисос во Атина, во Аргос, Дуга и Тимгет, но сепак имало привремени огради потпрени на столбови како и еден понизок парапет околу оркестрата кои обезбедувале единствена заштита на гледачите.

Таму каде што игрите во арената имале предимство над театарските престави оркестрата била во целост оградена со постојана ограда, како во Тиндарис, Цирена, Додона, Коринт и Стоби во последната фаза; во Мала Азија во Ефесос, Милетос, Термесос и Сагаласос; а во Галија и Британија амфитеатарскиот дел бил повеќе зголемен додека сцената била многу намалена.

Оградувањето на оркестрата, да би се направила арена, не се случувало само во II и III век од н.е. Како што некои заклучиле врз основа на зголемениот број на крволочни игри во тоа време. Напротив, заштитните огради веројатно потекнуваат од почетокот на ловот на диви животни како дел од свечената програма. Овие привремени огради понатаму биле проследени од перманентни оградувања во арената. Во два случаи театарот во Коринт и Августа Рорика, фазата на арената подоцна била поправена во некогашниот изглед наменет за сценски игри.

На овој начин, во овој труд се испитани повеќе методи поврзани со проблемот кој го проучува оградувањето на дивите животни во театарот кој бил користен и за други врсти на престави, може би во еден ист ден.

TECHNICAL OBSERVATIONS ON MOSAICS AT STOBI

by

RUTH KOLARIK and MOMČILO PETROVSKI

Technical analyses of mosaics are usually presented as mere appendices to studies concerned primarily with their style, iconography, or archaeology. Various methods have been used to examine mosaics "technically" ranging from simple observation and description to qualitative analyses of materials and sophisticated mathematical and statistical studies. The present article[1] is primarily a detailed study of the materials and methods used to lay some of the mosaics at Stobi and a standardized description of their motifs,[2] together with reconstructions of certain of their geometric patterns.

For the present we shall limit ourselves to the Stobi mosaics for which excavation has provided reliable dating and seek to relate them to other mosaics at Stobi which have not been archaeologically dated. This study has been limited to material at Stobi because the significance of technical comparisons in the light of present knowledge is restricted and there is a lack of published material from near-by sites that is precise enough to be used for comparison.[3] Our work is based

---

[1] We wish to thank the Co-Directors of the Stobi Project, James Wiseman and Djordje Mano-Zissi, *for asking us to write this article and providing access to the pertinent documentation.* Ruth Kolarik's work in the spring of 1974 was supported by a grant from the IREX Foundation. We are most especially grateful to Živojin Radošević who gave encouragement and support throughout our work and contributed stimulating ideas and interpretations.

The photographs are by Christopher Allen, Figure 9; Robert Black, Figures 27, 28, 29, 30, and 31; Tom Eals, Figures 8 and 32; Paul Gebhard, Figure 22; Ruth Kolarik, Figures 6, 12, 16, and 26; Julian Whittlesey, Figures 17 and 19; and various members of the Stobi staff, Figures 3, 7 and 21. Christopher Allen assembled the composite in Figure 17. Figure 23 was drawn by D. B. Peck and M. Prendžov; Figure 14 by Živojin Radošević. The mosaic drawings, Figures 1, 2, 3, 4, 5, 9, 10, 11, 13, 15, 18, 20, 24, and 25, are by Momčilo Petrovski, M. A., Senior Conservator of the Conservation Institute of Macedonia, who was assisted by Božidar Damjanovski, M. A., Veljo Tašovski, and Blaže Kuzmanovski, students at the Academy of Fine Arts, and Djordje Krsteski from the staff of the National Museum in Ohrid.

[2] The terminology used to describe the ornamental motifs of the Stobi mosaics is based on that adopted by the Association internationale pour l'étude de la mosaïque antique; *Répertoire graphique du décor géométrique dans la mosaïque antique* (Paris 1973). The stones were identified by Professor Tomislav Ivanov of the University of Skopje.

[3] A notable exception is the detailed study of the mosaic in the narthex of the Large Basilica at nearby Heraclea: M. Medić, "Technique and Materials," *Heraclea III* (Bitola 1967) 88—92.

on the assumption that similarities in the materials used, the shape, dimensions and manner of laying mosaic tesserae and the preparation of the mortar bedding can be used to supplement style analysis and archaeological evidence in relating mosaic floors from an individual site. Conversely, significant variation in the technique used in laying mosaics or differences within a single floor may distinguish various traditions or influences active within a locality or indicate remodelling or repairs during the use of the floor.

Although Stobi has several fine mosaic pavements, the current excavations are not concerned primarily with exposing the mosaics, but seek to examine the complete stratigraphy of the site. Therefore, the study of the mosaics is closely related to the investigation of the buildings in which they were laid. Technical examination of the mosaics often provides information which supplements our understanding of the architecture. Our investigations have, in fact, contributed new insights concerning a building below the Central Basilica and the Episcopal Basilica complex.

CENTRAL BASILICA COMPLEX: BUILDING TWO

Beneath the basilica referred to as the Central Basilica the floors of two superposed buildings have been identified.[4] The upper floor belonging to Building Two was paved with a mosaic which was discovered in 1963 during the excavations directed by Živojin Vinčić of the Conservation Institute of Macedonia.[5] This building was razed when the Central Basilica was built, but the lower parts of the N, E, and S walls of Building Two were preserved below the floor (Fig. 1).

---

[4] The Central Basilica is the name recently applied to the basilica formerly called the Synagogue Basilica, W—MZ (1972) 408—411; W—MZ (1973) 391—393; Wiseman, *Guide* 30—33. The hall-like building below it has been called Building Two, W—MZ (1971) 410—411; and Synagogue Two, W—MZ (1972) 409—410; W—MZ (1973) 391. The former is used here. The results of the 1974 excavations in this area, W—MZ (1974) 146—148, have not been incorporated in the present article. Our observations are not contradicted, but new material which requires further study was introduced. It will be treated in the projected final publication. This section of our article has been improved by the remarks of Dean Moe who is engaged in preparing the final publication.

[5] The mosaic is briefly mentioned by R. Pašić-Vinčić, "Poliharmosova Palata, Stobi," *Arch Preg* 5 (1963) 97—98; R. and Ž. Vinčić, "Sinagoga — bazilika," *Arch Preg* 7 (1965) 129—131 and fig. XLVIII; and R. Pašić-Vinčić, "Arheološki ispituvanja na 'Poliharmosovata palata rezidencija na crkovnite velikodostojnici vo Stobi," *Zbornik na arheološkiot muzej Skopje* (1961—1966) 67—75. We are especially grateful to Mr. Vinčić who generously put the more detailed unpublished report of his excavations at our disposal. An English summary of the results of the excavations of the Conservation Institute of Macedonia was published in W—MZ (1971) 410—411. The fragment beneath the N aisle was published as fig. 23. The same article appeared in French in *Arch Jug* 12 (1971) 25—28 and fig. 23. The fragments in the atrium and narthex were published in W—MZ (1972) 409; and W—MZ (1973) 391—392 and fig. 5. The floor was mentioned in Wiseman, *Guide* 31—32. The mosaic was discussed by Dj. Mano-Zissi, "Stratigraphic Problems and the Urban Development of Stobi," *Studies I* 209—210 and fig. 105. He was the first to compare the mosaics of Building Two to the Casino mosaics. See below, note 13.

Figure 1. Schematized plan of Building Two below the Central Basilica showing the location of the mosaics in relationship to the walls. The fragment below the atrium is at the top right, the fragment below the narthex in the upper center, and the main floor at the bottom. Stobi Grid Areas are indicated.

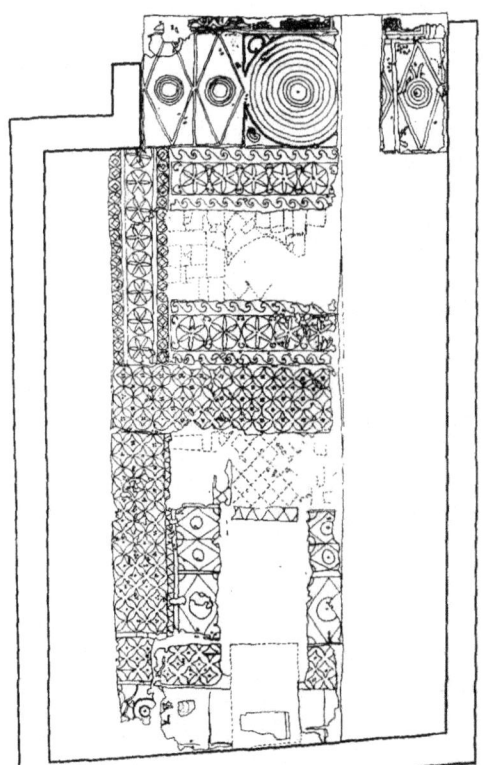

The foundations of the N stylobate and the nave-narthex wall of the Central Basilica were sunk below the level of Building Two, however, and cut through the mosaics. Although it is poorly preserved, most of the floor surface of Building Two E of the nave-narthex wall of the Central Basilica was probably covered with mosaic except for two areas paved with tiles or stones and a strip 1.25 m. wide along the S wall where the foundations of a bench were laid. The mosaic bounded by the N stylobate foundation and the nave-narthex wall of the Basilica and the S and E walls of Building Two was lifted and conserved[6] (Fig. 2). It is presently stored in a depot at Stobi and will eventually be returned to its place. Fragments remain *in situ* to the present time between the N stylobate foundation of the Central Basilica and the N wall of Building Two and below the narthex and the atrium of the Basilica.

There are two distinctly different kinds of mosaic in this floor. One, with extremely coarse and irregularly cut tesserae, comprises most of the pavement. However, a strip about 35 cm. wide along the nave-narthex wall and the two isolated fragments below the narthex and atrium are executed with smaller regularly cut tesserae.

The coarse mosaic is organized into four sections. The first section on the W is a strip approximately 2 m. wide which is divided into three nearly square fields. The central field is inscribed with a circle decorated with concentric rings. *Peltae* fill the two surviving corners of the square. The lateral sections are divided into halves and a diamond is inscribed into each resulting rectangle. Most of one of the diamonds and the edge of the circle was destroyed by the foundation of the N stylobate of the later Basilica. This section of the mosaic is centered between the SW Room and the N wall of Building Two.

Farther to the E is an area which was paved with tiles or flagstones, only the impressions of which were preserved in the mortar. This area is surrounded on three sides by panels of mosaic with rows of circles framing six-pointed stars. The E and W panels are bordered by a wave motif. *Peltae* fill the spaces between the circles and the frame. The panel on the S is bordered by two rows of quatrefoils formed by intersecting circles. These three panels do not form a unified border, but are simply juxtaposed at the corners. The six-pointed star against the E wall of the SW Room is incomplete as if it were intersected by the wall. The room is at least as early as Building Two,[7] however, so one must conclude that the mosaicist simply miscalculated the pattern. It seems probable that another panel of the same design framed this area on the N.

A second paved area E of the first is framed by a design of intersecting circles which form quatrefoils. Three sides of the border survive fairly intact and pieces of the fourth with the same design were found between the N stylobate foundation of the Basilica and the N wall of Building Two. The panels of the border vary in width and are not composed as a single frame. Each side is independently organized: the patterns simply end at the boundaries between two panels without continuity. The W part of the rectangular area surrounded by this design was paved with tiles or flagstones and the E part was set with a mosaic composed of diamonds

---

[6] The mosaic was lifted in 1969 under the supervision of Petrovski who prepared the drawing published as Fig. 2 in order to reassemble the mosaic when it is returned to its place.

[7] The N wall of the SW Room was built directly on top of an earlier wall, probably belonging to Building One.

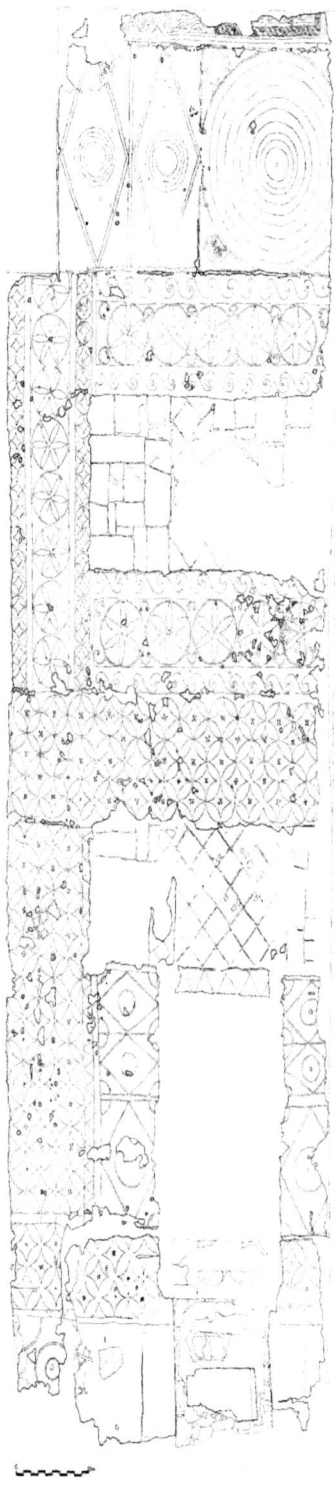

Figure 2. Mosaic from Building Two below the Central Basilica, showing the portion that has been lifted and conserved. The fields of fine mosaics are at the top.

inscribed in rectangular fields. It is similar to the westernmost section of the coarse mosaic. These diamonds and the W section of the coarse mosaic have tesserae up to 4 cm. on a side and contain roughly 15 to 20 tesserae per square decimeter.[8] The tesserae used for the intersecting circles and six-pointed stars are also very irregularly cut, but are somewhat smaller, about 1.5 to 2 cm. on a side. There are approximately 30 to 35 tesserae per square decimeter. Despite the differences in the size of the tesserae, the same materials are used throughout the coarse mosaic. The mosaic is made from a large variety of stones. The background of the designs is made of white marble for the most part; both calcitic and dolomitic marbles are present, but marbles veined in purple, gray, and green are also mixed in, as well as pieces of cipolin — a green marble with a high mica content — gray limestone, and even yellow quartz. The designs are for the most part executed in various shades of red and green: maroon jasper, pink marble, purple marble, gray limestone, green serpentine, green cipolin, and a hard green silicate. Some of the outlines are formed of black glass paste tesserae. The color areas are not pure, but are modulated with a sprinkling of other tesserae.

The floor does not appear to have been planned as a single composition; one field cuts the next; borders and patterns are interrupted. The mosaic is like a patchwork quilt. One might postulate that it was laid over some period of time or during several remodellings. The poor state of preservation of the mosaic, especially the weathering of the mortar, obscured any seams that may have existed in the mortar. But seams between sections of the mosaic are apparent in the tile underpinning beneath the mortar which was excavated under the N part of the mosaic (Fig. 3). What is more, there is a clear line between the tiles underlying the W section, which is composed of a circle and diamonds, and that beneath the immediately adjoining field with six-pointed stars in circles. A line is also visible at the point where two sections of this frame met each other. The W section itself was divided into areas that correspond exactly with the size and position of the preserved fields in the mosaic. Thus, it is clear that the work was divided and the design already planned in the first step of laying the mosaic.

There is no compelling evidence to suggest that the various fields of the coarse mosaic were laid at different times, however, so the seams merely indicate divisions in the work. In fact, the same types of stones are used for the entire mosaic, the underlying stratigraphy is the same, and the mortar bedding was consistent in color and construction. The bedding was laid on an underpinning of tile fragments and a few stones above a thin layer of sand. The tiles and stones were fitted together to cover the surface within each section as completely as possible. A layer of mortar, pink because of a substantial admixture of ground brick, was laid 4—7 cm. thick over the tiles. The rather thick tesserae (1.9—2.0 cm.) were set into a layer of white mortar with some ground brick fragments. This 2—3 cm. thick layer of mortar came up with the tesserae when the mosaic was lifted, leaving the layer of pink mortar in place. The entire profile can be seen only in the fragments presently *in situ* in the N aisle (Fig. 4).

Along the E wall of Building Two, part of the top of the bema and the floor on either side were covered with an even coarser mosaic of roughly cut white marble

---

[8] This measurement was taken by counting the number of tesserae enclosed within a square 10 cm. on a side. The tesserae only partly contained within the square were counted as fractions.

Figure 3. Tile underpinning of the coarse mosaic from Building Two. View from the W. On the left is the foundation wall of the N stylobate of the Central Basilica, on the right the N wall of the SW Room of Building Two. The strip of mortar along the nave-narthex wall is the bedding of the fine mosaic. The field with concentric circles was lifted from the area on the left, the diamonds from the area on the right, parts of two fields of six-pointed stars inscribed in circles from the strip on the E.

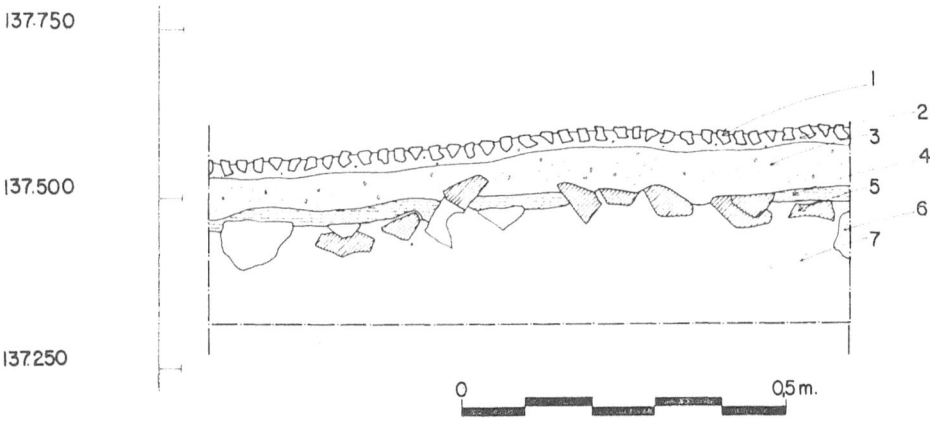

Figure 4. Cross section of the bedding of the coarse mosaic from Building Two. Legend: 1. Mosaic 2. Fine white lime mortar with a small admixture of ground brick 3. Pink mortar containing a large amount of ground brick 4. Sand 5. Tile fragments 6. Stones 7. Earth.

which was in a very poor state of preservation. Only traces of a linear design, perhaps a vine, could be seen on the S. The mortar bedding of this mosaic has not yet been examined.

The narrow fields cut by the nave-narthex wall of the Central Basilica are distinguished from the coarse mosaic by the manner in which they were laid (Fig. 5). Their much smaller, regularly cut tesserae and the varieties of stones that were chosen are likewise significantly different. The tile underpinning of the coarse mosaic had only a few stones, but more stones than tiles were set beneath the fine mosaic. A layer of coarse sandy lime mortar up to 4 cm. thick was poured over the stones to bind them together. Mortar with a substantial admixture of ground brick 3—6 cm. thick was laid over the coarse white mortar and covered with a 1.5 cm. thick coating of fine white mortar into which the tesserae were set. When the mortar of the coarse mosaic was dug away the mortar bed of the fine mosaic was left along the nave-narthex wall of the Central Basilica (Fig. 3). The edge of this 31—36 cm. wide strip of mortar was smooth and even, as if it had been laid up against a hard surface. When the seam between the coarse and the fine mosaics still *in situ* in the N aisle is examined it is clear that the fine mosaic was laid against and partly over the coarser mosaic which was already in place (Fig. 6). The small tesserae even extend slightly over the large ones in places.

The strip of fine mosaic below the N aisle is 37—36.5 cm. wide with quite regularly cut tesserae; most are square, 1.3 cm. on a side; there are about 48 tesserae per square decimeter. The field composed of two colors of scales is intersected by the nave-narthex wall of the Central Basilica.[9] Scales formed of green andesite, yellow tuff, and gray limestone alternate with scales of lustrous red and pink andesite. A border of slightly larger gray-green sandstone and white marble tesserae is set against the coarse mosaic across the whole width of the pavement.

A panel with a similar pattern composed of identical stones was lifted from the mortar backing along the nave-narthex wall that was described above (see upper right corner of Fig. 2). The tesserae of this field are much smaller, 0.7—0.8 cm. on a side; there are as many as 120 tesserae per square decimeter. The field with a scale design is framed with a *quilloche* border. One strand of the braid is composed of a row of white marble, two rows of ocher tuff, and one row of gray-green sandstone. The second strand has rows of gray-green sandstone, white marble, pink and red andesite. The scales of the field are of three colors: one of white marble, beige limestone, and gray-green sandstone; the second of white marble, pink and red andesite; the third of white marble and ocher tuff.

The adjoining field is arranged in a design of gray-green sandstone *peltae* alternately lying on their sides and set upright on a ground of white marble tesserae (see upper left corner of Fig. 2). The spaces formed along the frame are filled with semi-circles and stepped triangles of gray-green sandstone. The tesserae are 1.3 cm. square and closely set, 53 per square decimeter.

Two other fragments of mosaic with small, regularly cut tesserae of this size are still *in situ* W of the nave-narthex wall (see Fig. 1). The first is located beneath the narthex of the Central Basilica at an elevation of 138.394 m., about half

---

[9] We do not think it is a border design as stated by W—MZ (1971) 410, but part of a field cut by the nave-narthex wall.

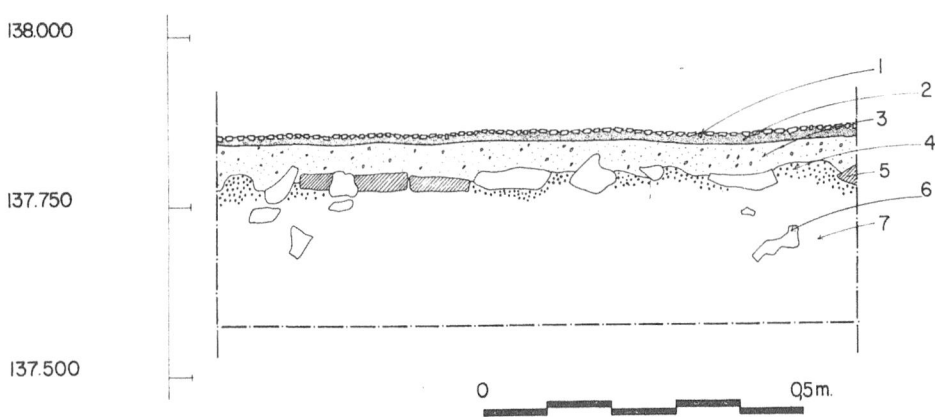

Figure 5. Cross-section of the bedding of the fine mosaic from Building Two. Legend: 1. Mosaic 2. Fine white lime mortar 3. Pink mortar containing a large amount of ground brick 4. Coarse white mortar 5. Tile fragments 6. Stones 7. Earth.

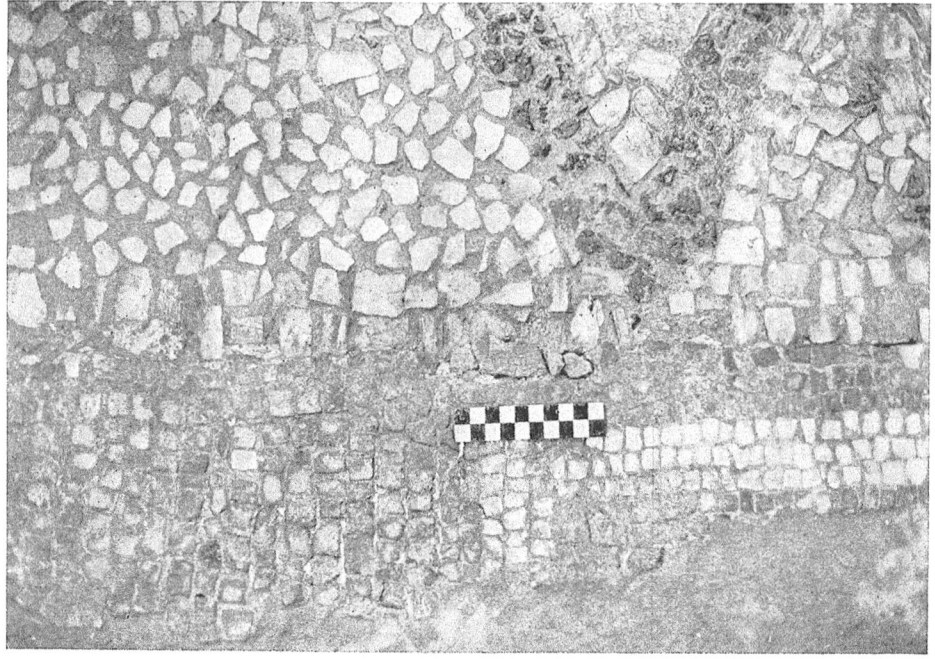

Figure 6. Detail of the mosaic from Building Two *in situ* below the N aisle of the Central Basilica. Note the seam between the fine and coarse mosaics. A few of the fine tesserae overlap the coarse mosaic just above the scale.

a meter higher than the main floor (the highest point on the mosaic still *in situ* below the N aisle is 137.869 m.). A section of this mosaic about 75 by 50 cm. is exposed. It is set in a checkerboard pattern of white marble and dark gray-green sandstone with an occasional red andesite tessera (Fig. 7). A frame of the same colors borders two sides of the design. Along the S side of the mosaic a border of smooth white mortar at the same level as the top of the tesserae indicates that the mosaic floor ended at this point, most probably against some structure of which no trace has been found. The mosaic extends into the scarp on the W and N.

Figure 7. Mosaic from Building Two *in situ* below the narthex of the Central Basilica. The border of white mortar is at the top of the picture.

Another fragment is preserved in a threshold on the N side of the peristyle and was cut by a drain running NE—SW across the atrium (Fig. 8). Its level, 138.921 m., is about a meter higher than the main floor. It has a design of *peltae* arranged as a border around two sides of a rectangular field. The *peltae* are outlined with gray-green sandstone and shaded with pink and red andesite tesserae which are also used for the semi-circles below the *peltae* and a lozenge which extended from the interior to the exterior corner of the frame. Part of one *pelta* and the concentric rings of the circle in the center of the field are set in tesserae of ocher tuff, white marble, and a blue-gray limestone not found elsewhere among the mosaics in

Building Two.[10] These tesserae are unpolished and more irregularly cut and laid than the rest of the fragment. The easily discernible and uneven boundary between the two sections indicates that this is a later repair.

These two fragments, excluding the patch, are identical in material and technique to the strip of fine mosaic which adjoins the coarse pavement. There is no doubt that they all belong to the complex of Building Two, which is thus

Figure 8. Fragment of mosaic from Building Two *in situ* below the atrium of the Central Basilica. The line divides the original mosaic from a repair on the right.

---

[10] It may be significant that these three types of stones are the same as those used for the three-color mosaics in the porticoes of the peristyle and a room of the Theodosian Palace. The date of these mosaics has not yet been archeologically established, but according to style they have been placed in the decades around 400 A. C. Kitzinger, "Survey," 127; Wiseman, *Guide* 47; and Dj. Mano-Zissi, "Stratigraphic Problems and the Urban Development of Stobi," *Studies I* 213.

shown to have extended some distance to the W of the main mosaic pavement. The fine mosaic below the nave was added sometime after the coarse mosaic was already in place. It surely represents a more technically proficient tradition than the rough, clumsy workmanship of the earlier pavement. One can only speculate about the circumstances that brought about the laying of such disparate mosaics adjacent to one another.

The relationship between the main pavement and the fragments in the narthex and atrium is problematic because no architecture that can be related to these mosaic fragments with any degree of certainty has been found, although several trenches have been set in the area. The associated structures were obviously at a higher level than the main part of Building Two: the checkerboard mosaic is 0.525 m. and the fragment preserved in the threshold is 1.052 m. higher than the large pavement. The architecture was evidently razed to the ground to build the atrium of the Central Basilica and only fragments of the mosaics survived by chance. Deposits of the 4th and 5th centuries lay directly above early Roman layers in the atrium and narthex areas so far excavated. The mosaics themselves, however, provide some tenuous evidence about the architecture. The fragment below the atrium is the corner of a field which would have just met the N wall of Building Two if it were extended to the W. The checkerboard fragment has a mortar edge which probably abutted some part of the structure.

The archaeological evidence for the date of the rough mosaic is extensive and consistent. Numerous trenches have been set in the nave and aisles of the Central Basilica below the level of the mosaic floor. The latest coin sealed beneath the mortar bedding of the mosaic, an issue of Licinius I, was found in the E part of the nave.[11] Coins and pottery of the late 3rd century A.C. were also found below the mosaic. The floor was therefore laid after 307—324, most probably in the first half of the 4th century A. C. The fine mosaics were added later, but could be part of the same building campaign or a later elaboration of the W part of the complex. The entire structure was destroyed and the Central Basilica was being constructed above it by the early 5th century A. C.[12]

Technically, the fine mosaic in Building Two relates very closely to the mosaic floor in the Casino.[13] The motifs of the mosaics differ, although both have small-scale geometric designs. They are made of identical stones: white marble, gray-green sandstone, ocher tuff, red and pink andesite. The tesserae are 1.3 cm. squares and there are about 50 tesserae per square decimeter in both cases. There seems little reason to doubt that they are contemporary.

---

[11] Coin 70—112, Field Notebook 11, p. 149. A coin of Constantine, 70—111, was found among disturbed mosaic tesserae below the level of the mosaic along the N wall of Building Two, Context Storage Lot 836, but was not sealed below the mortar.

[12] The fill below the floor of the Central Basilica produced large numbers of mid to late 4th century A. C. coins, and one of the early 5th century A. C. The latest coins were found below the floor of the narthex: Coin 71—114 dates from 383—395, 71—115 from 383—392, 71—119 from 395—408, 71—151 from 383—392. A. C. This material is contained in Context Storage Lot 127.

[13] See above note 5. Dj. Mano-Zissi, *Studies I* 210, fig. 106. We have no archaeological evidence for the date of the Casino mosaics.

THE EPISCOPAL BASILICA

The two superposed mosaics at the E end of the S aisle of the Episcopal Basilica have provided a basis for distinguishing the two major phases of the Basilica itself. The earlier mosaic exposed in 1970 and 1972[14] covered the entire width of the S aisle from the stylobate of the colonnade to the S wall (Figs. 9 and 10). The re-used theater seats which formed the base for a parapet in the second phase were laid on top of the mosaic. Parts of three fields of geometric ornament survive. The same color scheme, limited to white dolomitic marble, greenish-black serpentine, pink brecciated marble, and gray limestone tesserae, is used for all three fields.

The easternmost panel was donated by a "most pious deaconess" according to the votive inscription set into a *tabula ansata* in the lower left corner of the field.[15] It has a border of delicately tapering black vine scrolls on the N and W sides. The heart-shaped leaves are alternately filled in with gray and pink tesserae. An inner chain border of pink and gray links connected to form small circular fields, which contain Maltese crosses, surrounds a black diamond inscribed in a square panel. The diamond is framed with a *guilloche* border and filled with a white "arabesque" design. A pink and a gray *pelta* are set into the corners of the square. A broad band of white and gray tesserae separates this field from the second.

A vine scroll also borders the second and third fields on the N. This border is identical in design and color to the border of the first field, but more densely coiled. It is continuous along the two fields, although one of the tendrils is interrupted by the seam between them. Only the inner border of the second panel is preserved: it is a chain border identical to that of the first field.

The best preserved field, that on the W, is decorated with diamonds and squares. Rows of black diamonds set point to point lengthwise across the panel from E to W are filled with a white "arabesque" design formed of a Maltese cross with curved ends that are extended on the top and bottom with hearts and at each corner by a petal-shaped form. Gray and pink diamonds decorated with four-petalled designs alternate across the field from N to S. Squares are set between the lateral points of the diamonds. They contain a variety of motifs, an interlaced square with a Maltese cross, quatrefoils, an interlaced knot with eight loops and a double *pelta*. The chevron-shaped spaces between the squares and diamonds are filled in with pink or gray tesserae. The designs are bisected by the white border of the field. In the center of the W side of the panel is a votive inscription recording that the mosaic was donated by Peristerias.[16]

The tesserae of this mosaic are comparatively large; most are 2.2 by 2.4 cm., but pieces up to 3.2 cm. on a side are found. They are cut into rather irregular square and rectangular shapes which are closely fitted together. There are an average of 30 tesserae per square decimeter. The tesserae of the inscriptions, however, are much smaller. They are cut into quite precise squares from 0.8—1.0 cm. on

---

[14] W—MZ (1971) 398—400, fig. 1, ills. 3 and 4. French translation in *Arch Jug* 12 (1971) 17—19, figs. 3 and 4, plate I, 1. W—MZ (1973), figs. 11—12; Wiseman, *Guide* 59—60.

[15] Wiseman, *Guide* 59—60; W—MZ (1973) 397 give a reading of the inscription.

[16] W—MZ (1971) 399; Wiseman, *Guide* 59; give a reading of the inscription and suggest that either Peristerias or Peristeria are possible readings for the name. The latter possibility is favored by J. and L. Robert, "Bulletin Epigraphique," *REG* 85 (1972) 416—417.

Figure 10. Drawing of the earlier mosaic in the E end of the S aisle of the Episcopal Basilica showing location of walls and brick substructure. The E end is at the top.

Figure 9. Drawing of the earlier mosaic in the E end of the S aisle of the Episcopal Basilica. The E end is at the top.

a side. The tesserae are set into a 1.0 to 1.5 cm. layer of fine white mortar that was laid over a 5—6 cm. layer of pink mortar containing many brick fragments. Beneath the pink mortar is a layer of coarse white lime mortar, which was poured over a layer of stones. This was put over the layers of earth fill used to raise the level for the floor of the Basilica (Fig. 11).

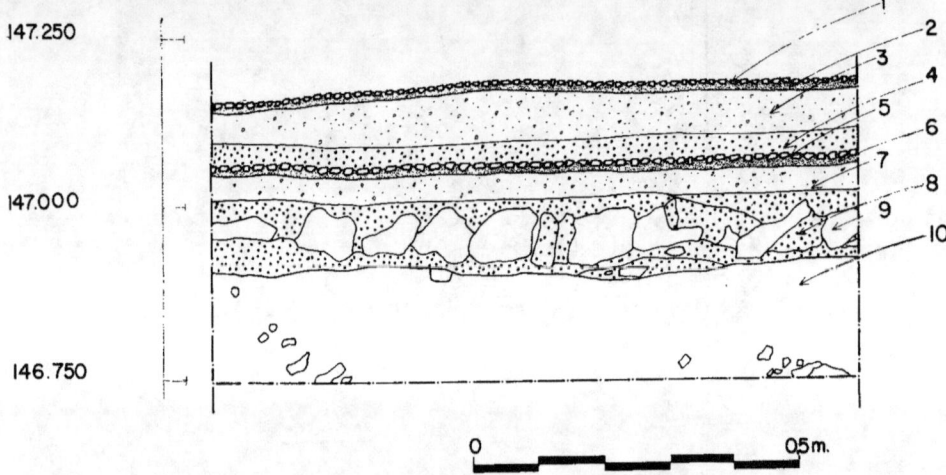

Figure 11. Cross-section of the mosaic beddings in the E end of the S aisle of the Episcopal Basilica. Legend: 1. Later mosaic 2. Fine white mortar with a small admixture of brick fragments 3. Pink mortar containing a large amount of ground brick 4. Coarse white mortar 5. Earlier mosaic 6. Fine white mortar 7. Pink mortar containing a large amount of ground brick 8. Coarse white mortar 9. Stones 10. Earth.

The seams visible between the fields were also clearly apparent in the mortar when the mosaic was lifted (Fig. 12). We can, therefore, be certain that each of the three fields was laid separately. This seems to be significant not only for the method used by the mosaicists, but also as an indication of the nature of the floor. The pattern of each field is independently planned and organized; even the dimensions vary. The first field is 3.25 m. long, the second is 3.50 m. and the third 7.10 m. The first and third fields have donors' inscriptions most probably of different individuals. The second field may well have also had an inscription, but nothing of it survives, or it may be included in the donation of Peristerias, with the seam representing simply a division in the work. The character of the floor as separately donated fields of various sizes is nevertheless clear.

The *terminus post quem* for this mosaic is indicated by the large number of coins sealed beneath it. Most of the legible coins are of the late 4th century A. C. but a few 5th century issues are also present.[17] Sealed in the deposit between

---

[17] W—MZ (1974) 144. Datable coins found below the mosaic include coins 73—58 from 383—392, 73—85 from 383—392, 73—94 from 364—378, 73—97 from 383—392, 73—98 from 383—392, 73—145 from 388—392, 73—153 from 383—392, 73—237 from 364—378, 73—247 from 5th century A. C. all from Context Storage Lot 588. Coin 74—383 from 383—392, 74—386 from 383, 74—387 from 388—392, 74—388 from 383—392, 74—396 from 393—395, 74—426 from 383—392, 74—428 and 74—429 from 5th cen. A. C., 74—430 from 367—375 A. C.

this mosaic and the second phase mosaic was a coin of Honorius (408—423 A.C.);[18] hence, the geometric mosaic can be dated securely to the early 5th century A. C.

The mosaic from the Cemetery Basilica had a geometric carpet identical to this earlier mosaic in the S aisle; they were doubtless laid at the same time.[19] A small fragment of another field of the mosaic from the Cemetery Basilica has been examined. The stones are identical to those of the earlier mosaic in the S aisle: white marble, greenish-black serpentine, gray limestone, and pink brecciated marble.

Figure 12. Earlier mosaic in the S aisle of the Episcopal Basilica as it was being lifted, taken from the N. Note the seam between the two mosaic fields both in the mosaic itself and in the underlying mortar.

The later mosaic in the S aisle of the Episcopal Basilica, a figural composition in a poor state of preservation, was discovered in 1972,[20] and certainly belongs to

---

[18] Coin 72—465, Context Storage Lot 796, W—MZ (1973) 397—398.
[19] W—MZ (1971) 404. A photograph of the mosaic now reportedly destroyed was published by H. Dragendorff, "Archäologische und kunstwissenschaftliche Arbeit während des Weltkrieges in Mazedonien," Kunstschutz in Kriege II, ed. P. Clemen, 158. The same article was published in Zeitschrift für bildende Kunst n. F. 30 (1919) 262. The fragment in a poor state of preservation was found, lifted, and conserved by Petrovski in 1969.
[20] W—MZ (1973) 397—398, figs. 10—11; Wiseman, Guide 60—61, illustrated in color fig. 12.

the same floor found and described by Saria[21] (Fig. 13). It was laid only from the base of the screen to the S wall of the Basilica, and is thus 1.30 m. narrower than the earlier mosaic. The tesserae are considerably smaller, averaging 1.5 cm. on a side, although pieces as small as 0.7 and as large as 2.3 cm. are also present. Most are square or rectangular, but triangular and irregular tesserae are quite frequent, especially within the figures, where there are 50 tesserae per square decimeter compared to 45 in the border ornament.

Before the later mosaic was laid the irregularly sunken surface of the earlier pavement was levelled with from 3 to 30 cm. of coarse white mortar and earth fill (Fig. 11). A layer of pink mortar about 4 cm. thick was laid on this surface. The tesserae were set in a 1 cm. thick layer of fine white mortar with a few brick fragments.

Remains of four fields of figural decoration arranged two by two across the aisle survive. Only a few tesserae of the eastern pair are preserved: one field contains the hind leg and tail of a quadruped, the other what may be a bird's head. More extensive parts of the next two fields on the E remain. The northern field contains a host of sea creatures, the other beasts that inhabit the earth. They are framed by a *guilloche* border, which is more colorful than the borders of the earlier mosaic. One strand is composed of deep yellow terracotta or tuff and white dolomitic marble tesserae, the other of purple limestone, pink brecciated marble, gray limestone and white marble. Both strands are outlined with dark gray-black limestone. The seascape is full of action: long legged birds and a water snake catch fish, various species of fish arch their backs and leap from the water or flee from the hungry predators, a squid and an octopus seize their prey, a crustacean and a shellfish rest peacefully. All the animals are rendered in outlines filled in with bright colors on a white marble background. A great variety

---

[21] A part of the border was evidently found by Egger, "Gradska crkva u Stobima," *Glasnik* 5 (1929) 38. He described a small piece of mosaic "in the left aisle" that was in the "simple black and white style decorated with circular strips." From the context it seems that he is probably refering to the S aisle, but it is not at all certain whether he is describing the earlier or later phase mosaic. It was probably the later phase, however, as Saria continued Egger's work and completely exposed several fields of that mosaic as is evident from the following description paraphrased from B. Saria, "Novi nalasci u episkopskoj crkvi u Stobima," *Glasnik* 12 (1933) 13—14. "The remains of six fields were still preserved in the S aisle. Only enough of the first field was left to indicate that there had once been representations. Just a bit of the braid surrounding the second field was preserved. One corner of the third field was exposed. It contained water creatures: a large polyp, a water snake, a red crab, a squid and various fish. In the fourth field were wild animals of the earth, a rhinoceros of gray tesserae with white incisors, two tigers in combat, a large yellow animal surely a lioness and other animals which cannot be identified. In the fifth field the remains of a deer's head were preserved and in the sixth various birds. In the western part of the S aisle the mosaics were destroyed, but they surely existed as the badly damaged backing of a floor mosaic was found over most of the aisle." After uncovering and photographing the mosaic Saria covered it with cardboard and earth. When he returned to Stobi in 1932 he noted that the mosaic was almost completely destroyed by visitors who took tesserae for souvenirs. Some fragments must have remained, however, as it seems that the mosaic which still survives is probably that which he described. W—MZ (1973) 397, note 21 are of the opinion that he found the fragments he described farther W. Without photographs or plans of the earlier excavations it is really impossible to be sure.

Figure 13. Reconstruction of the later mosaic in the E end of the S aisle of the Episcopal Basilica. Extant sections are heightened. The E end is at the top.

———→

of tesserae are used to portray the sea creatures: white dolomitic marble, light blue calcitic marble, pink brecciated marble, gray marble, a variety of limestones, gray, yellow-gray, reddish purple, brown, gray-black, a yellow to red tuff or terracotta, and red-orange terracotta. The same kinds of tesserae are used to depict the animals in the adjoining field. Two leopards in combat are executed in light blue marble tesserae, a wild boar in brown limestone. Fragments of other animals, perhaps deer, a fox, and a bear, are composed of ocher and dark gray-black limestone.

Along the E side of these two fields is a vine scroll border rendered in dark gray-black tesserae on a white marble ground and a fragment of a field of interlacing bands of the same colors as the *guilloche* borders. This field may be reconstructed as a design of intersecting cushion shapes that form curvilinear octagons (Fig. 13). The reconstruction seems reasonable in view of the fact that the dimensions of the aisle allow for a symmetrical development of this pattern from the surviving fragment, if one assumes that the vine scroll border framed all four sides of the field.

The mosaic of the second phase seems to be laid out according to a comprehensive plan, in contrast to the first phase mosaic which has clearly divided fields of unequal size, evidently donated by various individuals. The dimensions of the fields are constant and have been based on the length of the aisle. According to a reconstruction by Živojin Radošević, twelve such fields and their borders together with the repeated end panels correspond exactly to the total length of the aisle[22] (Fig. 14).

The mosaics of the narthex almost certainly belong to the same building phase.[23] Seven of the eight fields in the center of the narthex and parts of the lateral sections are preserved. Technically the narthex mosaics are virtually identical

---

[22] There may also have been a correspondence between the fields of the mosaic and the intercolumniations of the colonnade. According to Egger, *Glasnik* 5 (1929) 17, there were 13 columns on each side.

The brick and mortar substructure that cuts the earlier mosaic(see Fig. 10) is to be associated with the later mosaic as its position corresponds with the space within the frame of the third field from the E on the side along the nave. See Fig. 14.

[23] W—MZ (1971) 398, note 18, first associated the narthex mosaic with the earlier phase in the S aisle, but the re-discovery of the later mosaic has clarified the relationships of the mosaics in the Episcopal Basilica. W—MZ (1973) 397, described the style of the animal scenes in the S aisle as identical to the animal scenes in the mosaic of the narthex. Wiseman, *Guide* 60—61, noted the similarities in style between the narthex and the later phase mosaic in the S aisle, but also pointed out that the geometrical motifs in the earlier phase of the S aisle are identical to certain motifs in the narthex.

The narthex mosaic has an extensive bibliography: V. Petković, "Report on 1931," *Godišnjak* 40 (1931) 221—222; B. Saria, "Novi nalasci u episkopskoj crkvi u Stobima," *Glasnik* 12 (1933) 12—16, figs. 4—6; idem. "Neue Funde in der Bischofskirche von Stobi," *JÖAI* 28 (1933) 116—119, figs. 4—6; Dj. Mano-Zissi, "Mosaiken in Stobi," *BIABulg* 10 (1936) 277—279, 289—292, figs. 167, 170, 173—179; idem. "Mozaici u Stobima," *Umetnički pregled* 1 (1937—1938) no. 1, pp. 8—10, 2 illustrations; Kitzinger, "Survey," 107—108, 138, note 258, figs. 145—147, 210; Dj. Mano-Zissi, "Prolegomena uz probleme kasnoantičkog mozaika u Ilirikumu," *Zbornik* 2 (1958—1959) 93, 94, 96, fig. 8; idem. "La question des différentes écoles de mosaïques gréco-romaines de Yougoslavie et essai d'une esquisse de leur évolution," *La mosaïque gréco-romaine* (Paris 1963) 293, fig. 24; R. Hoddinott, *Early Byzantine Churches in Macedonia and Southern Serbia* (London 1963) 164—165, pls. 41, 42. The mosaics have been consistently dated to the late 5th century A. C. or ca. 500 A. C. A test trench below the level of the narthex mosaic in 1974 produced four coins, 74—245, 74—246, 74—251 and 74—252, none of which was legible, but one, 74—245, was a 5th century A. C. issue; it was embedded in the mortar.

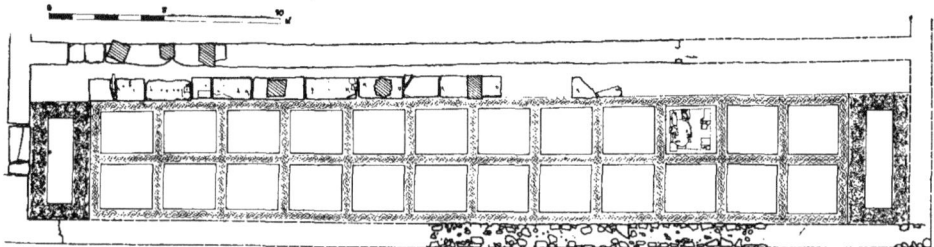

Figure 14. Reconstruction of the later mosaic from the Episcopal Basilica, entire S aisle, showing the location of the brick substructure. The E end is at the right.

to the later phase of the S aisle. The tesserae are of the same size and shapes; both are laid in white mortar with a few brick fragments (Fig. 15). Below the white mortar of the narthex mosaic is a 5—6 cm. layer of mortar with a substantial admixture of ground brick and from 10—11 cm. of a rough, sandy, white mortar with some small stones and loose mosaic tesserae mixed into it. This mortar overlies a 4 to 5 cm. thick layer of pink mortar which must have been the bedding of an earlier mosaic. The tesserae mixed into the rough mortar probably came from that mosaic. Below the mortar layers is an earth fill. The types of stones and terracotta used in the narthex mosaic are the same as those of the later mosaic in the S aisle with one exception. A few serpentine tesserae are found in the narthex mosaic, but this variety of stone does not appear in the preserved fragments from the S aisle.

Similarities are especially apparent in the composition and execution of the border ornament. Sections of the border of a field survive in the S part of the narthex. It is a *guilloche* identical to the borders of the panels in the S aisle. The

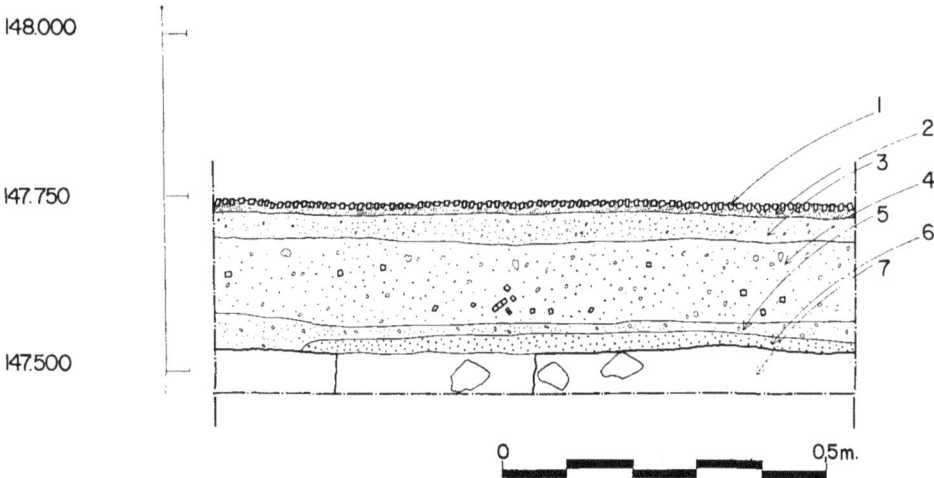

Figure 15. Cross-section of the narthex mosaic. Legend: 1. Mosaic 2. Fine white mortar with a small admixture of ground brick 3. Pink mortar containing a large amount of ground brick 4. Coarse white mortar with some stones and mosaic tesserae 5. Pink mortar containing a large amount of ground brick 6. Ash 7. Earth.

border of the central narthex panels is a different pattern; a linked chain forming circular fields. The links of the chain, however, are composed in exactly the same manner as the strands of the *guilloche* borders. That is, the links are made either of a row of gray-black limestone, a row of purple limestone, two to three rows of pink brecciated marble, two rows of white marble and a row of gray-black tesserae, or with yellow and ocher tesserae substituted for the purple and pink. These two colors of links are alternated around the fields.

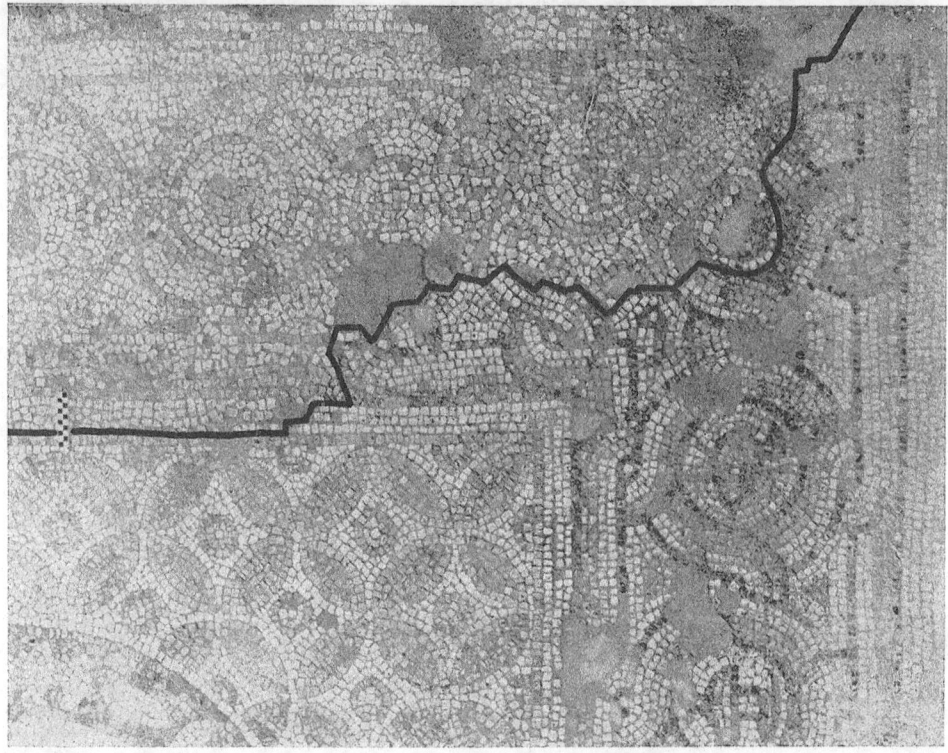

Figure 16. Detail of the NE corner of the narthex mosaic showing an ancient repair above the line.

Thus, we have rather strong evidence that the entire narthex and S aisle were paved with an extensive and elaborate mosaic in one campaign. No traces of mosaic have yet been found in the N aisle or nave.

These mosaics were laid after 408—423 A. C., the possible date of the coin of Honorius sealed beneath the S aisle mosaic. A rough sandstone floor was laid in the aisle sometime after mid 5th century, but probably not until the early 6th century A. C.[24] The narthex mosaics evidently remained in use for some time as they were repaired at least twice. They were patched with crude mosaic along the N side of the central section and near the threshold into the nave (Fig. 16), and again with mortar and tiles in front of the entrance into the nave.

[24] See above note 16. The dating is discussed in W—MZ (1973) 397—398 and Wiseman *Guide* 60—61.

THE BAPTISTERY OF THE EPISCOPAL BASILICA

The Baptistery of the Episcopal Basilica (Fig. 17), discovered in 1971,[25] is paved with a handsome floor mosaic. The color scheme is rather restricted, being limited to six colors: a fine-grained white dolomitic marble and a greenish

Figure 17. Composite photograph of the mosaic in the Baptistery of the Episcopal Basilica.

black serpentine predominate and are enlivened by a yellow-gray to gray limestone, pink brecciated marble, yellow marble, and red-orange terracotta. The tesserae are square or rectangular for the most part, although some triangular and irregularly

---

[25] V. McKeen, "A New Baptistery at Stobi," *AJA* 76 (1972) 215; W—MZ (1972) 422—424, figs. 41, 42 and 47; Wiseman, *Guide* 62—66, fig. 13; a discussion of the iconography is offered by I. Nikolajević, "Povodom najnovije diskusije o ranohrišćanskim krstionicama u Saloni," *Zbornik radova vizantološkog instituta* 14—15 (1973) 163—170.

shaped pieces are noticeable. Their edges are rather unevenly cut, and thus the interstices are a prominent element of the floor. Most of the tesserae range in size from 1.3—1.5 cm., although smaller fragments and an occasional larger piece are apparent. The tesserae cut from the yellow marble, however, are much smaller and quite irregular in shape, from 0.9—1.0 cm. In areas of background and ornament there are 50 to 55 tesserae per square decimeter, while within the figures there are from 58 to 66 per square decimeter. The tesserae are set into a 1.5—2 cm. thick layer of fine white mortar with a moderate admixture of crushed brick. This is laid over a 5 to 7 cm. thick layer of pink mortar with many brick fragments. Beneath the pink mortar is a layer of coarse white lime mortar. A few stones are set between the mortar and the earth fill (Fig. 18).

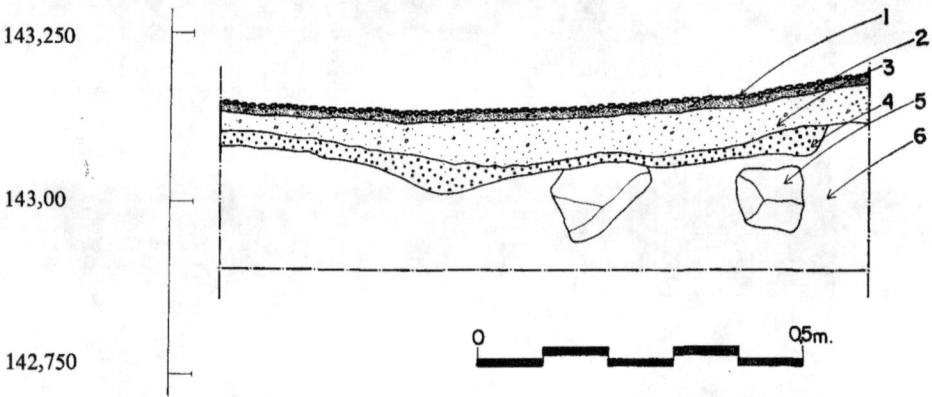

Figure 18. Cross-section of the bedding of the Baptistery mosaic. Legend: 1. Mosaic 2. Fine white mortar with a small admixture of ground brick 3. Pink mortar containing a large amount of ground brick 4. Coarse white mortar 5. Stones 6. Earth.

The five doorways of the Baptistery are paved with mosaic in a scale design. Each scale is framed by a double row of white marble tesserae that are bounded on either side by a row of black. The interior colors are gray and pink; the scales alternate in color. On the E and W sides of the piscina are niches paved with a design of rays around a semi-circle that has the same color scheme as the scales pattern. The E niche has ten rays, the W eight rays. Each ray is framed by white marble and outlined in black; they are alternately filled in by rose brecciated marble and gray limestone. The semi-circle is of gray limestone.

A *guilloche* surrounds the main part of the floor on both sides and divides it into four fields. The braids which separate the fields are continuous with the outer frame, but are continuous with the inner frame only on the N and probably the S sides; they are clearly separated from the inner frame on the E and W sides. One strand of the *guilloche* is always composed of three rows of gray tesserae and two of white marble bounded on either side by black. The second strand has two to three rows of pink breccia and two of white marble and is also outlined by black.

The braid is highlighted by a single white tessera placed on either side of the braid at each point where the strands overlap and in the middle of each loop.

The floor is composed of four main fields of irregular shape. Each field has an independent inner frame of black tesserae. Two peacocks face each other on either side of a kantharos in the NE and SW fields and a pair of deer frame a goblet-shaped vessel in the NW and SE fields.

The peacocks have black bodies and legs; the wings are yellow with a white border, the effect of feathers is given by black lines. The tails are pink breccia with the "eyes" outlined in black and filled in with yellow and white. Above the back of each peacock is a leafy branch of black tesserae which bears fruit and flowers of rose marble highlighted with yellow and shaded with red terracotta tesserae. Below the peacocks are a pair of ducks with yellow heads, rose breasts and tails, gray wings and red-orange terracotta beaks and feet.

The birds are arranged on either side of a large "candy-striped" kantharos. The vessel is emphatically outlined and the handles indicated by two rows of black tesserae. The base has a rose breccia rectangle at the bottom and a gray pyramid at the top. A pink circle connects the base with the bell-shaped body of the vessel, which is decorated by gray, pink, and yellow petal shapes outlined by black and framed with white marble. The straight neck of the kantharos is decorated by yellow and pink and red-orange petals. The lip of the vessel and the pine-cone fountain are rose breccia and the flowing water is indicated by black, white, and gray tesserae. The composition is gracefully fitted into the niche by two tapering leaves filled in with gray. The two fields with peacocks are virtually identical, except for slight variations in the branches and placement of the ducks and the addition of a plant in the NE field.

The NW and SE fields with their pairs of deer show more variation. The bodies of all the deer are firmly outlined with black and modelled with gray, yellow, pink, and white tesserae. The shading is accomplished by using the darkest color for the outline and progressively lighter colors towards the middle of the forms. Between colors a row of tesserae alternating the two colors on either side forms a transition. Sometimes the vari-colored tesserae are not arranged strictly according to rows, but randomly scattered in the areas with middle tones to produce a dappled effect. The tongues of the deer are red-orange terracotta. The foliage in these two fields is rendered with the same greenish-black as on the other panels. In the NW panel the deer on the right has a leafy branch over his back, as the peacocks do, while that on the left stands in front of a tree, as do both deer in the SE panel. Other sprigs of foliage are scattered across the fields to fill empty spaces. Below the deer stand two long-legged birds with yellow wings outlined with white, black bodies, red-orange beaks, combs and feet. The vessels in the centers of these compositions are nearly identical. The base is formed of a rose marble pyramid placed on a gray rectangle. A spindle-shaped form between two rose circles is filled in with red-orange terracotta framed by white marble. The bell-shaped body of the vessel is decorated by two rose breccia and three red-orange terracotta petals, framed by white and outlined with black tesserae. The upper part of the vase and the water are the same as in the peacock fields.

The niche in the NW panel is composed differently than in the other three fields of the Baptistery. The gray acanthus leaves on either side of the base do not follow the lines of the niche but curve out from the border and form small arched fields in which ducks are placed. The ducks both face towards the N, thus disrupting the symmetry of the field. The ducks have black heads, pink breasts and gray wings. This unique and rather awkward solution for the composition of the irregularly shaped field seems to result from fitting the design for a rectangular field, like that of the House of Psalms (Fig. 22), into a niche.[26]

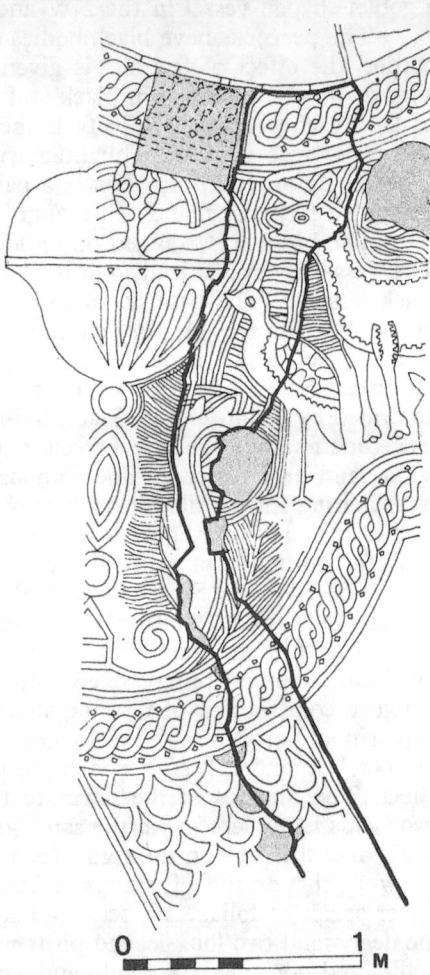

Figure 19. Repair of the Baptistery mosaic, SE field.

Figure 20. Drawing of the repair of the Baptistery mosaic, SE field.

The SE field is more successfully composed, the acanthus leaves follow the curve of the niche and the ducks are omitted. This field was damaged when

---

[26] This might be an example of the adaptation of a cartoon to a field of a different shape than that for which it was intended. Nikolajević, op. cit. (in note 25) 164, discusses the possibility that patterns or cartoons were used to transfer designs for mosaic floors.

the floor was dug up to remove the lead pipe which supplied water to the piscina.[27] An ancient restoration cuts across the field from above the head of the deer on the right to the SE doorway. It is 40 cm. wide along the piscina extending exactly from the location of the column base to the corner of the niche (Figs. 19—21). The long narrow shape of the patch might indicate the laying of a pipe to supply or drain water, but a test trench set outside the SE doorway failed to find any trace of it. The artisan who repaired the mosaic used the same kinds of stones as from the rest of the floor, but they are larger and more roughly cut and laid; they might be the original tesserae carelessly placed on their sides. There are approximately 33 tesserae per square decimeter in the head of the deer compared to 66 tesserae per square decimeter in the heads of the original deer. The tesserae are not laid in the approximately horizontal rows of the rest of the floor, but have been set vertically following the shape of the patch. The restorer attempted to reproduce the design of the original field, although the broad, crudely repaired head of the deer is easily distinguished from those of the original mosaic; the shape of the vessel is simplified; the end of the acanthus leaf ends not with a crisp spiral, but with a limp curve. The scales pattern of the SE entryway was restored using the wrong colors, pink rather than gray and gray in place of pink, so that three two-toned scales result. The most interesting "mistake" is in the upper braid border, where the restorer ended the braid with a loop up against the column base rather than continuing the pattern, and extended the black tesserae of the inner frame upwards, interrupting the continuous band of white tesserae. This indicates that the column base cemented to the mosaic surface was already in place when the restoration was made.

Other observations on the mosaic pavement offer some evidence for a sequence of remodellings in the Baptistery.[28] During the repair of the piscina it was noticed that the mosaic pavement extends beneath the slate and marble revetment of the piscina up to the brick structure of the basin itself in some places (Fig. 21). We may safely conclude that the piscina was faced after the mosaic was laid. This may be interpreted to mean that the piscina had a thinner revetment or covering when the mosaic was laid and that the first revetment was replaced by the slate and marble slabs or simply that the floor was laid before the revetment was put in place during a single phase of construction. The relation of the border to the piscina supports the former theory as the revetment overlaps nearly a third of the width of the border at some points. The border is also overlapped about 6 cm. by the wall frescoes still *in situ*. These simple geometric frescoes covered more elaborate figural compositions in some places. The relation of the mosaic to the earlier frescoes is not clear, but we can be sure the mosaic predates the outer layer of fresco. The addition of the revetment and/or the later fresco may or may not correspond with the placement of six columns with Ionic bases which were cemented onto the surface of the mosaic. The columns and revetment were both in place, however, when the mosaic was restored, because at the point of the repair the mosaic only extends up to the slate and marble slabs of the revetment. The mosaic was repaired with mortar patches at a still later date.

---

[27] W—MZ (1973) 398.
[28] Other points relative to the "phases" of the Baptistery are discussed in the article by W. B. Dinsmoor, Jr. in this volume.

The archaeological evidence for the date of the Baptistery mosaic is indirect. The early 5th century A. C. construction date of the Episcopal Basilica provides a *terminus post quem*. Excavations below the level of the mosaics on the S produced a large number of coins dating as late as the mid 5th century A. C., but they may have been deposited during the life of the Baptistery.[29] Excavations W of the Baptistery in 1973[30] revealed a number of walls which belonged to building phases earlier than the Baptistery and were dismantled after the late 4th or early

Figure 21. Detail of the relationship of the piscina, mosaic and ancient repair during conservation when the revetment of the piscina was removed. View from SE. Note the mortar which cemented a column base in place and how the restorer finished the braid border up against it with a row of black tesserae and a loop in the braid. The original mosaic extends nearly up to the brick structure of the piscina, while the repair extended only up to the revetment.

5th century A. C. Beneath the floor which overlay the dismantled walls a coin of Arcadius dating from 395 to 408 A. C. was found; 4th and 5th century pottery was found at lower levels.[31] Thus, the archaeological evidence suggests a 5th century A. C. construction date. The area was probably destroyed in the late 6th century. The latest coin below the debris was found S of the Baptistery and is an issue of Justin II, 565—578 A. C.[32]

---

[29] W— MZ (1973) 398— 399.
[30] W— MZ (1974) 144. A test trench E of the Baptistery below the level of the mosaic did not produce evidence helpful for a more precise date.
[31] Coin 73—25, Context Storage Lot 950. The pottery is contained in Context Storage Lots 951, 952, 953.
[32] Coin 72—63, Context Storage Lot 649.

The Baptistery mosaic matches the earlier mosaic in the S aisle of the Episcopal Basilica fairly closely in material, but it also has elements in common with the later phase. The same serpentine, pink brecciated marble, white marble, and gray limestone are used both in the earlier mosaic of the Basilica and the Baptistery mosaic. The black tesserae in the later phase of the S aisle and the narthex are different, being cut from a gray-black limestone. The drab color scheme of the earlier mosaic in the S aisle is supplemented in the Baptistery, however, with yellow marble and red-orange terracotta tesserae. Terracotta tesserae are also used in the later phase of the S aisle.

The technique of laying the bedding is similar for the earlier mosaic of the Basilica and the Baptistery because a layer of rough, sandy mortar and some stones underlie the pink mortar of both mosaics. This may be a workshop tradition significant in relating the two mosaics, but other factors may be responsible. This layer may have been omitted in the later phase of the S aisle because the earlier mosaic beneath made it unnecessary.

Figure 22. Mosaic in the triclinium of the House of Psalms.

The earlier phase in the Basilica has about 30 tesserae per square decimeter, the later phase 45 tesserae per square decimeter in background areas, and the Baptistery has 50 to 55 tesserae per square decimeter in the background areas. The size of tesserae is not an infallible indicator, however, varying as it does even between areas within the same mosaic. The closeness of the Baptistery and the later phase mosaic may simply reflect the fact that both have figural motifs of a similar scale.³³ The Baptistery mosaics, therefore, have technical characteristics in common with both mosaics in the S aisle of the Episcopal Basilica, and might be chronologically between them as well.

The Stobi mosaic most comparable to the Baptistery mosaic is unquestionably the composition of deer in the triclinium of the House of Psalms (Fig. 22). The mosaics are indeed strikingly similar,³⁴ but certain differences are apparent upon technical examination. The mosaic in the House of Psalms is composed of tesserae that are on the whole more evenly cut than those of the Baptistery. There are fewer small, irregularly shaped tesserae used, so that the mosaic surface has a more regular appearance and the number of tesserae is approximately 5 less per square decimeter than the Baptistery mosaic, i. e., from 45 to 50 in background and border areas. The material also varies slightly, the blackish-green serpentine, white marble, brecciated pink marble, red-orange terracotta and gray limestone, although somewhat lighter in color, are used in the House of Psalms as they are in the Baptistery. The yellow marble however, which forms the wings of the peacocks and models the bodies of the deer in the Baptistery is not used at all in the House of Psalms. An ocher limestone and a rose limestone together with the white marble and pink brecciated marble model the bodies of the deer in the House of Psalms, which is thus somewhat more colorful than the Baptistery mosaic. The mosaic in the triclinium of the House of Psalms is executed with a meticulous precision not seen in the Baptistery. This is especially apparent when one compares the rendering of the bodies of the deer. The careful alternation of colors is so pronounced that the white highlights across the body of the deer produce a comb-like effect compared with the more fuzzy dappling of the deer in the Baptistery. Nevertheless, there is little doubt that the two mosaics are rather close in date and that they represent the same tradition or school.

---

³³ The fact that the earlier mosaic in the S aisle is purely geometric and the Baptistery has a rich figural decoration is no reason in itself to consider them separately. The mosaic from the Cemetery Basilica had fields decorated with animals as well as fields of pure geometric ornament according to the description by H. Dragendorff in *Kunstschutz in Kriege II* 162; see above note 19.

³⁴ Wiseman, *Guide* 63. The House of Psalms has an extensive bibliography: V. Petković, "Report on 1932," *Godišnjak* 41 (1932) 208 –210; J. Petrović, "Report on 1932," *Godišnjak* 41 (1932) 234– 235; idem. "Stobi 1932," *Starinar*, 8– 9 (1933– 1934) 173—177, 182; Dj. Mano-Zissi, "Mozaici jedne kuće u Stobima," *Starinar* 8—9 (1933—1934) 249—254, figs. 7—13; idem. Mozaici u Stobima," *Umetnički pregled* 1 (1937—1938) no. 1, pp. 8—10, 1 illustration; Kitzinger, "Survey," pp. 134—138, figs. 193– 196; Dj. Mano-Zissi, "Prolegomena uz probleme kasnoantičkog mozaika u Ilirikumu," *Zbcrnik* 2 (1958– 1959) 93—96, figs. 6—7; *Idem*, "La question des différentes écoles de mosaïques gréco-romaines de Yougoslavie et essai d'une esquisse de leur évolution," *La mosaïque gréco-romaine* (Paris 1963) 293, fig. 23; Ž. Vinčić, "Poliharmosova palata, Stobi," *Arch Preg* 5 (1963) 97—98; R. Pašić-Vinčić, "Arheološka ispituvanja na 'Poliharmosova palata' rezidencija na crkovnite velikodostojnici vo Stobi," *Zbornik na arheološkiot muzej Skopje* (1961—1966) 67—75; W—MZ (1971) 406—411; J.—P. Sodini, "Mosaïques paléochrétiennes de Grèce," *BCH* 94 (1971) 747—748; K. Petrov, "Neobjasnete mesta na dve hristijanski alegoriski mozaični kompozicii," *Zbcrnik Skopje* 23 (1971) 299—305; Wiseman, *Guide* 34—36, fig. 4; I. Nikolajević, "Povodom najnovije diskusije o ranohrišćanskim krstionicama u Saloni," *Zbornik radova vizantološkog instituta* 14—15 (1973) 165—166, 169; Dj. Mano-Zissi, "Stratigraphic Problems and the Urban Development of Stobi," *Studies I* 209, 220, fig. 111; Kitzinger dated the mosaics to the first half of the fifth century and this dating has generally been accepted, although Vinčić dated the mosaic later 450—500 and W—MZ (1971) 411 associated it with the 4th century Building Two.

EPISCOPAL BASILICA SOUTH

During the 1971 and 1972 seasons a great number of mosaic fragments ranging in size from single tesserae to chunks 40 cm. on a side, was recovered S of the Episcopal Basilica and W of the Baptistery[35] (Fig. 23). Some of the mosaic fragments were found in a thick layer of destruction debris comprising large stones,

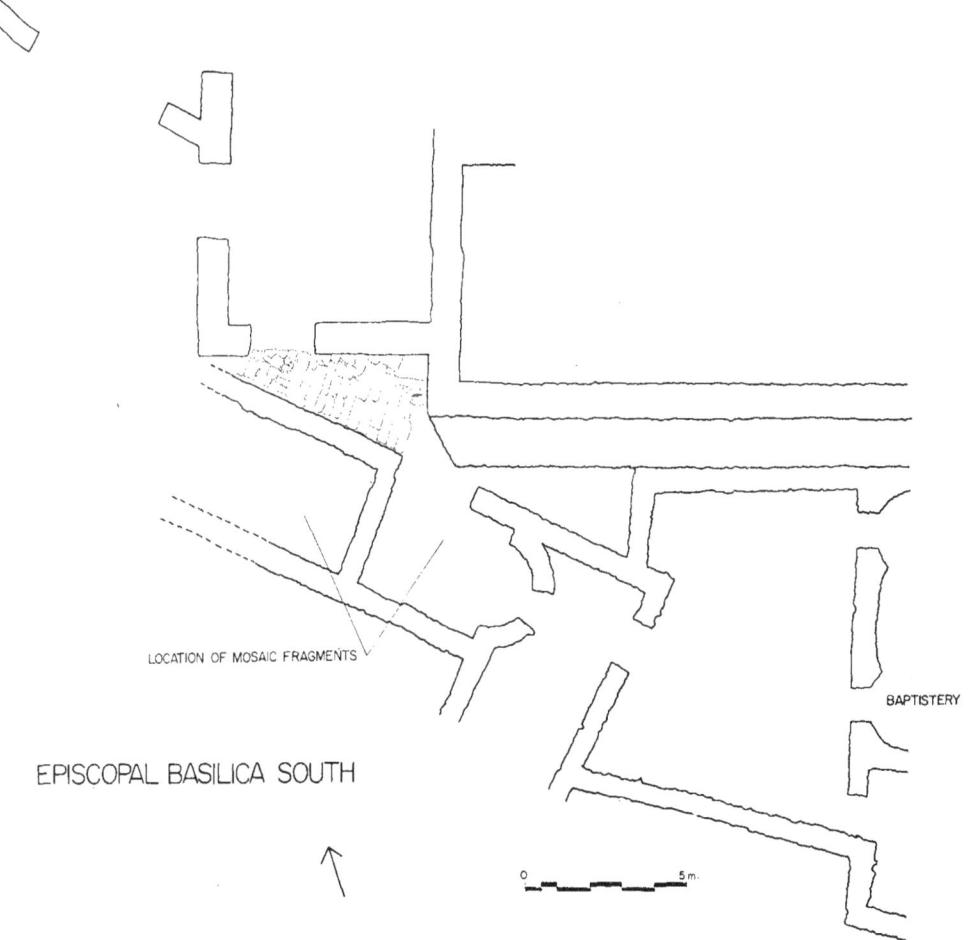

Figure 23. Plan of the area S of the Episcopal Basilica where fragments of mosaic were found.

---

[35] The area was divided approximately in half. The N half was dug in 1971 and S half in 1972. The E end of the apse, however, was dug in its entire width in 1971. The mosaic fragments found in the N half of the room were generally less well preserved than those in the S. Signs of burning were more intense in the N half. A few pieces of mosaic were also found immediately to the E of the apsidal room. Descriptions of work in the area were published in W—MZ (1972) 42 and W—MZ (1973) 398.

mortar, bricks, tiles, and many fresco fragments[36] and others were in a deposit of earth immediately beneath. The latter deposit contained ashes and large burned pieces of wood in some areas.[37] These mosaics are clearly parts of a pavement because the backing is a quite thick 6—10 cm. layer of pink mortar, the interstices are filled with mortar, and the tesserae have been smoothed--in some sections more than others-either as the result of traffic or a final polishing after the mosaic was laid. None of these features is characteristic of wall mosaics.[38] The deposit containing the mosaic fragments, however, overlay all the floors and possible use levels of the rooms in which they were found. The manner in which the pieces were evenly dispersed throughout the two rooms and stratified within the destruction debris eliminates the possibility that they were dumped. They must, therefore, have fallen from an upper floor. The shape and dimensions of the reconstructed mosaic[39] indicate that it belonged to a room or rooms directly above the rooms where the fragments were found. The large pieces of burned wood probably are the remains of timbers that formed part of the substructure of the floor of the upper story. The wooden beams burned and fell in, the floor above was weakened, the mosaic fell and broke into pieces, some fragments face upward, others face down, finally, perhaps after some time, the stones of the walls and the frescoes applied to them fell on top.

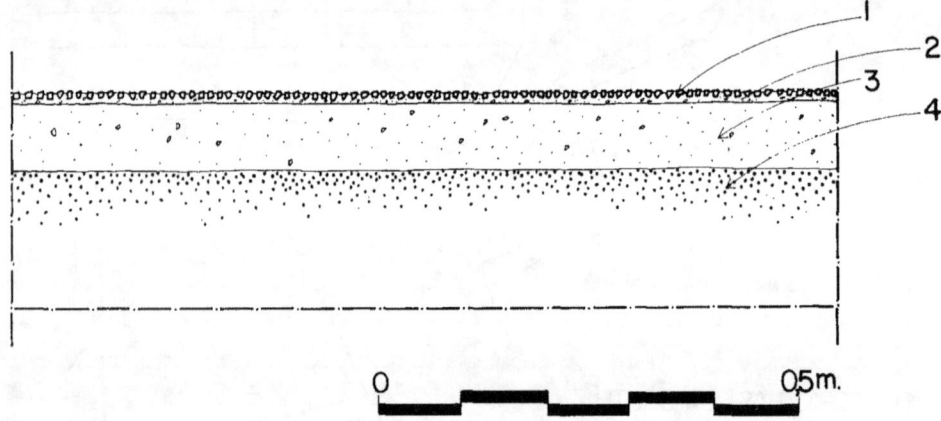

Figure 24. Cross-section of the bedding of the mosaic fragments found S of the Episcopal Basilica. Legend: 1. Mosaic 2. White mortar with an admixture of ground brick 3. Pink mortar containing a large amount of ground brick 4. Traces of coarse white mortar.

Although the mosaics were laid on the floor of an upper story, the technique is exactly the same as when a floor mosaic is laid directly on the ground. When the mortar is preserved in its entire thickness several layers are apparent (Fig. 24).

---

[36] Context Storage Lots 318, 321, 322, 323, 732.
[37] Context Storage Lots 324, 325, 328, 336 and 733 in the apsidal room, Lots 350 and 746 in the rectangular room to the W.
[38] See below, Appendix on Wall Mosaics, pp. 105—106.
[39] See below, p. 101.

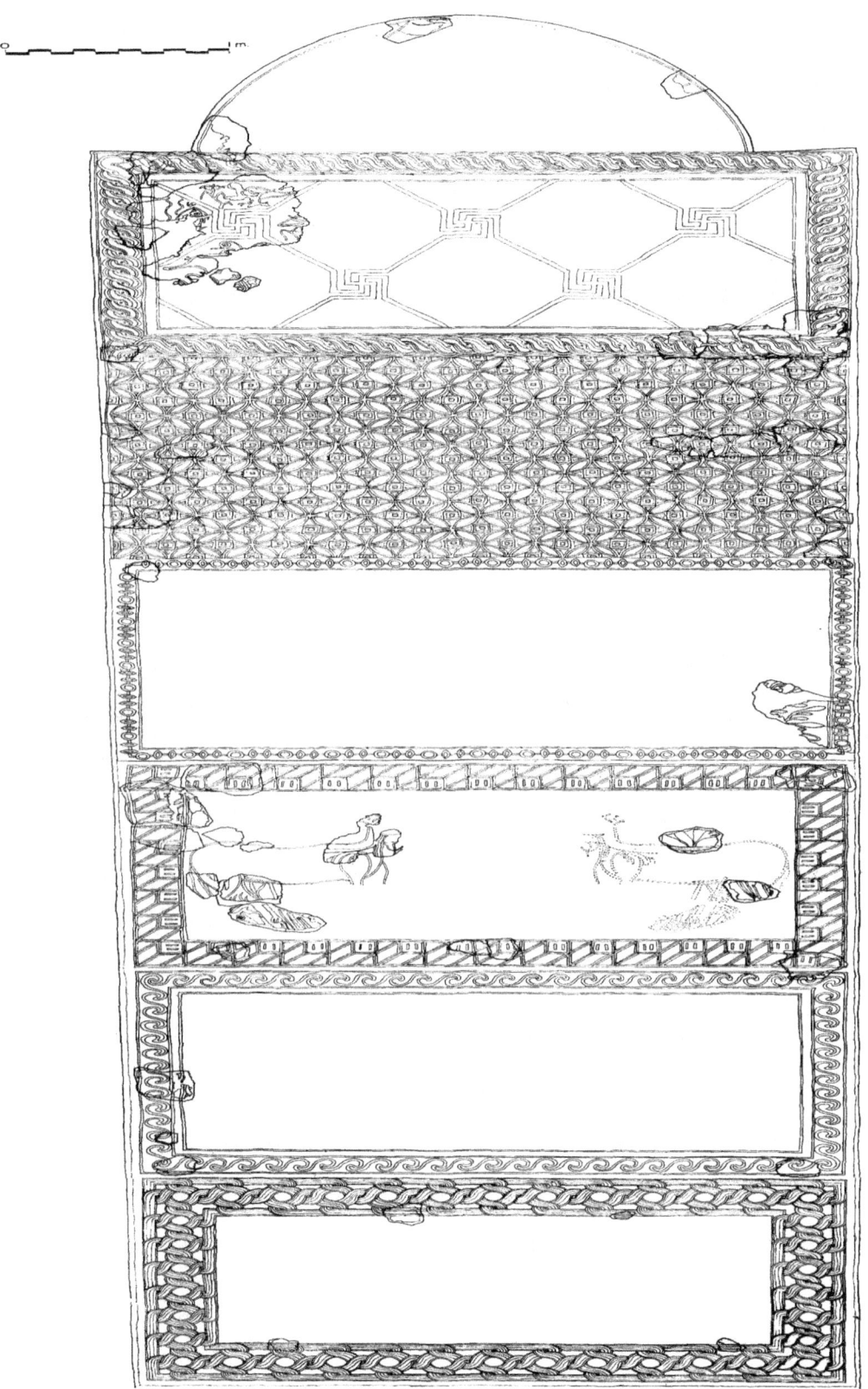

Figure 25. Proposed reconstruction of the mosaic from S of the Episcopal Basilica. Important extant fragments are included and heavily outlined.

The upper layer of fine white mortar has a moderate amount of broken brick fragments and ranges from 1.0 to 1.8 cm. in thickness.[40] The lower layer of pink mortar is from 4 to 9 cm. thick and is much rougher in texture with a greater

Figure 26. Mosaic fragment found S of the Episcopal Basilica. The smooth curved edge indicates that it is from an apse.

---

[40] Several fragments with smooth straight edges which originally abutted walls are preserved; the mortar layers are always thickest where they met the wall.

quantity of brick fragments, some up to 2 cm., and pieces of undissolved lime. Bits of a layer of coarse, white sandy mortar still adhere to the reverse of some of the fragments. The tesserae are smaller and more closely set than those of other mosaics from the Episcopal Basilica. There is a good deal of variation in size among the different materials and designs, but most areas have from 70 to 80 tesserae per square decimeter. The glass paste tesserae are the smallest; there are as many as 120 tesserae per square decimeter.

Figure 27. Mosaic fragment found S of the Episcopal Basilica. The fragment has a curved edge which abutted an apse wall and a rectangular hole for a structure around which it was laid, on the right.

Although only a small fraction of the floor is preserved in pieces large enough to be legible, it is possible to reconstruct the general composition with some degree of accuracy using the pieces that join, the dimensions of the geometrical patterns, and the archaeological documentation of the fragments (Fig. 25).

A large piece of mosaic 43 by 25 cm. was found just E of the apse (Fig. 26). The fragment has a smooth curved border where it was laid up against a wall. If the arc of the edge is continued, a circle with a diameter of approximately 2.5 m. results. This measurement compares closely with the dimensions of the apse, which is 2.45 m. across, and supports the hypothesis that the mosaics were originally located in the room directly above. Two other pieces with curved edges were found, one of which preserves the edges of a hole in the mosaic pavement of the central part of the apse (Fig. 27). This indicates that the mosaic was laid around some structure permanent enough to be in place before the mosaic was laid. The field of the apse has a background of white dolomitic marble tesserae with bright green grass and leaves executed in green glass paste. Several fragments of the field are preserved, all with floral motifs. A single row of red terracotta tesserae outlines the curve of the apse and extends across the field laterally at the front of the "base". The mosaic tesserae did not extend right up to the wall, but a 2.5 cm. wide strip of mortar was left as an edge, perhaps to allow for the thickness of the frescoed plaster on the walls.

The lower portion of the large apse fragment (Fig. 26) has part of a *guilloche* border below the curve of the apse which joins with the border of the adjoining field. This field has been sufficiently restored to be certain that it was composed of a double row of meanders with diagonal arms forming octagonal and elongated hexagonal fields containing birds, fish, and probably other fauna. A section of the N part of this mosaic has been restored and it is large enough to be certain of the dimensions of the pattern which could be repeated exactly three times across the width of the floor (Fig. 28). A section of another corner of the field, but without the diagonal of the meander, indicates that the field must have been composed of an even number of rows of meanders and ended with a row of octagons. The location of the pieces on the reconstruction is based on their connection with adjoining fields and the fact that some of these pieces have a border of mortar and smooth edges which abutted the wall.

The background of the meander field is of the same white marble as the apse. The tesserae are somewhat irregularly cut; most are square, ca. 1 cm. on a side. They, like the tesserae from the apse fragments, are laid in approximately horizontal rows which are interrupted to follow the outlines of the elements of the field. The lines of the meanders and borders are composed of a gray-black limestone. Leaves are indicated by green glass paste, a flower with pink brecciated marble. The fish is made of red terracotta and pink brecciated marble and outlined with a brownish-black glass paste. The birds are composed of brown, green, and blue glass paste, ocher limestone, gray marble, and red-orange terracotta. The feet of all the birds are composed of a distinctive shiny, bright-red glass paste.[41] The glass paste tesserae are much smaller than those of stone or terracotta, ca. 0.7 cm. on a side.

This field was surrounded by a *guilloche* 21 cm. wide. One strand is composed of two to three rows of blue-green glass paste, one row of gray marble, and a row of white marble. The second has one to two rows of red-orange terracotta, two rows of pink brecciated marble, and a row of white marble; both strands are outlined on either side with gray-black limestone.

---

[41]. A piece of the glass raw material from which tesserae of this color were cut was found in the S aisle of the Episcopal Basilica and inventoried as MF—72—39 A, B. It is irregularly shaped, black on the exterior and bright red with orange and yellow streaks on the interior. It measures about 4 cm. across. Another piece for making light green tesserae was found in the Episcopal Basilica and inventoried as MF—72—40. B. Saria reported finding fragments left over after the manufacture of glass tesserae in fill dumped into the cavea of the Theater. "Novi nalasci u episkopskoj crkvi u Stobima," *Glasnik* 12 (1933) 17; Neue Funde in der Bischofskirche von Stobi," *JÖAI* 28 (1933) 119; "Pozorište u Stobima," *Godišnjak muzeja Južne Srbije* 1 (1937) 4.

Figure 28. Mosaic fragments found S of the Episcopal Basilica, joined to form a field of a meander with figures

The border of the meander field was directly adjoined by a field of intersecting circles that form quatrefoils (Fig. 29). A square is inscribed in the center of each curvilinear square. The inscribed squares and quatrefoils are of white marble, and the negative design, which can be read as Maltese crosses, is in gray-black limestone. Four gray-black tesserae enliven the center of each white square. The tesserae of this field are cut and set like the background and ornamental areas of the second field. Fragments of the field of intersecting circles were found on both sides of the apsidal room and thus must have extended the full width of the room. Many fragments with this design have smooth finished edges where the mortar was laid against a form or wall. Some pieces have a single

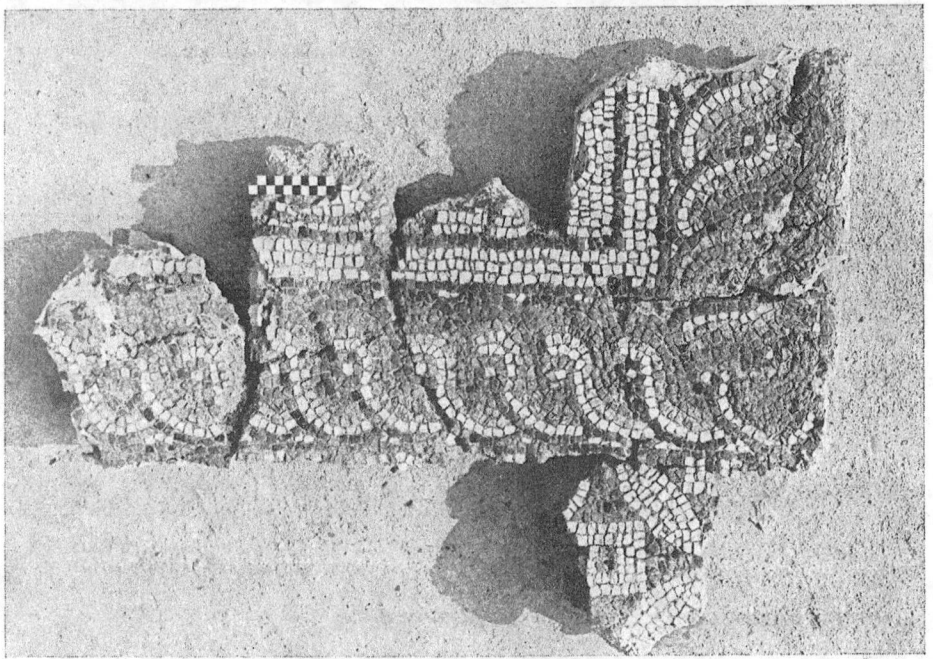

Figure 29. Mosaic fragments found S of the Episcopal Basilica, joined to form a section of the guilloche border of the meander field as it meets the field of intersecting circles. It abutted the wall on its right side.

row of red terracotta and a 2 to 3 cm. margin of mortar on the edge and probably abutted a wall. Others have no border and the tesserae extend up to the edge at the end of the pattern. These edges represent the seam between two sections of mosaic and most probably the end of the field on the W.

Fragments of a fourth field with a border of a stylized bead and reel design were also found on both the N and S sides of the apsidal room. Quite a large fragment which abutted a wall was found just N of the center of the S wall of the room (Fig. 30). From the location of this fragment we may conclude that this field was immediately W of the intersecting circles, although no fragments survive that have parts of both. This is only logical since there seems to have been a division of the work between these two fields. The border is composed of circles alternating

Figure 30. Mosaic fragment found S of the Episcopal Basilica, border of a bead and reel design which abutted a wall.

with a pair of egg-shaped forms; both are made of an ocher limestone and are "strung" on a row of red terracotta tesserae. Fragments of three corners are preserved so that we know it surrounded all four sides of a field. This field was decorated with a floral scene set in green glass and red terracotta tesserae on a white marble ground. It must have been rather similar to the apse composition. The tesserae are of the same size and material. Thus, parts of four separate fields were found in the apsidal room. The dimensions of the apse field are determined by the architecture, the size of the first field by the pattern itself. The third and fourth fields have been restored hypothetically with the same dimensions as the second. This corresponds roughly with the dimensions of the apsidal room.

Many mosaic fragments were also found W of the wall in the rectangular room (Fig. 31). They can be reconstructed to form other fields of this elaborate mosaic floor, which on the upper level was probably not divided by a wall. The fifth panel was surrounded by a border of boxes or solids in perspective. The front of each box is white marble with two lines of red terracotta tesserae. There are three colors of boxes represented among the fragments preserved: the first has a top of pink brecciated marble and a side of red terracotta with a lower border of a single row of pink breccia; the second is made of light green glass paste above and dark blue green glass paste on the side; the third is a box with a light gray marble top and an ocher limestone side. Although no long sections of the border are preserved, it seems that they alternate pink-green-gray-green-pink, that the bright glass paste boxes alternate first with the pink and then the gray ones. The background of the border is gray-black limestone. Enough fragments of the composition have been preserved to reconstruct the main outlines of a large animal, probably a deer, but with a long tail, standing in a grassy meadow with a tree growing behind him and a flower in front of him. Judging from the measurements of the animal and the width of the room there was most probably another animal on the other side as in the compositions of the House of Psalms triclinium and the Baptistery. Some fragments of the body of the other animal have been recognized. The surface of this mosaic is more finely polished than that of the other panels; perhaps it was more carefully smoothed when it was made, being the most prominent figural composition on the floor, or perhaps it was located where much traffic passed across it. The background is of white marble tesserae, the vegetation of green and blue glass paste. The body of the animal is outlined by a row of gray-brown glass paste tesserae. The predominant color is an ocher limestone, shading is rendered by various dark green and brown glass paste tesserae. Highlights are indicated by light gray marble, light green glass paste, and white marble tesserae. The tesserae are laid in lines which strongly emphasize the contours of the body. This, together with the subtle and varied coloring, produces a more three dimensional effect than the schematized shading of the Baptistery and especially the House of Psalms mosaics.

Adjoining the animal field is another field bordered with a wave pattern in ocher limestone and red terracotta. A piece containing sections of both the border of solids in perspective and the waves confirms the arrangement. A few fragments with pieces of another border were also found. This border seems to be a chain which forms circular fields like that in the earlier phase mosaic in the S aisle of the Episcopal Basilica and in the narthex mosaic, but only small fragments have been found. Perhaps future excavations will enable us to reconstruct the decoration of these fields. The rectangular room is not completely cleared, and mosaic fragments are still visible in the unexcavated scarp.

Figure 31. Mosaic fragments found S of the Episcopal Basilica. The fragments form a field with a deer framed by a border of solids in perspective.

The method of laying the tesserae and the stones used associate these mosaics with the later mosaic in the S aisle and the narthex mosaics. They are distinguished, however, by their extensive use of glass tesserae. The mosaic of the Palace of Peristerias is the only other floor mosaic at Stobi with substantial numbers of glass tesserae, but there only two colors, light blue-green and dark blue, are used. The two mosaics have little else in common, however, as the small regular tesserae of the fragments from S of the Episcopal Basilica are not comparable to the rough, irregular shapes of the Peristerias mosaic.

An approximate date is provided for these mosaics by the archaeological evidence.[42] The apsidal walls served as the foundations for the apsidal room on the upper story which was paved with mosaic. Sections of these walls are built without mortar, but are nevertheless quite thick and could have supported an upper story. The construction date of these walls provides a *terminus post quem* for the mosaic. The walls were built during a remodelling of the area, probably some time after the construction of the Episcopal Basilica. They are associated with a pink mortar floor which just overlies the foundation courses of the apsidal wall and part of the S lateral walls. The latest coin found below the floor is an issue of Valentinian II dated 383 to 392 A. C.[43]

The area was destroyed in the same 6th century A. C. collapse as the Baptistery.[44] It seems most probable that the mosaics were laid in the late 5th century A. C. on the basis of their similarities with the later phase in the S aisle and the narthex. Many of the same kinds of stones are used: light blue calcitic marble, white dolomitic marble, gray marble, pink brecciated marble, gray-black limestone, brown limestone, ocher limestone, and red-orange terracotta. The mosaic fragments are, however, brighter and more colorful because of the addition of so many glass paste tesserae.

Although the entire substructure of the room has not yet been cleared and the W wall has not been found, it is certain that the room could not have been entered from the aisle of the church and probably not from the narthex, unless via the landing of the stairway just S of it. Access was most probably from the atrium or the street. A richly decorated room with such a route of access and a proximity to the Baptistery may have been a catechumanate.[45]

CONCLUSION

Examination of the mosaic pavements at Stobi has indicated that the procedure used to prepare the bedding for a mosaic remained fairly uniform through the fourth and fifth centuries A. C. The area to be paved was levelled, a layer of rocks or tiles was set over it, and then layers of mortar were laid. The first layer is usually a rough sand and lime mortar, covered by pink mortar with a large quantity of brick fragments, and finally a finer layer of white mortar with or

---

[42] The brief published accounts, see above note 35, were supplemented by the unpublished season reports and field notebooks of the area supervisors, Virginia Anderson and Carolyn Snively.
[43] Context Storage Lot 741.
[44] Context Storage Lot 649.
[45] The architectural explanation for the function of this room was offered by Živojin Radošević.

without a small admixture of crushed brick. Such deviations as do occur may be significant for distinguishing different phases in a single mosaic floor or similarities may be used to associate pavements that have other features in common, but no pattern of development can be seen using such a small number of examples. The preparation of the mosaic bedding seems to remain uniform although the mosaics themselves may vary in material or technique. The uniformity of the mosaic beddings, however, cannot be used to support the theory of a Stobi mosaic school, without systematic comparisons with techniques in other centers. The concept of a "mosaic school" is met frequently in the literature, but evidence for the actual organization or degree of specialization in the manufacture of mosaic floors is mostly inferred.[46]

We may summarize the line of development in the technique of laying mosaic floors at Stobi from the pavements we have examined, although these conclusions will no doubt be modified as other floors are discovered and studied. In the first half of the 4th century A. C. a floor of roughly cut tesserae made of many kinds of stones was laid in Building Two, beneath the Central Basilica. The floor was planned and laid out in the bedding, but some of the patterns were not symmetrically and regularly worked out. Some time before the beginning of the 5th century and probably rather soon after the first floor was made, a fine, well-made floor of regularly cut tesserae was set next to it on the W. This mosaic is comparable to another Stobi mosaic, that in the Casino. The fine mosaic in Building Two was in use long enough to be repaired once, but with different kinds of stones.[47] It would seem that in the course of the 4th century A. C. a superior method of mosaic making was introduced to Stobi. This "workshop" made at least two pavements, but did not have a lasting influence as the mosaic was repaired with a different technique.

In the early 5th century A. C. an ornamental mosaic was laid in the E end of the S aisle of the Episcopal Basilica, evidently paid for by subscription. A floor with identical motifs and the same kinds of tesserae was laid at about the same time in the Cemetery Basilica. The simple color scheme and patterns of the earlier phase of the S aisle were enriched by the introduction of more colorful tesserae and figural motifs in the mosaics of the Baptistery and the triclinium of the House of Psalms. These mosaics were probably laid somewhat later, but are part of a single developing and evolving tradition.

---

[46] In *The Edict of Diocletian on Maximum Prices*, ed. by E. Graser in T. Frank, *An Economic Survey of Ancient Rome V* (Baltimore 1940) 338—339, the daily wages for workmen of various occupations are listed. Among them are χαλικοκαύστης, *calsis coctor*, a lime burner — 50 Den.; μαρμαράριος, *marmorarius*, a marble worker — 60 Den.; μουσιάριος, *musearius*, a mosaicist — 60 Den.; ψηφοθέτης, *tessellarius*, a maker of tessellated decoration — 50 Den.; τοιχογράφος, *pictor parietarius*, a wall painter — 75 Den.; and εἰκονογράφος, *pictor imaginarius*, a figure painter — 150 Den. are mentioned. There is nothing in the list itself to suggest that these craftsmen worked together, although obviously lime must be burned to produce the mortar for mosaics and frescoes, etc. Some of them probably had nothing to do with floor mosaics, the *pictor parietarius*, for example. Only the *tessellarius* and the *musearius* could definitely, although not necessarily exclusively, have worked on floor mosaics. The elaborate organizational schemes that Medić and other have derived ultimately from this list are at best educated guesses; *Heraclea III* Bitola 1967) 93.

[47] These stones are the same as those used for the mosaics in the Theodosian Palace, which were laid probably towards the end of the 4th or early 5th century A. C.; see note 10. These mosaics are related to the earlier mosaic in the Episcopal Basilica and the mosaics of the House of Psalms by their motifs.

In the later 5th century A. C. the S aisle and narthex of the Episcopal Basilica were paved with an elaborate figural and geometric mosaic. The room S of the Basilica was decorated at about the same time, but its mosaic is even more richly adorned with glass tesserae, which were certainly cut and probably manufactured at Stobi. The more varied and colorful tesserae of these mosaics markedly differentiate them from the earlier pavements, but a certain continuity of motifs suggests that there is some degree of dependence on the earlier tradition.

After these fine pavements were made the art of laying mosaics declined at Stobi, as witness the poor repairs in the Baptistery and the narthex of the Episcopal Basilica. Towards the end of the life of the city even these crude repairs could not be had and mosaic floors were patched with mortar and bricks.

APPENDIX: WALL MOSAIC FRAGMENTS

The techniques used for making wall mosaics differ markedly from those for floor mosaics. A fine white plaster with an admixture of straw or chaff, similar to the backing for frescoes,[48] is used for the bedding of wall mosaics, while mortar with more sand and varying amounts of ground brick like that used for marble floors is also used for floor mosaics because of its water resistant qualities. The tesserae of wall mosaics are not laid exactly parallel to the surface, but at angles to enhance the effect of light and shadow. They are seldom polished and protrude from the surface of the mortar.[49] The interstices in floor mosaics, on the other hand are filled with mortar and the floor is often polished to produce a smooth surface. For these reasons fragments of floor mosaics, as those from the room S of the Episcopal Basilica,[50] are easily distinguishable from pieces of wall mosaic, and technical comparisons between floor and wall mosaics have a very limited value.

It has long been supposed that at least parts of the Episcopal Basilica were decorated with wall mosaics. Egger reported the discovery of many colorful stone and glass tesserae in the apse. He associated them with a hypothetical mosaic in the conch of the apse.[51] As is evident from the floor mosaic fragments from S of the Basilica, glass tesserae cannot be assumed to be from wall mosaics. Gold tesserae are almost exclusively used for wall mosaics, however, and several have been found in the debris S and E of the Basilica during the recent excavations. Five have been inventoried as G-71-93, G-72-59, G-72-60, G-73-17 and G-73-35. The gold tesserae are fairly consistent in size, averaging $0.9 \times 0.7 \times 0.4$ cm. but are irregular in shape. They are made of transparent glass that has aged to iridescence; one side has a sheet of gold leaf sealed under a thin coating of glass.

---

[48] See the article by Dj. Georgievski and J. Wiseman in this volume.

[49] These same features are characteristic of other fragments of wall mosaics from this period found elsewhere in Macedonia: the mosaics of the dome of H. Georgios in Salonica, the fifth century fragments from H. Demetrios in Salonica, a fragment found at Bargala, B. Aleksova, "Bargala-Bregalnica vo svetlinata na novite arheološki istraživanja," *Glasnik instituta za nacionalna istorija* 3 (1967). An as yet unpublished fragment has been found at Scupi by M. Garašanin. Mr. Petrovski plans a study of the Yugoslav material.

[50] See above page.

[51] R. Egger, "Gradska crkva u Stobima," *Glasnik* 5 (1929) 30; also discussed by Dj. Mano-Zissi, "Mozaiken in Stobi," *BIABulg* 10 (1936) 277—278; Kitzinger, "Survey," 108; R. Hoddinott, *Early Christian Churches in Macedonia and Southern Serbia* (London 1963) 165.

Decisive evidence for the existence of wall mosaics in the Episcopal Basilica is provided by pieces of wall mosaic still attached to their mortar backing. The fragment inventoried as A-73-51 was found in debris SE of the apse. A piece of fine white plaster with an admixture of straw has three glass paste tesserae embedded in it. One is black, the other two are light blue-green. They are 0.9 cm. square and 0.6 cm. thick and protrude 0.3-0.5 cm. from the plaster surface. The impressions of seven or eight other tesserae are preserved in the plaster.

Figure 32. Fragment of wall mosaic from the Episcopal Basilica.

Two other fragments with slightly larger tesserae were found between the presbytery and the N aisle of the Basilica (A-70-94) and SE of the apse (A-72-4) (Fig. 32). The tesserae are approximately 1.4 × 1.0 cm. and are cut from white marble and blue-black or brown glass paste. They protrude slightly from the backing. The plaster was painted before the tesserae were set. The dark tesserae were placed in the areas covered with dark gray paint which served as a kind of cartoon and to strengthen the effect of the colors. It is clear, therefore, that the Episcopal Basilica did indeed have mosaics both on the floors and some walls and it is possible to make clear distinctions between the fragments on technical grounds.

ТЕХНИЧКИ НАБЉУДУВАЊА ВРЗ МОЗАИЦИТЕ ВО СТОБИ

РУТ КОЛАРИК И МОМЧИЛО ПЕТРОВСКИ

Истражувањата на мозаичните подови во Стоби покажуваат дека начинот на кој се вршела подготовка на местата за обликување на мозаик останал прилично непроменет во текот на 4 и 5 век од н.е. Земјата — носач на просторот во кој требало да се изведе мозаик била набивана и нивелирана. Врз неа најнапред се редел еден слој крупен камен — дренаж или парчиња од керамиди, а потоа се ставале пластови од малтер — подлога. Првиот пласт обично се состоел од крупен песок и вар, вториот е хоросан малтер со голема количина на парчиња од тули и третиот, пастуозен слој од бел малтер со или без мала количина на ситно толчени тули во кој се поставувани и редени мозаичните камчиња.

Таквиот начин во припремање на носачот и подлогата е значаен за идентификување на различните фази во еден еднороден мозаичен под, а сличностите можат да се користат за поврзување на подовите кои имаат други заеднички црти. Меѓутоа, засега не постои модел што би можел да се забележи, користејки го така малиот број на примери. Подготвувањето на местата за изведување на мозаик изгледа останало непроменето иако самите мозаици можат да се разликуваат по материјалот, изработката или техниката. Единственоста во припремање на носачите и подлогите кај повеќе мозаични подови сепак, не може да се користи за оправдување на теоријата за постоење на мозаична школа во Стоби, без анализа на систематски споредби со техниката во другите центри. Концепцијата на една „мозаична школа" често пати ја сретнуваме во современата литература, меѓутоа од античките извори не можеме да утврдиме, дека се работи за една школа, иако постои документ[46] список за исплатување на уметници сликари и мајстори за повеќе видови работа, но не сме убедени дека посебно работеле на проектирање и изведување на мозаични површини. Нашето повеќегодишно искуство од конзервацијата на мозаичните површини покажува дека е сосема во ред ако се има комплетна група на специјализирани соработници за повеќе видови на работа.

За подните опуси кои се истражени во кратки црти можеме да дадеме приказ за начинот на развојот во усовршувањето на техниката за изработка на мозаични подови во Стоби, иако овие заклучоци без сомнение ќе бидат надополнети кога ќе се откријат и проучат други подови.

Во првата половина на 4 век од н.е. во Втората зграда под Централната Базилика направен е мозаичен под од камчиња со неправилни форми од повеќе видови камен.

Со истражувањата во наосот, под подлогата се утврдени кршени керамиди редени во полиња. Формата и димензите на полињата подоцна биле пренесувани во декорацијата на мозаичниот под што зборува за нивно сукцесивно поставување. Тоа го потврдува различниот степен на цврстината на подлогата (сл. 1—3).

Овој податок укажува на специфична постапка во поставувањето на подлогата и слободниот третман во обликувањето на мозаикот. Во композиционата поставка некои геометриски мотиви не се доследно симетрично оформени како целина.

Врз основа на изнесените податоци сметаме дека мозаикот, во технички поглед, не е квалитетно изработен. Извесно време пред почетокот на 5 век, веројатно прилично наблизу после изведувањето на првиот под, бил изработен друг мозаичен под во продолжение од западната страна (сл. 6—8), далеку поквалитетен во ликовен и технички поглед. Камчињата се мали, правилно сечени, поставувани и редени едни до други. Подот бил доста долго во употреба, а едаш е поправан со различни видови на камчиња. За овој мозаичен под може да се рече и тоа дека е во потполност идентичен со мозаичниот под во коцкарницата.

Се чини дека во текот на 4 век од н.е. во Стоби бил применуван поусовршен метод за правење на мозаици. Групата на мајстори направила најмалку два мозаични пода (Коцкарница и Централна Базилика) меѓутоа, нивниот квалитет воопшто не влијаел врз подоцнежните интервенции така што сите поправки се впечатливи. Во почетокот на 5 век од н.е. во јужниот кораб на Епископска Базилика бил изработен мозаик со орнаментални мотиви. Од фрагментарно сочуваниот мозаик на источниот дел, спрема составите на подлогите и композиционите решенија, се утврдени три полиња. Од натписите со сигурност се знае дека првото и третото поле биле подарок од две различни личности.

Мозаик идентичен на овој, со еднообразни мотиви и видови на камчиња, бил приближно истовремено изработен и во Гробната Базилика. Едноставната палета и орнаменталните мотиви се карактеристични за двата мозаика. Нешто подоцна во Крштелникот на Епископска Базилика и триклиниумот во Куќата на Псалмите се изработени мозаици со исти орнаментални мотиви, меѓутоа, се разликуваат по тоа што тие имаат побогата палета и фигурални претстави. Анализирајќи ги споменатите четири мозаика произлегува сигурен податок дека тие се дел од една единствена развојна традиција.

Кон крајот на 5. век од н.е. Епископска Базилика била обновена и притоа збогатена со мозаици во јужниот кораб и нартексот. По техничката обработка, извонредниот колорит, решавањето на композициите, геометриските мотиви и фигуралните представи, овие мозаични површини делуваат импресивно.

Јужно од оваа базилика, во рушевините на една апсидална просторија во текот на ископувањата се пронајдени фрагменти од мозаичен под. За него се мисли дека бил приближно истовремен со мозаиците во нартексот и јужниот кораб на Епископска Базилика. Постои разлика во колоритот, поради употребените камчиња од стаклени пасти во неколку бои. Овие камчиња биле сечени од грутки на стаклени пасти веројатно произведувани во Стоби. Со проучувањето на пронајдените фрагменти направена е и реконструкција на целосниот изглед на мозаичниот под (сл. 25). За него може да се рече дека бил на спрат, веројатно во нивото на нартексот од Епископска Базилика, а самата просторија може би имала функција на катихуменион.

Мозаичните подови од најмладата фаза на комплексот на базиликата се разликуваат од останатите мозаици во Стоби како комплетна целина гледана од повеќе аспекти во смисол на квалитет.

Меѓутоа, континуитетот на мотивите веројатно до извесен степен е во зависност од поранешните традиции.

За Епископската Базилика треба уште да се рече дека некои нејзини простори биле декорирани со ѕиден мозаик. Такви фрагменти се пронајдени и идентификувани според нивните технички карактеристики.

Во најголемиот процут на градот се изработувале мозаици со особени уметнички квалитети.

Подоцна, со промената на економските прилики и неговото опаѓање, опаѓа и квалитетот за што зборуваат видливите поправки на мозаиците во Крсталникот и нартексот од Епископска Базилика.

Кон крајот на животот на градот, дури и овие поправки ги нема, така што оштетувањата на подовите биле крпени со малтер и тула.

OBSERVATIONS ON THE CONSERVATION AND PRESENTATION OF THE MONUMENTS AT STOBI

by

DJORDJE MANO-ZISSI

The results both of geological[1] and archaeological[2] research indicate some of the changes that have taken place in the history of human environment in the region of Stobi. Analyses at the geological laboratory at the University of Skopje (Ivanov), the analyses of pollen and of other botanical remains, and the study of the skeletal remains of fauna and of humans are enlarging our understanding of the ancient environment.

We might say that the site of Stobi was predestined to become the center of the region in which it is located because of its geographical situation at the confluence of two rivers and at the intersection of routes of trade leading in the direction of the four cardinal points. Both military and commercial interpenetrations resulted from the political issues in the area involving tribal border controversies and conflicts among the neighboring states, cultures, and civilizations.[3]

The Paeonian tribal population whose presence in this area, according to historical sources, goes back as far as the 8th-7th centuries B.C., may have built a "refugium" of the "Gradina" type, a sort of hideout, on the narrowing ridge of the plateau of Stobi near the bank of the Vardar. No trace of such construction, however, has yet been found. Greek merchants from nearby Stenae (Demir Kapija) could have visited the area in the 5th century B.C.;[4] fragments of bronze vessels of that period were found in excavations in 1955—1957.[5]

---

[1] Robert L. Folk, "The Geologic Framework of Stobi," *Studies* I, 37—59; idem, "Geologic Urban Hindplanning: An Example from a Hellenistic-Byzantine City, Stobi, Yugoslavian Macedonia," *Environmental Geology* 1 (New York 1957) 5—22.
[2] See, e. g., the changes in the lower city: W—MZ (1974) 121—128.
[3] F. Papazoglu, *MGRD* and *Srednjobalkanska plemena u predrimsko doba* (Sarajevo 1969).
[4] D. Todorović-Vučković, "Antička Demir-Kapija," *Starinar* N. S. XII (1961).
[5] Dj. Mano-Zissi, "Stratigraphic Problems and the Urban Development of Stobi," *Studies* I, 187—190.

Graves dated to the 3rd—2nd centuries B.C. in the Hellenistic period, during which the Macedonians invaded the territory, were preserved below the complex of the House of Peristerias and its exterior S courtyard; they contained coins of Philip V.[6] Graves from the Early Roman period extended along the road to Palikura,[7] but no other Hellenistic burials have been found within the later city; they may have been destroyed by later constructions. On the other hand, N and E of the Central Basilica-Synagogue, within the area of the ancient Polis and Acropolis, the remains of a settlement from the same period were found including walls with fresco and stucco decoration, imported and domestic ceramics, and evidence of pottery kilns: in its lowest layers, coins of Philip V were also found.

Next followed a long period of favorable climate which lasted into the 3rd century A.C. and contributed greatly to the economic development of the city. During that period Stobi attained great prosperity and its greatest spatial extension. The monuments from that epoch, which have been completely or partially excavated, include the Theater, the Baths, the Casa Romana on the bank of the Crna River, part of the House of the Fuller, and an important complex of buildings cut through by the Inner City Wall, which was erected in the late 4th century. Architecture, statues, and inscriptions denote a high degree of refinement, reached partly, perhaps, because of the area's rich natural resources in clay, woods, reeds, possibly beeswax (used in bronze foundries), and quarries of stones of a variety of color and hardness (tuff, andesite, serpentine, marble, limestone, sandstone, and breccia). The historical sources refer to Stobi as a salt emporium. And livestock was abundant.

After the conquest of Macedonia by the Romans, the relatively well-organized Roman administration, based on a slaveholder social system, contributed to the rapid decline of the autochthonous population in favor of Roman and Greek elements. They developed an urban community possessing its own mint. The tribal names *Aemilia* and *Tromentina* indicate the presence of Roman citizens. The inscriptions on tombstones and votive offerings provide evidence for the presence of settlers from different regions from Pannonia to Asia Minor.[8] Evidence of customs and cults indicates both the persistence of domestic characteristics and of unbroken ties with Greek civilization.[9] It is possible that economic interests are also represented by some indications of ties with Chalcidice and Amphipolis (terracotta figurines, architecture), or Pergamon (ceramics), Clarus (cults of Apollo and Artemis) and Sagalassos (construction of theaters). The peristyles, nymphaea, and palace basins, on the other hand, reflect broader Hellenistic styles that may have developed in Syria (Antiochia). Coins minted at Stobi circulated in Moesia and Pannonia, and ceramics and lamps from Stobi were exported to Scupi.[10] The role of Jews and their Stobi community increased steadily.

However, those ties also had tragic consequences brought by oriental wars.[11] For instance, by the end of the 2nd century, they may have resulted in heavy epi-

---

[6] W—MZ (1973) 401—402.

[7] I. Mikulčić, "The West Cemetery: Excavation in 1965," *Studies* I, 61—95.

[8] James Wiseman, "Gods, War and Plague in the Time of the Antonines," *Studies* I, 143—184.

[9] W—MZ (1971) and (1972). Mano-Zissi, op. cit. in note 5. Al B. Wesolowsky, "Burial Customs in the West Cemetery," *Studies* I, 97—142. Mikulčić, op. cit. in note 7.

[10] I. Mikulčić, "Teritorija Skupa," *ŽA* 21 (1971) 463—484.

[11] Wiseman, op. cit. in note 8.

demic diseases which could have caused economic and spiritual crises and a prolonged standstill of the city's development. Another disaster occurred towards the end of the 3rd century: a new period of heavy rains caused the inundation of the lower quarters of the city. The inhabitants were obliged to move away from the Crna. By the end of the 4th century, the whole area between the Inner and Outer City Walls was abandoned and turned back to agriculture. It is worth mentioning that the lower part of the partially excavated Casa Romana on the bank of the Crna is still penetrated by water.[12]

The city of Stobi rose in the 4th century to its greatest prosperity and political importance.[13] During that period many large palaces, residences, and cult buildings were constructed. The resources of the region were exploited to that end, and the economic and ecological exhaustion of the whole region resulted. From that time to the 6th century, the hills were deforested and the quarries exploited, not solely for construction purposes but also in order to strengthen the ramparts against possible assaults during this period of migrations. Two Gothic plunders paralyzed the development of the city whose citizens grew ever more devoted to the construction of Christian buildings. During the 6th century, the surroundings and the city itself were often subjected to heavy plunderings. During the period between the arrival of the Slavs and the Turks the ecological conditions deteriorated even more; settled community life in the city ended before the end of the 6th century.

What is more, beginning with the 6th century, winds covered the denuded hills surrounding the barren plains of the valley with ever thicker layers of dust. The weather conditions even today are often marked by a surprising succession of periods of rain and drought, burning heat and chilling cold, brought by S and/or N winds, unlike the winds prevailing in the Danubian basin, which blow from E to W and vice-versa. The region of Stobi is very often struck by sudden thunderstorms which carry red sand particles brought from the African or Near Eastern deserts. Even nowadays, the sight of Stobi conveys to the visitor a painful impression of an abandoned, ruined city. In spite of conservation work and tidying of the site, one cannot avoid the overwhelming feeling of desolation produced by the neglected state of the natural environment.

Slightly more to the W — towards Pletvar — and to the S — around Kavadarci and Demir Kapija — success has been achieved recently in the reforestation of hills and the intensified cultivation of orchards. From the beginning of this century only cotton and poppies have been cultivated in the Vardar valley at Pusto-Gradsko. The irrigation systems that are now being installed in the Vardar and Crna basins, thanks to the dam constructed at Kavadarci, will however transform Stobi and its surroundings; the new woods and orchards will surely mitigate the climate.

The water supply was always a most important problem of the city of Stobi. Its soil, which consists of grey sandstone, brown tuff, and green clay, is not at all suitable for the construction and maintenance of wells in the vicinity of two capricious rivers. For that reason, it will be necessary to utilize the Klepa springs which supplied Roman Stobi through an aqueduct of which remains are still visible at Sirkovo and Rosoman. Water was brought to a water tower or pyrgocastellum

---

[12] W—MZ (1972), (1973), and (1974) 121—128.
[13] Papazoglu, op. cit. in note 3. James Wiseman, *Guide* 13—19.

near the Porta Heraclea. By means of a network of water pipes[14] all the consumers were supplied with water: the Central Fountain, nymphaea, peristyle basins, water fountains of the triclinia, and private and public baths. The use of hypocausts was indispensable in the winter in private houses as well as in the *thermae*.

The ancient aqueduct should be reconstructed and put into operation if the maintenance of the site and the organization of technical, scientific and tourist activities are to be secured. This would also make possible the reforestation of the surrounding areas and the development of horticulture within the site itself, and would have a beneficial influence on the climate. Fruit-bearing and decorative plants should be cultivated, particularly species known from historical sources as characteristic of this area. Fields of poppies and cotton would fill adequately the areas between the Outer and Inner Walls or outside them, while slim poplars and willows might mark the banks of the rivers and grow around the walls. The fence of the site could consist of thorn, red dogwood, and myrtle shrubs. Weeds should be exterminated except for the thistles that resemble acanthus. Examples from Delphi, Olympia, Italian sites and even Mogarjelo could be useful, with certain reservations. Is it not interesting to note that a fig tree sprouted from the ruins of the House of Psalms, or an almond tree within the area of the House of Peristerias? The region surrounding the site and the residental areas of the archaeological and administrative teams could be embellished by horticulture; what is more, flower beds, hedges, bushes and rose shrubs, evergreen plants, vine, ivy, and so on, would certainly add to the attractiveness of the excavated buildings. Decorative plants should be skillfully used in order to enhance the appearance of atria, peristyles, basins, streets, and the ruins in general, taking care however that their roots do not destroy them. Mossy plants can be planted for decorative purposes on wall tops, that have been coated with cement and covered by a layer of earth.

Furthermore, priority should be given to the cultivation of plants that can endure the severe climate of Stobi. In spite of that circumstance, aromatic plants always grew there. Hothouses and vegetable patches would be desirable, as well as orchards. Why not establish a tree nursery close by, outside the City Wall? Apiculture which was quite prosperous in antiquity should be revived. Songbird colonies should also be encouraged. Fishing has survived, and the picturesqueness of the panorama would be enhanced by the casual silhouette of a grazing donkey.

Sightseeing paths should be laid out and the names of the streets and the plans of the city adequately displayed on signs and placards. The measures for renewal recommended here, together with the establishment of a central park, would greatly enhance the impression the city produces on visitors. Pleasant rhythms would result from the alternation of green lines, bands, and geometrically shaped fields, on one hand, and from the parallel or transverse strokes of the walls, floors, plastic bulges and recesses of apses and niches, pools, hypocausts, furnaces, and aqueducts, combined with a profusion of color nuances of stones, bricks, and tiles. Within such an environment, the mosaics, and the opus sectile of the halls would impress the visitor as beautiful carpets, while the marble columns, capitals, tables, and fragments within the ruins, as well as the ocher pithoi resting

---

[14] K. Petrov, "Istražuvanja na vodovodniot sistem vo ranovizantskiot Stobi," *Zbornik Skopje* 19 (1967) 267—306. Mano-Zissi, op. cit. in note 8.

on yellow sand or greenish grey stone floor would represent the decorative plastic elements giving contrasting accents to those rhythms. The damaged or missing parts should be repaired or replaced using earth coated with ocher mortar and sand or grass.

As far as the maintenance, conservation, documentation, and presentation of monuments are concerned, the problem of uncovered and partially preserved horizons of life of different levels and periods causes serious difficulties at Stobi. The archaeologist needs the cooperation of architects and naturalists in order to achieve an ecologically ordered presentation; that cooperation, indeed, is indispensable. The city's development was disproportionate in the different areas of the terrain it covers. The changes did not take place at determined horizon levels. Within some complexes of an *insula* only certain parts underwent large changes and the erection of superstructures. Certain buildings show several phases of destruction and/or construction; in the latter case, the new basement almost regularly reached the virgin soil so that the layers of the earlier horizons were destroyed. On the other hand, it is difficult for the excavators to single out the contextual material corresponding to the respective construction and horizon of life. They are facing therefore a heavy responsibility since they have to find the right answer to the question: how do we preserve and present the witnesses of different epochs?

The case is rather simple if an important complex of buildings has been preserved which has been built approximately at the same time and has later undergone only minor repairs. The most important task will be to preserve the main urban lines and traffic arteries, as well as the most representative style of the construction period, by singling out the most valuable buildings, regardless of the timetable, in order to preserve the ambience as a whole and present it as a vision of the past grandeur. But it has to be done without romantic sensitiveness or professional pettiness.

In the course of excavations it is often necessary to remove certain layers, to empty stores or *horrea*, after having conscientiously documented the contextual material and having sent it to the laboratory, the store-room, and/or the museum. Graves or any small structures are also removed after precise measurement and description, if they represent an obstacle to deeper penetration into the past. In such cases care must be taken to preserve the most characteristic features of the construction and/or of some detail of the walls. We are sometimes compelled to reconstruct only partially the most remarkable features of a phase, sacrificing the less important ones.

We are endeavoring to conserve smaller wholes from each layer and/or horizon. Experiments of reconstruction have been undertaken with removable, artificial top surfaces of buildings, which could be lifted in order to disclose some details of the lower layer. More difficult and expensive would be the complete reconstruction of the superposed layers of two epochs in the same place, as it is done at Cologne, Trier, Budapest, and Vienna. If complete decorative artifacts are conserved in situ, the authenticity of the documentary whole will be reinforced.

Reconstruction should be carried out when fragments and bases are preserved. It is desirable — and it has been undertaken already several times — to erect the columns in their original places. When documents or proofs are available, the arches should also be erected or their original position partially suggested. A successful conservation of conchae has thus been carried out in the Baptistery of the Episcopal Basilica, for instance.

The best method of conservation of mosaics is to lift them and set them in concrete blocks. Quite satisfactory results have also been obtained by removing fragments of stucco and/or fresco ornaments which could no longer remain in situ or when they covered stucco or fresco layers of an earlier period. They must be strengthened and preserved. Ancient techniques should be used if possible, even in mortar, by means of silicone injections. The conservator should remodel monuments only as a last resort, and always in compliance with the ancient technique, after having, of course, documented the smallest details. The buildings in which valuable wall paintings, mosaics, and/or exceptionally fine stucco ornaments are preserved in situ should be roofed in order to protect the artifacts from the storms which frequently rage at Stobi. The use of esthetically attractive panels of plexiglass or transparent plastic for the construction of light roofs supported by thin but strong metal frameworks would be too expensive. The example of the glass shelters of the palace at the Piazza Armerina, where scaffolds and staircases are at the disposal of the visitors of mosaics, is tempting enough but induces us to look for a simpler solution which would not rob the visitor of the illusion of his presence in a far-off past. Architect R. Findrih built at Stobi a functional, temporary wooden roof above the Baptistery of the Episcopal Basilica; however, it arouses an oppressive impression and deprives the visitor of the possibility to imagine what the original construction, about which Architect William B. Dinsmoor, Jr. has contributed such a fine study,[15] was like.

Conserved mosaics that must endure the winter in an open space must be covered with sand. The wall paintings and stucco ornaments in situ should be protected by means of plastic or nylon covers, wooden shutters, or roof constructions. Humidity and cold weather are not the only enemies of unearthed artifacts but also, especially at Stobi, changes of air pressure, temperature, and humidity.

Some important sculptures or inscriptions should remain in situ at Stobi. Preparatory work can adapt the stone monuments to the severe weather conditions. However, it cannot be done with the bronze artifacts made of thin sheet metal. For that reason, such valuable artifacts are kept in museums and store-rooms. The example of Pompeii and Herculaneum could perhaps be followed and some statues and statuettes reproduced and exposed at the places where the original sculptures stood or were found. Of course, such reproductions should be done only in cases when the original can endure the treatment without being damaged.

In order to explain the history of the ancient city to visitors and help them to understand and enjoy the tour of its ruins, several means are available: a guidebook,[16] explanations given by guides, traffic signs indicating which directions to follow, large plans of the site, plans of monuments, enameled signs bearing the names of the monuments. The tour of the site will help them memorize the knowledge acquired in the Museum, thanks to the written explanations concerning the finds that include references to the monuments they will visit. Professional

---

[15] William B. Dinsmoor, Jr., "The Baptistery: Its Roofing and Related Problems," *Studies* II.

[16] James Wiseman, *Stobi. A Guide to the Excavations* (Beograd 1973) English, Serbo--Croat and Macedonian editions.

visitors will be given the required information by the personnel of the Museum, which should include at least a custodian, a conservator, a civil engineer, and a horticulturist. They will find most of the answers they seek in the contextual collections, the laboratory, and the library.

Let us remind the reader that the parallel conservation of unearthed monuments was started already in 1930 and was continued up to 1940 (Bošković and Duhač). If we cast a critical glance on the actual situation of the site, we may say that a great deal has been done with the restricted means available in order to protect the site and resume the excavations, which were neglected during the long war and post-war period. Thanks to the efforts of Čipan, Tomovski, Vinčić, and Černjakov, among others, the Conservation Institute of Macedonia has undertaken in the 50s and, 60s two short-term conservation programs involving the Theodosian Palace, North Basilica and its Baptistery, Large and Little Bath, Central Fountain, Synagogue and the so-called Polyharmos' Palace (House of Psalms). Conservation of unearthed mosaics was also carried out.

New excavations (Project Stobi, 1970—1975) extended the area of uncovered monuments, brought new worries, and increased the need for conservation work. For the time being, the major problem is the conservation of the lowest excavation layers where a Hellenistic horizon of life has been ascertained. Unfortunately, the fragments of fresco ornaments from below the Civil Basilica which had been transferred with other contextual material into the Archaeological Museum at Skopje (Kale) were destroyed in the catastrophic earthquake of 1963. The earliest layers of fresco and stucco ornaments in the Casa Romana near the left bank of the Crna are drenched by water; so their salvation remains one of the crucial problems. That building is one of the major concerns of the Stobi Project, although panels have been strengthened and many of them removed from the walls and documented.

The Domus Fullonica[17] is one of the monuments which are most difficult to conserve and reconstruct. Its numerous phases range from the 1st to the 6th centuries A.C. The most interesting of its earliest phases are marked by the workshops in the N—W part of the upper terrain, a hall which contained the remains of fresco paintings (now removed) dated to the Flavian era, and a hypocaust. That building had its most seigneurial appearance in the 3rd and 4th centuries with its big apsidal hall, the atrium with adjoining rooms, a smaller apsidal exedra, a kitchen, a pantry, and the management premises. After its third destruction, in the 5th century, the building was transformed into a *ginaeceum*, a fuller's workshop. It was completely destroyed in the 6th century.

The complicated history of the building will be a major obstacle to the conservators of the earlier phase in the upper terrain and of the later phases (hall, atrium, and apsidal rooms) in the lower terrain. From a corridor which separated the atrium from the big hall, pre-war conservators left a column erect, with its capital.

Still more complicated is the case of the so-called Central Basilica-Synagogue. It contains preserved parts of layers from the Hellenistic and early Roman periods and from the 3rd and 4th centuries (Synagogue), as well as a Christian basilica. In spite of the documentation available, it is extremely difficult to single out the

---

[17] W—MZ (1971), (1972), (1973), and (1974) 138—141,

most characteristic elements because of the inevitable destructions caused by the digging of deep test trenches. At any rate, in addition to the preserved south nave, the two rows of stylobates and the atrium of the Christian basilica, we shall have to prepare for presentation two layers of the Synagogue in the naos and in the north nave as well as the earliest phases of the narthex and of parts of the naos and apse. The access of visitors to these structures will be a difficult problem. On the other hand, already before World War II, that building and its reconstructed atrium attracted attention. The North Basilica, the House of Psalms, the Central Fountains, and the two Baths have already been successfully conserved (Vinčić), and there has been a partial reconstruction of the Theodosian Palace and the House of Parthenius. For the latter, however, the anastylosis of the peristyle, which is a crucial need, remains an unsolved problem.

The conservation of the House of Peristerias, already underway, whose east part, with its peristyle, triclinium, and bath, is evidently characteristic of the late 4th century, while its west part, which was remodelled several times, represents a complicated *insula* with stores and workshops.

There still remains to be finished (since 1940) the excavation and conservation of the Episcopal Residence and of the Casino with bath. It is a pity that the excavation of those buildings could not be included in one of the post-war plans or in the Stobi Project. The first buildings is contiguous to the north side of the Episcopal Basilica, and the second to the Theater. Their locations fully justify the claim for their urgent uncovering.

Two of the most important buildings with which the Stobi Project is concerned are the Theater and the Episcopal Basilica with their contiguous south complexes. Research in the Theater has progressed to the point that the situation regarding the conservation needs of that monument are clear, but the restoration of the huge complex will have to await a more favorable moment and, more importantly, greater financial means. The Theater is perhaps the best preserved theater in Yugoslavia and will some day attract and impress visitors as do other theaters of the Mediterranean Coast. Even in its present state it is a monument deserving careful maintenance and, within the limits of possibility, presentation to the visitors. It would be particularly difficult to reconstruct the structures that support the cavea, as well as the radial and circular corridors.

Thanks to the excavations executed according to the program of the Stobi Project, it is possible to penetrate deeper into the past of the Episcopal Basilica. An important fact has been ascertained: it was constructed above the ruins of an earlier building, probably an oratorium or martyrium, whose axis slants slightly eastwards. Also important are the two construction phases of the Basilica itself, whose apse was partially built on the ruins of the outer circular corridor of the Theater. The earlier cult building can best be presented in the south nave where a colorful fresco is preserved on the wall, provided the Basilica's earlier mosaic, which bears significant inscriptions, can still be placed in its original position.

The complex south of the Basilica's narthex, comprising the stairway leading to the ground floor and an apsidal room with its first story, which was ornamented with mosaics (catechumeneum), is an area that should be restored jointly with the Baptistery and its complex in order to form a vivid unity with the Basilica.

Finally, the complete uncovering and conservation of the Porta Heraclea, Via Sacra, and the Semi-circular Court, as well as of the staircase descending from the Basilica narthex to the lower level on which the Baptistery is situated, should be carried out. The same task awaits us with the staircase north of the Basilica, which leads from the street to the corridor and the exedra of the Episcopal Residence.

Such, for the time-being, are the problems and responsibilities regarding the preservation of the results achieved within the city during the last half-century. Outside the city, there are two monuments which should be taken care of and conserved: the Cemetery Basilica with its large tomb-mausoleum, with preserved vaults and *arcosolii*, and the Palikura Basilica with its octagonal baptistery or mausoleum.

The research of the site of Stobi will remain a durable need and responsibility of future generations. For that reason, the Stobi Project must be followed by the foundation of an Institute of permanent research, conservation, reconstruction, and presentation of the ruins to the public of Yugoslavia and the world, who will always admire the work and the arts of classical civilizations.

(*Written in 1975, in the year of international protection of cultural monuments*).

ОПСЕРВАЦИЈА НА КОНЗЕРВАЦИЈАТА И ПРЕЗЕНТАЦИЈАТА НА ОБЈЕКТИТЕ ВО СТОБИ

ЃОРЃЕ МАНО-ЗИСИ

Геолошките и археолошките испитувања укажуваат на некои моменти од историјата на човековата средина на ова место. Анализите на Геолошката лабораторија на Универзитетот во Скопје, полен-анализите и флотациите на флората и на фауната, како и антрополошките испитувања, ќе ја надополнат нашата претстава за крупните еколошки промени. Географски и сообраќајно, инаку, на устието на две реки и на крстосувањето на проодните премини од четирите страни на светот, ова место било предестинирано за клучна точка за населување. Во воена и во трговска смисла токму во него како да се достасуваат продорите и судирите на племенските граници, на државните аспирации, на културата и на цивилизацијата.

Во одделни временски периоди локалитетот на Стоби имал мошне поволна клима и добри економски услови за поттикнување на населувањето, во милот на пониската почва на терасата. Пеонскиот период може би со својата градина, и македонскиот, со својата хеленистичка полиса, акропола и некропола, сведочат за повлекувањето кон покаменестиот повисок дел од терасата.

Од хеленистичкиот трети век пред нашата ера до римскиот трети век од нашава ера, се задржал релативно најпогодниот период на климата и на добрите еколошки услови, со урамнотежена флора и фауна и со богата економика. Тоа бил процутот на класичниот Стоби — во проширен обем. Каменоломите и трговијата со сол ги надополнуваат богатствата во стопанството и во шумите. Ковницата на римскиот Муниципиум ги шири своите пари во Мезија и во Панонија, а економските врски со Халкидик и со Амфиполе, со Мала Азија и со Сирија (Пергамон, Сагаласос и Карос) одат напоредно се културните манифестации и со архитектонско-уметничките влијанија. Сè повеќе се чувствува улогата на Евреите и на нивната општина во Стоби.

Меѓутоа, веќе од втората половина на вториот век од нашава ера, се појавува стихијата на болештините, како последица од војните на Исток, и таа стихија носи со себеси економска и духовна криза, како и една тешка цезура. Втората тешка природна стихија доаѓа со новиот период на дождови кон крајот на третиот век од нашава ера — со поплавувањето на долниот дел на градот. Тогаш се повлекуваат внатрешните бедеми. Во крајот на четвртиот век од нашава ера целиот простор меѓу внатрешните и надворешните бедеми луѓето го напуштаат и тој служи за земјоделско обработување.

Меѓутоа, во четвртиот век од нашава ера настапува и период на највисок процут и политичко значење на Стоби, со развиен урбанизам и со градба на големи палати, со користење на сите околни придобивки но, и период на едно економско и еколошко исцрпување на овој крај. Отогаш до шестиот век од нашава ера се засилува сечењето на шумите и користењето на каменоломите и заради зајакнување и зацврстување на бедемите, поради сè посилните навалици на преселбите на народите. Двете готски пљачкосувања го уназадуваат градот, кој и онака тоне во мистицизам, зашеметен сè повеќе од христијанските градби. Од шестиот век на нашава ера почнува пустосувањето на градот и на неговата околина. Од доаѓањето на Словените до Турците, денизден се распипуваат и еколошките услови. Турскиот мост на Црна уште потсетува на потребата да се има пат кој поминува низ Пусто Градско. Оголените ридишта ја опкружуваат исушената котлина, врз која ветриштата пластат песок. Климатските услови сè повеќе и повеќе предизвикуваат ненадејни промени во атмосферата, изненадувања поради дождови или поради суша, поради жежтини и поради студови, и поради ветришта од југ и од север. Ете зошто и денеска Стоби, потонат некако во своите урнатини, остава мачен впечаток на напуштен град и покрај сите чистења и сите конзервации на ископините.

Токму затоа се пледира за обласнување на природните услови на околината и на самиот локалитет, со наводнување, со обновување на дамарот на римскиот водовод, со пошумување и со обновување на природноисториски документираната флора и агрикултурата на овоштарството, градинарството, цвеќарството и расадниците во непосредната близина на Стоби. Од мошне поголемо значење е, напоредно со конзервацијата на ископините, во нивни состав и во нивни рамки да се преземат и агротехнички мерки, кои ќе припомогнат за нивното одржување. Кон тоа би одело и архитектонското и естетското планирање, како и формирањето на хортикултурниот амбиент, како придружник на презентацијата на ископините. Тешко е да се прикаже и да се презентира целата историја на развојот на еден град.

Кратката анализа на проблемите на конзервацијата ја истакнува тешкотијата кај обекти со повеќе животни хоризонти, со повеќе висински нивоа и со повеќе стратиграфски датуми. Градот се развивал несразмерно, а промените не настапувале по определените висински нивоа. Повеќето фази на уривање и на новоградби (со темели што се спуштаат до самти здравица) ги оштетувале слоевите на поранешните хоризонти. Треба да се направи обид да се најдат решенија за зачувување на позначајните едновремени градби во својот блок или комплекс, но да се сочуваат притоа и позначајните резервати од секоја епоха и од секој слој. Покрај тоа да се сочуваат главните урбанистички решења, сообраќајниците, стилот на најрепрезентативниот и на најдобро сочуваниот градежен период. Да се сочува амбиентот и визијата на минатото.

Со анастилоза и со чување на спомениците и натписите, како и на декоративните елементи, фреските и подните мозаици in situ поверодостојно делува инаку со документација научно утврдениот карактер на објектот.

Продискутирани се прашањата во врска со одржувањето на мошне чувствителните делови, или во врска со нивното симнување, како и со презентацијата на копиите од прибраните пластични дела. Суровата атмосфера со своите промени ги загрозува на самиот терен.

Со анализа на конкретните проблеми на одделни откриени објекти, во смисла на нивното одржување и презентација, се забележува широка скала на потреби и на . . . можности, кои уште постојат и кои чекаат да бидат решени. Уште кон триесетите години се беше дошло до сознанието за потребата од споредбена конзервација со ископувањата (Бошковиќ — Духаќ). Во педесеттите и во шеесеттите години, Заводот за заштита на спомениците на Македонија, презема големи работи (Чипан, Томовски, Винчиќ, Саржоски, Чорњаков). Од седумдесеттите Георгиевски, Петровски, Пренџов и Винчиќ имаат уште поширок комплекс на одговорности на таа работа во врска со работите на Проектот Стоби. Подводноста на долните слоеви на Casa romana покрај реката Црна, повеќе фази градба на Domus fullonica, а особено компликуваните надградувања на Синагогата од првиот век на нашава ера до шестиот век, при што треба да се истакнат двата периода на Синагогата, во третиот и во четвртиот век и христијанскиот, во петтиот век. Театарот со својот огромен комплекс при тоа создава тешкотии со обработувањето на подградбата на Cavea, со нејзините радијални и циркуларни коридори.

Епископската базилика, со својот комплекс, на конзерваторот му презентира многу изненадувања. Со пронаоѓањето на темелите на постарата зграда на *ораториумот*, со поисточно скршната оска, и на двете фази на епископската базилика, којашто во постарата апсида била зидана над зидовите на циркуларниот коридор на Театарот, — се појавија тешкотии околу одржувањето на самото место на двете нивоа поден мозаик со натписи, и на двете слоја фрески на зидот на најстарата зграда. Со катехуменонот, ситуиран јужно од нартексот, се испречува прашањето на конструкцијата на катовите(етажната конструкција), а со сочувани скали Баптистериумот се појави со две фази, со подоцнежно президување на сводовите, со два реда временски различни столбови, носачи на сводовите на куполата над писцината (кршталникот), во која се крштавало, во четвртиот век со *имерсија* (потопување), а во петтиот век со *аблуција* (миење). И мозаиците и фреските, со своите преправања, временски се разликуваат.

Со сугестија за едно интегрално зафаќање за одржување на локалитетот, се чувствува потребата за напоредна соработка на организацијата за истражување и конзервација, во 1975, во меѓународната година за заштита на спомениците на културата.

INVESTIGATIONS IN THE HOUSE OF PERISTERIAS

by

VIKTORIJA SOKOLOVSKA

The House of Peristerias is one of the least investigated buildings at Stobi. Early published reports convey only general data about it and are without extensive deductions and datings.[1] Moreover, the structure has not yet been completely unearthed; there are whole complexes still awaiting the excavators. Investigations undertaken by the Archaeological Museum of Skopje in 1965 and 1966 had some important and unexpected results,[2] which are presented in this study.

DESCRIPTION OF THE BUILDING[3]

Bounded by the streets Via Principalis Superior on the NW, Via Principalis Inferior on the SE, Via Axia on the NE, and Via Theodosia on the SW, the structure is a complex of buildings of various types. That fact alone indicates that the house was not constructed originally as it stood before its final destruction, but was enlarged and remodelled during its existence.

The central part of the house complex (see Plan, Fig. 15) consists of two apsidal rooms facing a peristyle court which is bordered by corridors on all sides. There is a large quadrangular fountain at one end of the peristyle. The east corner of the house contains a small bathing complex.

Storage rooms with pithoi preserved where they had been set into the floor, as well as a kitchen complex, are located NW of the peristyle. Since there are remains of staircases in Rooms 19, 25, and 26, we may be certain that an upper story existed once in that part of the house. Along the Via Principalis Inferior, in the SE part

---

[1] J. Petrović, "U Stobima danas," *Glasnik Sarajevo* (1943) 482—483.
[2] Conservation work planned at that time required preliminary archaeological investigation; work in the house was undertaken for this reason.
[3] A description of the house is given in Kitzinger, Survey, 128; B. Josifovska, *Vodič niz Stobi* (Skopje 1953) 26—28; Wiseman, *Guide* 40—44.

of the house, there are five solidly built small rooms. The NW and SW wings are occupied by small rooms which probably served as shops and workshops.

Near the central peristyle with the large fountain there are two more courtyards. One (No. 17) is located S of the apsidal rooms where remains of earlier walls are preserved. The other courtyard (27) leads to the shops and workshops and has direct access on to the Via Axia.

ROOM 1

The principal entrance into the complex is on the NE side, from the Via Axia (see plan, Fig. 15).[4] That street descends from the NW to the SE, past the Central Fountain, the Large Bath, and the House of Psalms. A canal existed along the whole street; it carried the sewage to the Crna River.

Room 1 is the vestibule of the house. In the middle of the 3 m. wide entrance a threshold of greenish sandstone, of which one side is carved, is preserved (dimensions: 1.93 m. × 0.54 m. × 0.22 m.). One doorjamb of the entrance is preserved to a height of 0.45 m. The NW wall has an opening ca. 1.35 m. wide which provided for communication with the NW part of the house. That opening, however, is so damaged that its original width cannot be determined. A doorway which originally led directly into Corridor 5 was later walled up and communication between Room 1 and the central part of the complex was secured through Room 20.

The walls of Room 1 are of rubble stones, greenish sandstone for the most part, cemented with lime mortar. The greatest preserved height is 1.65 m. The floor is paved with flag-stones.

ROOMS 2, 3, AND 4

Rooms 2, 3, and 4 are parts of the bath complex. From Corridor 5, an entranceway 1.56 m. wide gave access to a rectangular room (dimensions: 5.80 × 3.50 m.). On the NE side of that room there is a 1.28 m. wide entrance leading over a step into a small room (1.16 m. × 4.46 m.) where a small niche is preserved. A layer of pink mortar and traces of black slate (with which that room was paved) indicate that it must have been exposed to moisture.

The flag-stone floor of Room 2 is relatively well-preserved. Its walls are identical to those of Room 1; their greatest preserved height is 1.80 m. The SE wall, which has an unusually wide opening leading into Room 3, has undergone major changes. The end parts of the walls on both sides of the entrance are coarsely patched with bricks; this circumstance suggests that before it was repaired the entrance was much narrower or, perhaps, did not exist at all.

The changes caused by the opening of such a wide entrance are probably in connection with the construction of Room 4 which, as will be seen later, belongs to a later phase of the complex. It should also be noted that the NE wall of Room 2 did not exist originally; in an earlier phase there was an entrance into those rooms from the street. Access to Room 3 was through the wide entrance mentioned above. Since the floor level of Room 3 is much lower, a step was required. The NE, NW,

---

[4] Photographic documentation of the house is by I. Mikulčić; the plan was drawn by Lenče Mihajlova.

and SW walls of this room seem to have been built at the same time. However, the SE wall, or at least its upper part, was constructed later; it was probably built at the same time as the walls of Room 4, which was entered from the SW corner of Room 3. There was an opening in the NW wall also, but it was walled up later when the room was transformed into a bath. Also at that time an embankment was set into the NW corner, the entrance was enlarged, and a stepped wall constructed on the NE side leading to a small basin. The basin did not occupy the entire width of Room 3. The basin itself is coated with three layers of hydraulic mortar, of which the first is very coarse and the others somewhat finer; the surface is very smooth. The room has a flag-stone floor and the embankment too is built of stone with a row of bricks on top. While tidying up the debris in that room, we found remains of a thick layer of mortar which had fallen from the ceiling; among them were fragments of stucco ornaments as well as of fresco paintings of red, black, and green.

Figure 1. Firebox below Room 4, *caldarium*.

Water was drained from the basin by a water pipe which emptied into a brick-lined canal. A stone grating was found in the canal; it has circular holes to admit water and a rosette decoration (Fig. 6). The canal extends into Corridor 5 where it emptied into a shaft which also received the sewage from a canal that leads from the apsidal room with the mosaic floor (Room 15). The sewage flowed from that shaft into the street sewer.

Room 4 contained a firebox (Fig. 1) and was hence the *caldarium*. Through a small chamber, which may have been the *tepidarium*, it communicated with

Room 3. In my opinion, this complex was a private bath of reduced dimensions, but it consisted of all the compartments which completed such a set of rooms: *apodyterium, frigidarium, tepidarium*, and *caldarium*. However, a problem remains to be resolved: there is a difference of level between the *tepidarium* (Room 4a) and the *caldarium* (Room 4), since the latter undoubtedly was located above the level of the arch-shaped openings. The difference of level was probably compensated for by means of a staircase, which has not yet been found. The reconstruction of the *caldarium* would be a difficult problem. Its small dimensions and cross-like shape suggest that a basin for warm water existed there, analogous to the basins of the Large Bath.

THE PERISTYLE

The asymmetrical peristyle, which represents the central part of the house is bordered on all four sides by corridors (5, 6, 7, and 8). The walls are 0.60—0.64m. thick. The peristyle was built of cut stones and rubble consisting chiefly of friable green sandstone.

A nymphaeum (dimensions: 7.80 m. × 2.45 m. × 1.25 m.) is in the NE part of the peristyle. It is enclosed on three sides by a balustrade (0.75 m. high) and consists of 15 large marble blocks which seem to be re-used. A tombstone, also re-used, is set into the center of the balustrade. The stone basin was cemented with a rather coarse hydraulic mortar.[5] Eleven openings are preserved in three walls (N, S, and W) of the basin; the lower portion of several ceramic vessels were found set into the holes. The vessels were of no evident practical use since water did not flow through them; their function remains uncertain. They were disposed at different levels, but all are below the water level.

The basin was supplied with clean water from water pipes which protruded from the still preserved holes in the balustrade. The 0.85 m. wide space between the balustrade and the three neighboring walls was cemented with hydraulic mortar and enclosed at both ends with two stone slabs. That space too, then, was part of of the nymphaeum and received clean water from the main conduit.

The peristyle was paved. The preserved columns belong to the wide entrance to Corridor 7.

ROOMS 10—14

Rooms 10—14 are arranged along the SW wall of the complex. These rooms were constructed between two parallel walls set 3.40 m. apart. The walls are built of cut stones cemented with a strong lime mortar. Rooms 10, 11, and 12 communicate with Corridor 6, while Rooms 13 and 14 were entered from (apsidal) Room 15, although the entrance to Room 13 was later walled up. Room 14 also opened through a narrow passage into the SW courtyard. The floor of these rooms was of crushed bricks.

APSIDAL ROOM 15

The sumptuous triclinium, one of the most attractive rooms of the house, is ornamented with a mosaic pavement and an octagonal fountain.[6] It was built

---
[5] Wiseman, *Guide*, Fig. 5.
[6] For the mosaic see Dj. Mano-Zissi, "Mosaiken in Stobi," *BIABulg* 10 (1936) 279—280, 283—289, 296—297; Kitzinger, Survey, 138, note 258; Wiseman, *Guide* 40—43, Fig. 6.

so solidly that it stands out in that respect from all the other structures of the house. The walls are carefully chosen, cut stones cemented in the manner of *opus mixtum* with one row of stones alternating with four rows of bricks, of which only one zone has been preserved. The thickness of the mortar layer is equal to that of the bricks.

The triclinium with the mosaic floor is organically related to Rooms 10—14; their construction technique is identical. One may conclude that they were constructed simultaneously.

APSIDAL ROOM 16

Apsidal Room 16 is much smaller than Room 15. What is more, the two rooms differ greatly in their principal characteristics. The construction technique of Room 16 is conspicuously poorer; no bricks were used. The floor was paved with stone slabs.

ROOM 19

A 1.46 m. wide entrance leads from Corridor 8 into Room 19 where the walls are poorly preserved. There is an L-shaped pier 1.40 m. thick in the SW corner; it is built chiefly of cut stones and rubble along with some bricks cemented with mortar. The SE wall, built of rubble, was added later. A 1.55 m. wide entrance existed originally in the SW wall, but was later walled up with a staircase set against it. The floor of the room was paved with bricks which are poorly preserved.

ROOM 20

At the very entrance into the house from the Via Axia, one may enter Room 20 from Room 1. This small apsidal space was probably a work area.

ROOM 21

This room of irregular shape was a late addition.

ROOMS 22, 25, AND 26

Rooms 22, 25, and 26 comprise a unit which, judging from the presence of wall niches and pithoi in the floor, served as a storage area, perhaps for food, in the final phase of the complex. The unit, however, may not always have served such a purpose. The perimeter walls of the 4—room complex, as well as three sections of the N—S interior wall, were built of rubble and cut stones bonded with mortar. Such is not the case with the other partition walls, which are thinner and were bonded with mud. Rectangular niches (Fig. 2) were found only on these later walls. It would be difficult to say at present what purpose the complex served earlier.

Stairways are preserved in Rooms 25 and 26, indicating that an upper story existed at one time (Fig. 3).

ROOM 24

Another room deserving special attention is Room 24, which includes the poorly preserved remains of a circular kiln. The kiln was built of stone except for four arched openings of brick. It is difficult to determine the use of the kiln; it may have been for ceramics. A number of over-fired, deformed sherds were found throughout the house and especially in adjacent Corridor 40.

Figure 2. Later walls with niches in Room 22.

OTHER ROOMS

Rooms 28—46 are arranged along the SW and NW walls of the house. Almost certainly they were the shops and workshops. They communicated with the interior of the house as well as directly with the Via Theodosia and Via Principalis Superior.

THE AQUEDUCT AND DRAINAGE SYSTEM

It is not possible at present to determine precisely the organization of the water supply and drainage systems of the House of Peristerias. Parts of both networks were destroyed at the time of the abandonment of the house. What we could find out in the course of our investigations may be summarized as follows.

We were unable to state how clean water was brought into the octagonal fountain of the *triclinium*. At any rate, a conduit must have been installed under the mosaic floor. Water from the fountain flowed out through a canal that passed

Figure 3. Stairway and pithos in Room 26.

Figure 4. Drainage canal in Corridor 6. View from S.

along Corridor 6 (Fig. 4) and emptied into a shaft at the end of that corridor (Fig. 5). That shaft also received the water emptied by a canal leading from the large fountain of the peristyle, as well as from the pool of the *frigidarium* (Room 3) (Fig. 6). From that shaft water flowed into the street sewer.

A canal in the SW wing of the house passed through Rooms 41 and 43 (Figs. 7, 8). Another canal which passed through Room 38 emptied sewage into Courtyard 17.

Figure 5. Drainage collecting tank in Corridor 6.

OBSERVATIONS

The House of Peristerias has not been completely excavated, and we offer here only preliminary remarks concerning the construction phases and their chronology.

It is self-evident that the House of Peristerias underwent important changes during its existence. In the first place, it should be emphasized that the apsidal rooms (15 and 16) were not built simultaneously, though the time interval separating the two events was perhaps not long. The east room (15) is a solid structure built of carefully set, cut stones in *opus mixtum* technique, quite unlike Room 16. The former has a mosaic floor with a fountain, and the second, a common stone-paved floor. In addition to these fundamental differences, we note that Room 16 has much smaller dimensions. Test Trench b confirmed that the two rooms were constructed separately, since the foundations could be examined. The question arises: which room is older? In my opinion, there is an acceptable answer. The SE wall of Room 16 is much thinner than the other walls of that complex and suggests that the contiguous wall of Room 15 already existed when the wall for Room 16 was constructed. That is, the wall of Room 15 could have served to support the wall of Room 16, for which reason the latter wall could be less substantial.

Figure 6. Water canal in Room 3 (right) and a cover slab with circular openings and rosette decoration.

The construction technique of the *caldarium* (4) is similar to that of the room with the mosaic floor. For that reason, we may suppose their construction to have been contemporaneous.

In the bath complex, on the other hand, the *caldarium* itself (4) is the latest structure. The lower courses of its walls are remains of earlier walls whose construction technique corresponds to that of the walls in the other rooms of the bath. There are other visible remains of those earlier walls in Room 4a (Fig. 9). The wall behind the firebox was destroyed while the new *caldarium* was being constructed and an exterior corner was formed by adding contiguous walls along the Via Axia.

These observations indicate at least three construction phases. The first phase would include the lower parts of the walls of Rooms 1, 2, 3, and 4 (See Plan, Fig. 15). The firebox and its contemporaneous room with the mosaic floor (15) would belong to the second phase, while the third phase would be represented by apsidal Room 16.

Figure 7. Drainage canal in Room 43.

With regard to the two construction phases stated for the bath complex, the question arises as to the role of that building during its first phase. Test Trench d, dug in the firebox of the *caldarium*, resulted in the discovery of an earlier floor of hydraulic mortar. A water channel, which was later sealed up, was also found within the N wall of Room 3. Taking into account these two facts we might deduce that even in its first phase that complex served as a bath, but that it was located at a lower level and the disposition of its rooms was different.

Rooms 10—14 along the SE side of the house might be ascribed to the second construction of Room 16, though perhaps in another form.

The complex of storage rooms also underwent important changes. Let us emphasize, however, that partitions built with mud do not always mean a later date of construction.

As mentioned above, the SW part of the house has many small rooms which were probably used as shops and workshops. These rooms are set between two parallel walls, which are solidly built, while their transversal partitions are of a much weaker construction (mud mortar). Some of these walls contain spoils of constructions which must themselves date to late antiquity (Fig. 10).

Figure 8. Drainage canal in Room 47.

It would be difficult to determine with precision the datings of the construction phases. The complex is still insufficiently investigated and there is little useful data for dating available. Nevertheless, taking into account some of the more reliable information thus far ascertained, we shall try to establish approximate dates and time intervals in the House of Peristerias.

Apsidal Room 15 has a mosaic floor with an octagonal fountain; it is the only mosaic found in the structure. Dating it to the end of the 4th century A.C. and the beginning of the 5th[7] would be in accordance with the *opus mixtum* technique used in the construction of the *triclinium*.[8] As already mentioned above, Rooms

---

[7] Dj. Mano-Zissi, op. cit. in note 6.
[8] S. Bobčev, *Smesenata zidarija v rimskite i ranovizantijskite stroeži* (Sofia 1952) 46.

Figure 9. Traces of earlier phase of walls in Room 4a.

Figure 10. Re-used capital in wall of Room 37.

10—14 and the firebox of the bath are contemporaneous with Room 15. Our first phase, stated for the complex of the bath, could be older by several decades and might be dated to the middle of the second half of the 4th century. Apsidal Room 16, which we find to be later than Room 15, represents our third phase. Such was the appearance of the house during the 5th century A.C., if we admit as evidence a gold *solidus* of Anastasius I[9] (491—518 A.C.) found in Corridor 6 (Fig. 11). After the Gothic invasion in 479 A.C. the house must have undergone important changes. The NW rooms with their deteriorated construction technique, as well as many repairs and remodellings of the house, might be ascribed to that period.

Figure 11. Gold *solidus* of Anastasius I (491—518 A.C.) found in Corridor 6.

---

[9] H. Goodacre, *Handbook of the Coinage of the Byzantine Empire* (London 1928) 61.

TEST TRENCHES

The results of test trenches in several parts of the House of Peristerias are summarized below.

Trench a. This trench was dug in Courtyard 17 with the aim of investigating that unoccupied area where some earlier walls had been uncovered. Under a deposit of yellow earth and gravel we found a layer of stones and small slabs that represent the level of the courtyard itself.

Trench b. Set between the walls of the two apses, this trench provided evidence that the two apsidal structures were constructed separately, as discussed above. A grave with the remains of a skeleton was discovered beneath the substructure of Apsidal Room 16. In addition to iron nails, the grave contained a pyxis with a high foot. The pyxis was coated with a rather thin brown varnish. Its lid is ornamented with a raised circular band with 12 pale yellow palmettes arranged around it. The pyxis is a rare example from Stobi of "West Slope" ware (Greek Hellenistic period).[10] The grave may be dated to the late 3rd century B.C. (Fig. 12).

Figure 12. Pyxis (West Slope Ware) from grave found in Test Trench 6.

The discovery of that grave, together with other data from investigations below the Civil Basilica,[11] indicate that the area in which the large houses of late antiquity were constructed at Stobi was used as a cemetery in the Hellenistic period.[12] More recent excavation by the Stobi Project has resulted in the discovery of four other graves in the Peristerias Courtyard (17).[13]

---

[10] V. Blavatskij, *Istorija antičnoj raspisnoj keramiki* (1953) 57.

[11] Dj. Mano-Zissi, "Stratigraphic Problems and the Urban Development of Stobi," *Studies* I, 191—200.

[12] I. Mikulčić, "Stobi — (Peristerija) — Kasnohelenistički grobovi," *ArchPreg* 8 (1966) 113—114.

[13] W—MZ (1973) 401—402.

A burial urn with lid (Fig. 13) was found near the remains of an earlier wall in Courtyard 17. Soot, ashes, and remains of partially burnt bones were found in the vessel.

Trench d. A floor cemented with hydraulic mortar was uncovered below the final floor of the firebox of the *caldarium*. Our opinion that even in an earlier phase that complex was used as a bath was thus given added strength.

Trenches g and h. They were dug in Rooms 11 and 13 and resulted in the discovery of the floor of crushed brick.

Trench m. This test was dug in Room 18 and resulted in the discovery of a grave pit containing several stones. The pit was filled with black earth in which were found numerous animal bones and pottery fragments belonging to rather large amphoras coated with pale yellow engobé.

Trench n. A fire-place constructed of stone slabs was found below Corridor 7. Besides a large quantity of soot, there were several fragments of rather coarse ceramic vessels, with horseshoe, ribbon, and band-shaped handles. Precise dating is difficult at present.[14]

 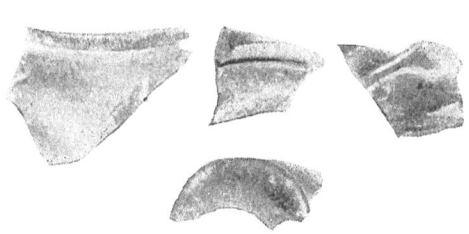

Figure 13. Burial urn from Courtyard 17.   Figure 14. Partially vitrified and deformed pot sherds from Corridor 40.

Several fragments of dark-gray pottery, partially vitrified and deformed by excessive heat, were found during the cleaning of Corridor 40 (Fig. 14). The sherds suggest that the kiln in Room 24 was used for the production of pottery.

Future investigations in the House of Peristerias will hopefully lead to new results which will enlarge our understanding of this building of late antiquity at Stobi.

---

[14] We shall include the ceramic finds from the 1965—1966 test trenches in the House of Peristerias in a separate work in which all the pottery from Stobi now in the Archaeological Museum in Skopje will be published.

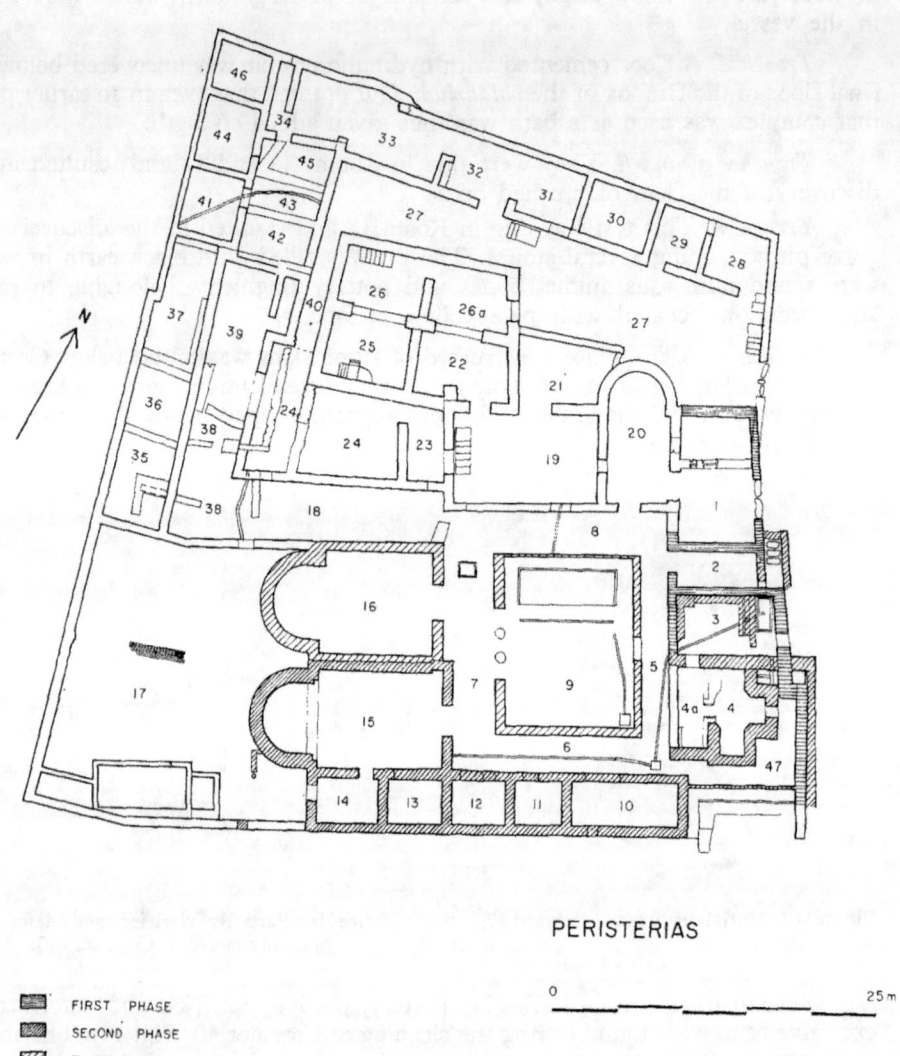

Figure 15. Plan of the House of Peristerias.

ИСТРАЖУВАЊАТА НА КУЌАТА ПЕРИСТЕРИЈА

ВИКТОРИЈА СОКОЛОВСКА

Куќата Перистерија е една од најмалку проучените градби во Стоби. За неа во литературата се среќаваат само основни податоци, без поопширни разгледувања и датирања. Истражувањата што ги презеде Археолошкиот музеј од Скопје во 1965 и 1966 година дадоа извесни значајни резултати, дотогаш речиси непознати.

Ограничена со улиците Via Principalis Superior на северозапад, Via Principalis Inferior на југоисток, Via Axia на североисток и Via Theodosia на југозапад, оваа куќа претставува цел еден комплекс од разнородни градби. Самиот овој факт зборува дека куќата не е првобитно изградена како таква, туку дека со текот на времето се вршени доградувања и преправки за да се дојде до последната фаза, комплетната градба што сега ја имаме.

Централниот дел на куќата го претставуваат две апсидални сали — триклиниум, свртени кон главниот перистил со трем на столбови, обработен со коридори на сите четири страни. На едниот крај на перистилот се наоѓа голема четириаголна фонтана. Источниот агол на фонтаната е исполнет со комплекс од бањи, коишто, иако со помали размери, ги содржеле сите придружни простории.

Северозападно од перистилот се наоѓаат остави со зачувани питоси, вкопани во земјата, како и кујнски простории (сл. 2). Судејќи според остатоците од скалилата во просториите 19, 25 и 26, може да се заклучи дека на овој дел од куќата постоел кат (сл. 3). На југоисточната страна од куќата, по должината на Via Principalis Inferior, се наоѓаат пет помали простории, мошне солидно градени. Северозападното и југозападното крило е исполнето со помали простории, коишто најверојатно служеле како дуќани и работилници.

Покрај централниот перистиал со големата фонтана, во куќата се наоѓаат уште два двора. Едниот е зад апсидалните сали каде што се зачувани остатоци од постари ѕидови како и една мошне плитка фонтана. Другиот двор води кон дуќаните и работилниците и има директна врска од Via Axia.

Макар што куќата Перистерија сè уште не е во целост истражена, ќе се обидеме да изнесеме некои свои забележувања што се однесуваат на определувањето на градежните фази, како и на нивното временско вклопување, до кои дојдовме во текот на нашите истражувања.

Паѓа в очи дека куќата Перистерија претрпела големи промени во текот на своето егзистирање. Пред сè треба да се нагласи дека апсидалните сали 15 и 16 (види го планот 15) не се градени истовремено. Можеби временското растојание во изградувањето на едната и другата градба не е големо, но е очигледно дека тие се градени одвоено. Источната сала 15 е градена мошне солидно, од грижливо реден делкан камен, со примена и техниката opus mixtum со четири реда цигли, додека кај другата сала (16) ова не е случај. Кај првата, имаме мозаичен под со фонтана, кај втората пак, обичен поплочен под. Освен овие основни разлики, се забележува дека салата 16 е значително помала и по своите димензии. Сондата b покажа дека двете градби се градени одвоено уште од самите темели. Се поставува прашањето која од овие градби е постара. За одговор на ова прашање се чини дека имаме еден доказ на кој би можеле да се потпреме. Југоисточниот ѕид на салата 16 е значително потесен од другите ѕидови на оваа градба. Тоа значи дека севернот ѕид којшто ѝ припаѓа на салата 15 претходно постоел, па служејќи му како потпирка на јужниот ѕид од салата 16 е изграден значително потесен. Со други зборови, салата со мозаичен под е постара, а малку подоцна е изградена и салата 16, којашто во технички поглед значително заостанува зад првата.

Адекватна на триклиниумот со мозаичен под е градбата на калдариумот (4) (сл. 1). Техниката на градењето кај двата објекта е мошне блиска, така што би можеле да ги сметаме за истовремени. Меѓутоа, самото одделение на калдариумот во целиот комплекс од бањи е понова градба. Во долните слоеви на неговите ѕидови се забележуваат остатоци на постари, пренебрегнати темели, коишто конструктивно им соодветствуваат на ѕидовите на другите одделенија на бањата, а над кои е иззидан нов калдариум (сл. 9). Во одделението 4а се наоѓаат видливи остатоци од овие постари ѕидови, а зад ложиштето, помладиот ѕид којшто овде формирал агол, при подигањето на новиот калдариум е уништен и дополнително направен надворешниот агол формиран од ѕидовите кон улицата Via Axia.

Според досега изложеното, можат да се издвојат три градежни фази. Кон првата фаза би спаѓале ѕидовите на одделенијата 1, 2, 3 и 4 во своите долни партии (види го планот). Втората фаза е застапена со градбата на ложиштето од комплексот на бањите и со салата со мозаичен под додека кон третата фаза би спаѓала салата 16.

Во врска со констатираните две фази на комплексот на бањите, се поставува прашањето каква намена оваа градба имала во својата прва фаза. Сондата d поставена во самото ложиште на калдариумот, откри уште едно подно ниво од хидрауличен малтер. На северниот ѕид од просторијата 3 постоел канал којшто подоцна е заѕидан. Врз основа на овие две индиции, можеме да констатираме дека и во првата фаза овој комплекс бил користен како бања, и имал поинаков распоред и на значително пониско ниво.

Просториите од 10—14, распоредени по должината на југоисточната страна на куќата, би можеле да ѝ се припишат на втората градежна фаза. Нивната конструктивна поврзаност со салата 15 упатува на овој заклучок.

Подигањето на перистилот концепциски би требало да се врзе со двете апсидални сали, меѓутоа и пред подигањето на градбата 16 перистилот морал да постои, можеби во поинаква форма.

Комплексот на просторниите каде што се наоѓаат оставите на куќата, исто така претрпел значителни промени. Меѓутоа, треба да се нагласи дека преградните ѕидови врзани со кал, не означуваат секогаш подоцнежен датум. Како што веќе споменавме, југозападниот дел на куќата е исполнет со помали одделенија, каде што најверојатно се наоѓале дуќаните и работилниците. Сите овие одделенија се формирани од два паралелни ѕида, поцврсто градени, додека нивните напачни ѕидови се од кал. Во некои од овие ѕидови се вградени сполии од доцнаантичките градби, што мора да се доведе во врска со нивната подоцнежна фаза.

Прецизно временско определување на констатираните градежни фази е тешко да се изведе. Куќата сè уште не е доволно истражена, така што недостигаат многу податоци потребни за датирањето. Па сепак, потпирајќи се на извесни посигурни елементи, досега констатирани, ќе се обидеме приближно да ги определиме временските граници на егзистирањето на куќата.

Апсидална сала 15 има мозаичен под, единствен мозаик во целата куќа. Неговото датирање во крајот на IV и почетокот на V век би одговарало на техниката на opus mixtum применета во градењето на триклиниумот. Како што порано забележавме, истовремени со салата 15 се просториите од 10—14, како и калдариумот во комплексот на бањата. Нашата прва фаза констатирана во просториите 2, 3 и 4 би можела да биде неколку децении постара и временски би можела да се постави во средината на втората половина од IV век. Апсидалната сала 16, за која утврдивме дека е помлада од салата 15, претставува наша трета фаза. Во оваа форма куќата егзистирала во текот на целиот V век, за што ни сведочи златниот солид на Анастазиј I (491—518 н.е.), откриен во коридорот 6 (сл. 11). По наездата на Готите од 479 година од н.е. куќата морала да претрпи значителни промени. На ова време би можеле да му се припишат северозападните простории, градени на значително послабо техничко ниво, како и многу поправки и пресидувања што се видливи на куќата (сл. 10).

Сондажните испитувања во куќата дадоа видни резултати, од кои ќе ги наведеме најзначајните.

Во сондата b, под темелот на апсидалната сала 16, откриен е еден гроб во кој се констатирани траги од скелет. Покрај железните клинци, во гробот е откриена една пиксида со висока нога. Пиксидата е премачкана со поредок црн фирнис, а нејзиниот капак е украсен со испупчен кружен прстен, околу кој се распоредени 12 палмети изведени со бледо жолта боја. Таа претставува подоцнета варијанта на класичните пиксиди, чијшто орнамент е изведен во техниката на west stope стилот (сл. 12). Гробот би можеле да му го припишеме на касниот III век пред нашата ера.

Наодот на овој гроб, како и другите податоци добиени од истражувањата на Цивилната базилика, покажуваат дека просторот што сега е опфатен од касноантичките поголеми куќи во Стоби, во хеленистичкото време бил користен како некропола. Новите ископувања од Проектот Стоби открија уште 4 гроба во просторијата 17 на куќата на Перистерија.

Покрај остаците на стариот ѕид во дворот 17, откриен е еден мешлест сад со капак (сл. 13). Саѓите, пепелта и остатоците од нагорените коски откриени во садот, зборуваат дека се работи за урна, слободно закопана во земјата. Временски таа би можела да се постави во I—II век н. е., што би зборувало дека закопувањето овде се вршело и во раниот римски период. Во прилог кон ова одат и наодите на рано царска керамика, откриени во оваа и во другите соседни куќи.

Во сондата m, на длабочина од 0,60 м, откриена е гробна јама, исполнета со црна земја, во која имаше многу животински коски и фрагменти од керамички садови што им припаѓаат на поголемите амфори, премачкани со бледо жолта енгоба.

Во сондата n, на длабочина од 1,60 м, откриено е огниште формирано од плочи. Покрај големата концентрација од саѓи, најдени се неколку фрагменти на погруби керамички садови, веројатно грнци, со потковичести, врвчести и лентести рачки. Оваа керамика би можела да му се припише на постариот автохтон елемент, меѓутоа, попрецизно временско опеределување засега е тешко да се даде.

PATHOLOGY OF HUMAN REMAINS FROM STOBI, 1970—1973

by

AL B. WESOLOWSKY

INTRODUCTION

The human skeletal remains recovered during the 1970—1973 excavations at Stobi, in Yugoslavian Macedonia, possess some lesions of paleopathological interest. Almost all of the skeletons were found during the joint United States-Yugoslav work at the site; the remainder are from a series of disturbed graves salvaged early in 1973 by the National Museum of Titov Veles. The skeletal remains and their primary documentation, like all the materials from the 1970—1973 excavations, are stored on the site. A more complete study of the skeletal remains is in progress; the present report is a consideration of the utility of these remains in assessing the health of the early inhabitants of the city.

To date 251 graves have been located in various areas of the site, and skeletal remains have been recovered from 125 of them. Of the remainder, fifteen have been only partly exposed and await future excavation, and 111 were so damaged by pipeline-laying activities that no bones could be certainly associated with them. The earliest graves (four in number) are dated to the early 2nd century B.C. while the remainder date from the turn of the era through the 4th century A.C. Table I summarizes the distribution of the graves.[1]

---

[1] Earlier accounts of the cemeteries of Stobi are in W—MZ (1971), W—MZ (1972), and W—MZ (1973). There are also two papers in *Studies I*: A. Wesolowsky, "Burial Customs in the West Cemetery," (pp. 97—142), and I. Mikulčić, "The West Cemetery: Excavations in 1965," (pp. 61—96).

TABLE I

Graves*	Area	Total Graves	Total Graves Opened	Total of Graves Yielding Any Skeletal Remains	Dating
1—6, 8, 10—86, 88—96	West Cemetery	93	82 (55 cremations: 67%)	81	Augustan (*ca.* 25 B. C. — 25 A. C.) through late 3rd-early 4th centuries A.C.
7, 9	West Cemetery II	1	1	1	Roman Imperial
87, 97	Theater, East Parodos	2	2	2	Late 4th century A.C.
98	Fossa	1	1	1	Roman Imperial
99—102	Peristerias Court	4	4	4	Late 2nd century B.C.
103—114, 244—251	Basilica Cemetery	20	20 (13 cremations: 65%)	19	1st-2nd centuries A.C. Late 4th century A.C.
115—243	West Cemetery Salvage	129	129	17	Uncertain, likely 3rd-4th centuries A.C.

* Starting in 1970, all graves were numbered sequentially as they were found or, in the case of the West Cemetery Salvage, entered into the Grave Index. Column 1 lists *all* graves whether excavated, merely located, or disturbed by ditch-digging machines.

PALEOPATHOLOGY

Paleopathology is the study of the diseases that can be demonstrated in earlier human and animal remains[2] or through more indirect means. This report is limited to the pathological processes apparent in the human skeletal materials from Stobi and as yet cannot utilize any indirect assessment of disease as, say, from ancient texts.[3] The lesions (injuries to tissues or organs) in archeological samples can serve as indicators of the health status of earlier peoples and frequently illustrate the history of certain afflictions. For example, D. R. Brothwell[4] and J. Lawrence Angel[5] have produced accounts of disease in skeletal samples that may represent population-level responses to environmental fluctuations. The archeological implications of such studies is evident although the disease processes are difficult to quantify.

---

[2] M. S. Goldstein, "The Palaeopathology of Human Skeletal Remains," in D. Brothwell and E. Higgs (eds.), *Science in Archaeology* (London 1969) 480—489.

[3] J. Wiseman, "Gods, War and Plague in the Time of the Antonines," *Studies* I, pp. 143—183 illustrates the potential for textual studies in the paleoepidemiology of Stobi, but the diseases referred to in that report leave no apparent trace on excavated bone.

[4] "Palaeodemography," in W. Brass (ed.), *Biological Aspects of Demography*, Symposia of the Society for the Study of Human Biology 10 (1971) 111—130.

[5] "Porotic Hyperostosis, Anaemias, Malarias, and Marshes in the Prehistoric Eastern Mediterranean," *Science* 153 (1966) 760—763; "Early Neolithic Skeletons from Çatal Hüyük: Demography and Pathology," *Anat St* 21 (1971) 77—98.

Paleopathology can be studied through at least three different media which, like other manifestations in the archeological record, are subject to the dual vagaries of preservation and interpretation. These media are lesions in the physical remains of earlier humans, literary evidence, and representations in art.

The most direct evidence — lesions preserved in the biological remains of individuals — can be equivocal from the standpoint of modern clinical diagnosis. Ordinarily, when studying pathology in a skeletal series there is no recourse to the comparative wealth of data that today's physician relies upon for his diagnosis: clinical symptoms, histological examination of fresh specimens, biochemical assays of physiological processes, et al. Archeological materials usually preserve only the gross appearance of dried bones for diagnosis, though roentgenography has long been recognized as a useful tool in the identification of certain disorders in early material.[6] When soft tissues have been preserved a greater range of disorders can be examined.[7] Soft tissue preservation is limited to so few areas of the world, however, that paleopathologists are generally restricted to bone for their investigations.

When only bones and teeth are preserved the only diseases that can be demonstrated are those which affected the bony structures of the body. A cleanly healing fracture or a dental carie present little problem in diagnosis. On the other hand, virulent epidemic diseases were known in antiquity but these did not involve the skeletal tissues. Between these two extremes there are different pathological processes that can produce similar lesions on bones.[8]

Ancient texts are another source of information on diseases in ancient times and their impact on society. Here, also, there are differentials in preservation and interpretation with the additional complication of translating the descriptions of symptoms of disease into modern terms. Adam Patrick[9] has illustrated some of the problems associated with the medical literature of the Greek and Roman world.[10]

Finally, representations of disease and malformation are known in ancient art. Wall paintings, sculpture, and anthropomorphic vessels have illustrated abnormalities that may rarely be preserved in skeletal remains.[11] Attention should be

---

[6] E. A. Hooton, *The Indians of Pecos Pueblo* (New Haven 1930); J. E. Moseley, "Radiographic Studies in Hematologic Bone Disease: Implications for Palaeopathology," in S. Jarcho (ed.) *Human Palaeopathology* (Yale University Press 1966) 121—130.

[7] For examples of examination of soft tissues in paleopathology see A.T. Sandison,"Diseases of the Skin," (449—456) and J. T. Rowling, "Respiratory Disease in Egyp," (489—493), both in D. Brothwell and A. T. Sandison (eds.) *Diseases in Antiquity* (Springfield 1967). A number of other papers in that volume mention soft-tissue lesions.

[8] Examples of approaches to the diagnosis of such diseases are D. Morse, "Tuberculosis," in Brothwell and Sandison, op. cit. (in note 7) 249—278; and W. G. J. Putschar, "Problems in the Pathology and Palaeopathology of Bone," (57—65) and the discussions by H.L. Jaffe and L.C. Johnson (65—81) in Jarcho, op. cit. (in note 6). Infectious disease is only part of the spectrum of human misery. Paleopathology is also concerned with biological senescence, physiological disorders, trauma, and idiopathic lesions.

[9] "Disease in Antiquity: Ancient Greece and Rome," in Brothwell and Sandison, op. cit. (in note 7) 238—246.

[10] Difficulties of interpretation exist for much more recent texts as well. Owsei Temkin "Palaeopathology and the History of Medicine," in Jarcho, op.cit.(in note 6) discusses the problems of the identification of syphilis in Europe in the last decade of the 15th century A.C.

[11] D. Brothwell, *Digging Up Bones* (London 1965) 164 shows some Egyptian statuettes of achondroplastic dwarfs. A.T. Sandison and C. Wells, "Endocrine Diseases," in Brothwell and Sandison, op. cit. (in note 7) 521—531 and C. Wells, *Bones, Bodies and Disease* (London 1965)

called to votive offerings, found in Asklepieia, in the image of a stricken limb or organ. Although these stone or ceramic effigies rarely possess traits that reveal the precise etiology of the ailment they are of interest in the history of medical treatment.[12]

In summary, the effects of disease in earlier times can be studied in preserved biological tissue, literary commentaries, and artistic representations. Like other archeological data, evidences of pathology are subject to differentials in preservation and interpretation. More critically, when paleopathology attempts to assess the health status of earlier groups it evaluates negative factors. When a bone is visibly affected we can be certain that some disorder was involved, and whether or not the condition was fatal, or apt to have been, can be a quite different question. The adaptive ability of the human frame to continue living with multiple and spectacular lesions can be astonishing. But when a skeleton is apparently free from lesions few statements about the health at the time of death can be made; the person could have suffered from disease or trauma that affected only the softer, more perishable tissues of the body. Whatever the life expectancy of an earlier group was, those individuals dying before middle age did not die from natural causes.

Despite this host of shortcomings and sources of error, paleopathology can contribute to an appraisal of the health of earlier human populations. This is particularly true with large, well-preserved samples from cemeteries. With smaller, less well-preserved collections the health (or perhaps more precisely, the lack thereof) of the population from which the sample was drawn is correspondingly more difficult to evaluate.

CLASSIFICATION

Classification of diseases in the living may vary in detail from one survey to the next, but there is a measure of general agreement in the medical literature on the taxonomy of pathological processes. Although lack of information on soft tissues complicates paleopathological diagnoses, the classification of these processes is somewhat simplified. The simple scheme used in this report is similar to those in other publications.[13]

A. Trauma.
B. Developmental anomalies.
C. Degenerative joint disorders.
D. Hematologic disease.
E. Inflammation.
F. Dental pathology.

These categories are a reflection of the specimens present and are not necessarily mutually exclusive.

---

depict representations from the New and Old Worlds showing a range of such disorders. Morse op. cit. (in note 8) makes a convincing case for the diagnosis of tubercular spinal deformities in artwork from the Americas and Egypt.

[12] H. Sigerist, *Civilization and Disease* (Ithaca, New York 1944) 204—206.
[13] Brothwell, op. cit. (in note 11) 133; H. W. Neumann, *The Paleopathology of the Archaic Modoc Rock Shelter Inhabitants*, Illinois State Museum Report No. 11 (1967) 7; J. S. Miles, "Diseases Encountered at Mesa Verde, Colorado," in Jarcho, op. cit. (in note 6) 92.

A. TRAUMA

Traumatic lesions involving the skeletal tissues were identified for certain in only two instances. Curiously, both were almost identical fractures of the lower leg that developed into localized fusion of the tibia and fibula. They resemble Pott's fractures[14] with complications of healing although there seems to have been little injury to the ankle joint.

Grave 3, dated to the late 3rd or early 4th century A.C., was an inhumation preserved only from the groin down. The bones were those of a robust adult, likely a male, but a more precise estimate of age at the time of death could not be made. Some time prior to the time of death the left tibia and fibula had been frac-

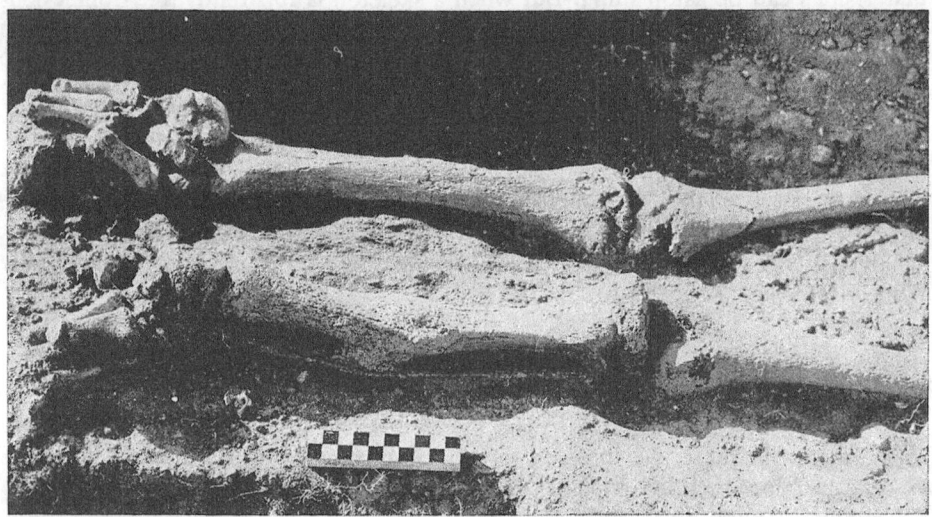

Figure 1. Grave 3. Fracture of left lower leg *in situ*.

tured near their distal ends and the formation of bony callus was well advanced (Fig. 1). During the healing process of bone remodelling the two bones fused in an area between 110 mm. and 140 mm. from the distal tip of the fibula. The shaft of the tibia inferior to the callus is very slightly displaced laterally. Judging from the plane of displacement the fracture in the tibia was ca. 130 mm. from the tip of the medial epicondyle. The region of remodelling presents an abnormal appearance, with gross cortical swelling and some interior elaboration of cancellous bone. The bones were quite fragile in the affected region because of the disproportionate amount of cancellous tissue. When the specimen was removed from the soil it broke into several fragments.

There is a difference of 18 mm. in the maximum length of the tibiae (right, 325 mm.; left, 307 mm.) that may have introduced some limp into the gait. The

---

[14] A type of fracture occurring immediately above the ankle joint and which may involve the bones of the ankle.

fusion of the tibia and fibula would have interfered with normal movement of the lower leg. The bones of the ankle and foot and the knee joint seem little affected, if at all.

Certainly the bones were viable at the time of death. No abnormal sinus or exposure of cancellous bone was noted that would suggest a suppurating bone infection shared with the soft tissues. The elaboration of cancellous bone may indicate an inflammation of bone tissues of uncertain severity.

Grave 17 contained an adult inhumation, doubtless a male, who appears to have died late in the 3rd or early in the 4th decade of life. The grave is dated to later Augustan times, from the turn of the era to ca. 25 A.C. The right lower leg was fractured (Fig. 2), resulting in fusion of tibia and fibula in an area between

Figure 2. Grave 17. Fracture of right lower leg *in situ*.

90 mm. and 130 mm. from the tip of the medial epicondyle of the tibia. There is slight medial displacement of the shaft of the fibula superior to the fracture line. No accompanying displacement of the tibial shaft is apparent; this suggests that the original trauma resulted in nothing more serious than a greenstick fracture of the tibia which merely compressed the medial side while slightly fracturing the lateral side. Alternatively, this could be the result of an expertly set and well-healed separated fracture of the tibia but the fusion with the fibula resulted from inadequate medical care.

This specimen presents a less pronounced callus and less elaboration of cancellous bone than in the case of Grave 3. The loss of mobility must have been the same in both cases.

There are at least 70 inhumations represented in the total collection from Stobi, and lower legs were preserved in 56 of these (17 non-adults, 39 adults). It is conceivable that a fragment displaying a localized fusion of the lower leg could be preserved in a cremation, but none was noted. Calvin Wells[15] mentions that Pott's fractures are "common" in Anglo-Saxon skeletal series and that they may have resulted from stumbles in rough, plowed ground while the persons were wearing clumsy footwear. He cites data that indicate a relatively low frequency of Pott's fractures in groups that ordinarily went barefoot. At present, we can only speculate on the reasons for the low incidence for these fractures at Stobi.[16]

B. DEVELOPMENTAL ANOMALIES

Three examples of congenital developmental anomalies were observed in the collection, all in the spinal column of inhumations.[17]

Grave 20 is that of a female who died in the 4th decade of life and is dated to early Augustan times. The dorsal portion of the neural arch of the 1st cervical vertebra remains unfused. The other vertebrae present were normal.

Grave 141, from the West Cemetery Salvage excavations, is that of a male who died in the 4th decade of life. The grave dates from the Roman Imperial period. The left portion of the neural arch of the 5th lumbar vertebra failed to unite with the body of the vertebra. Although it has been suggested that a combination of genetic predisposition and activity-specific stresses may be responsible for such failures of ossification,[18] others are inclined to discount the stresses on living bone and consider such cases as strictly a function of genetic endowment.[19] A survey of 513 5th lumbar vertebrae in collections from British Neolithic through 19th century A.C. sites[20] noted fusion failures ranging from 0% (Medieval) to 11.1% (Romano-British).

Skeleton B of Grave 160 is that of an individual 10—15 years of age at the time of death and displays an open sacral canal. The canal is almost bridged over at the first sacral vertebra but nothing of the remainder of the spinal column was preserved to show if they were normally developed. In the same survey mentioned above, Brothwell and Powers found the frequency of open sacral canals in 943 specimens ranging from 0% (Post-Roman Dark Age) to 7.3% (Romano-British).

All three of these anomalies are minor from the clinical standpoint and it is doubtful whether or not the first two individuals were even aware of their defects. Likewise, the adolescent of Grave 160 probably suffered no loss of vitality from his open sacral canal. The inheritance of these traits is not completely understood

---

[15] Wells, op. cit. (in note 11) 50—55.

[16] Several cremations in the West Cemetery (Graves 38, 46, 47, 48) yielded quantities of small nails (ca. 1 cm. long) that could have belonged to "heavy" footwear or to some wooden artifact burned with the corpse. Grave 244 (a late 1st century A.C. inhumation) and Grave 113 (a triple inhumation of the late 4th century A.C.) produced small nails in quantitites similar to the cremations (between 20 and 47). Grave 38: female? adult; Grave 46: juvenile, ca. 6 years old; Grave 47: adult; Grave 48: adult male; Grave 113: two adult females, one juvenile; Grave 244: adult female.

[17] Tooth impaction, which could be considered a developmental disorder, is dealt with in the section on oral pathology.

[18] Miles, op. cit. (in note 13) 96.

[19] Brothwell, op. cit. (in note 11) 110.

[20] D. Brothwell and R. Powers, "Congenital Malformations of the Skeleton in Earlier Man," in D. Brothwell (ed.) *The Skeletal Biology of Earlier Human Populations, Symposia of the Society for the Study of Human Biology* 8 (1968) 173—203.

and, in general, archeological materials are hardly the place to search for genetic links in earlier groups. Still, under certain circumstances statements of probability can be made concerning familiar links among excavated skeletons. A convincing case has been made for close genetic ties between the two occupants of a single grave at Ancient Corinth,[21] and there is a likelihood of familiar ties among a series of Roman graves from England.[22] These examples are exceptional, and it is more common to encounter occasional observations of congenital anomalies in skeletons from graves of uncertain contemporaneity. Under such circumstances it is difficult to demonstrate that the presence of these anomalies is more than happenstance.

C. DEGENERATIVE JOINT DISORDERS

Degenerative joint disorders can be particularly troublesome to diagnose specifically because of the lack of soft tissues, particularly cartilage. Also, not all joint disorders are a concomitant of advancing age. Some pathological processes that are traumatic in etiology may resemble more "normal" aging processes.

"Osteoarthritis ... is a consequence, at any given period of adult life, of injury, deformity, or disease, or arises spontaneously in the elderly .... the morbid anatomy of all osteoarthritis is fundamentally the same, no matter what disorder may have been the primary cause."[23]

In addition, there is a distinction between two of the more common manifestations of chronic joint disorders, chronic osteoarthritis and spinal osteophytosis *(spondylosis deformans)*,[24] and confusion has arisen from the indiscriminate use of these terms in descriptions.

In excavated skeletal materials these diseases appear as bony elaborations on the margins of articular surfaces, most commonly those of the vertebrae. Part of the distinction among the different kinds of disorders depends on the type of joint involved, but the specimens from Stobi are so incompletely preserved that it will not serve to belabor the point.

These bony elaborations, or "lipping", begin as slight growths that exaggerate the normal contours of the edges of the joint surface. They may enlarge into more elaborate bony formations and even combine within a joint and immobilize it. Vertebrae are particularly prone to this immobilization, from degenerative disorders and other diseases.

The generally poor preservation of the remains from Stobi certainly affects examination of degenerative changes. The articular ends of long bones, having less cortical bone per unit volume than the shafts, are not as likely to be preserved as the shaft. Vertebrae are particularly prone to such post mortem disintegration. An additional bias is introduced by the large proportion of cremations, in which a complete vertebra, not to mention an articular end of a long bone, is a rarity.

---

[21] Nils-Gustaf Gejvall and F. Henschen, "Two Late Roman Skeletons with Malformation and Close Family Relationship from Ancient Corinth," *Opuscula Atheniensa* 8 (1968) 179—193.
[22] Brothwell, op. cit. (in note 11) 110.
[23] D. H. Collins, *The Pathology of Articular and Spinal Diseases* (London 1949) 74.
[24] A. E. Hertzler, *Surgical Pathology of the Diseases of Bone* (Philadelphia 1931) 73—77; Collins, op. cit. (in note 23) 307—308.

Skeletal remains representing at least 141 individuals from 125 graves yielding bones were examined in 1973. Cremations accounted for more than half of these graves (68 cremations; 56%); and of the 71 individuals from inhumations, 49 were adult. Only a few complete spinal columns were preserved so observations were usually limited to noting an occasional lipped vertebra. Even so, there were evidences of degenerative joint changes in only eight individuals, seven of which were cremations. All cases were recorded as "slight"[26] and with one exception all were cervical or lumbar vertebrae (occasionally both were involved in the same individual).

These frequencies of the site of lipping in the spinal column are consistent with some other studies,[27] and the suggestion has been made that lipping is apt to be most pronounced in the areas of greatest spinal mobility (the neck and the lower back).

Most of the cremations had several vertebral bodies present but ordinarily identification was limited to whether they were cervical, thoracic, or lumbar. Segments and more complete spinal columns were present in only 21 of the 51 adult inhumations. Only one of these, a 30—40 year-old male from Grave 141, displayed any appreciable lipping. There is some anterior elaboration that increases slightly from L1 through L5 and some slight lipping on three preserved cervical vertebrae.

There are at least two factors operating to obscure the incidence of degenerative joint disorders in this sample of inhumations.

1. *Preservation.* The tally of 21 adult vertebral columns present include even those with just a few vertebrae present. Only half a dozen spinal columns can be classed as "fairly complete."

2. *Age at the time of death.* Only five of the 21 adults have been aged in excess of 30 years at the time of death. However, three of the well-preserved spines belong to individuals aged 30—40 years; very likely incomplete and poorly-preserved skeletons are being given ages somewhat lower than their true age at the time of death. Several surveys agree that there is apt to be little involvement of vertebrae prior to the age of 30 years.[28] One individual also has slight lipping on the margins of the humerus-ulna articulation in the right elbow. The left elbow seems normal.

Grave 42, an adult cremation, had two thoracic vertebral bodies fused together. Not enough of the remainder of the spinal column was preserved to indicate whether this was an age-associated degeneration or the result of a more localized fusion. The preserved portions of the intervertebral articular surfaces of the fused vertebrae (the superior surface of one, the inferior surface of the other) showed no appreciable lipping. This suggests that the etiology is more likely a localized defect, possibly traumatic, rather than an age-associated change.

---

[25] J. B. Bourke, "A Review of the Palaeopathology of the Arthritic Diseases," in Brothwell and Sandison, op. cit. (in note 7) 352—370, present an intelligible discussion of the different forms of arthritis.

[26] Brothwell, op. cit. (in note 11) Pl. 14.

[27] T. D. Stewart, "Some Problems in Human Palaeopathology," in Jarcho, op. cit. (in note 6) 43—55.

[28] T. A. Willis, "The Age Factor in Hypertrophic Arthritis," *Journal of Bone and Joint Surgery* 6 (1924) 316—325; T. D. Stewart, "The Rate of Development of Vertebral Hypertrophic Arthitis and its Utility in Age Estimation," (abstract) *American Journal of Physical Anthropology* 15 (1957) 433; Bourke, op. cit. (in note 25).

D. HEMATOLOGIC DISEASE

Hematologic diseases have received attention in recent studies of paleopathology[29] and efforts have been made to correlate certain forms of anemia with population-level responses to environmental change in earlier times.[30] One instance of a condition likely resulting from some blood disorder was observed at Stobi. The age of the adult male from Grave 140 is difficult to assess, but the 3rd molars have erupted and there is only slight synotosis of the preserved cranial sutures. Dental attrition suggests an age in the 3rd or early 4th decade of life.

The cranium is fragmentary, but portions of the frontal and parietals are as much as 7 mm. thick. This abnormal thickening appears to be limited to the diplöe, and only very slight involvement of the outer table is apparent. In addition, the innominata are abnormally thickened; here also, the thickening is in the cancellous bone. The cortical bone appears to be normal. The cancellous tissues of the long bones appear to be present in normal amounts. There are several forms of anemia which could be responsible besides thalassemia.[31]

E. INFLAMMATION

One individual was diagnosed as having a non-dental bone inflammation. Another displayed lesions that may be inflammations, but this identification is by no means certain.

Grave 112, that of an adult male of uncertain age at the time of death (perhaps the 3rd or early 4th decade, judging from dental attrition and synotosis of cranial sutures), is dated to the 2nd or early 3rd century A.C. The medial surfaces of both tibiae are slightly swollen and the cortical bone is striated.[32] This bilateral osteitis[33] of the tibiae has been noted in a number of skeletal series[34] and can range from the barely perceptible lesions of this example[35] to more severely swollen tibiae with attendant bowing.

The wide geographical distribution of this peculiar lesion and the range of its "severity" suggest that more than one etiology is involved.[36] It is not impossible that trauma, in addition to bacterial infection, may play a role.

The lesions on the 18—19 year-old, perhaps a male, from Grave 99 are even more obscure (Fig. 3). Both radial tuberosities are malformed, the left a little more so than the right. The central portions of the tuberosities are depressed (about 2 mm. in the left) and in the left some cancellous bone is exposed. Otherwise the tuberosities seem normal.

---

[29] Moseley, op. cit. (in note 6).
[30] See note 5.
[31] Brothwell, op. cit. (in note 11) 160—161; Moseley, op. cit. (in note 6) 123—129.
[32] Recall that of the 70 (at least) inhumations, lower legs were preserved in 56 (17 sub--adults, 39 adults).
[33] Osteitis is the name given to infections of bone tissue.
[34] Usually termed "periostitis" to indicate that only the tissue on the exterior of the bone is involved.
[35] Mentioned in Wells, op. cit. (in note 11) 76—80.
[36] A. M. Brues, "Discussion," in Jarcho, op. cit. (in note 6) 107—112, considers it a manifestation of a single disease. She is careful to note, however, that there is little transition between the cases of slight swelling and gross porous involvement of bone. If, as she indicates, the lesions have a bimodal distribution of severity, the possibility of multiple etiology should be entertained.

The left ulna is normal except for a small (*ca.* 1 mm. long) bony elaboration on the proximal end of the interosseus crest, where the connective tissue from the radial tuberosity would have been sited. The right ulna is normal.

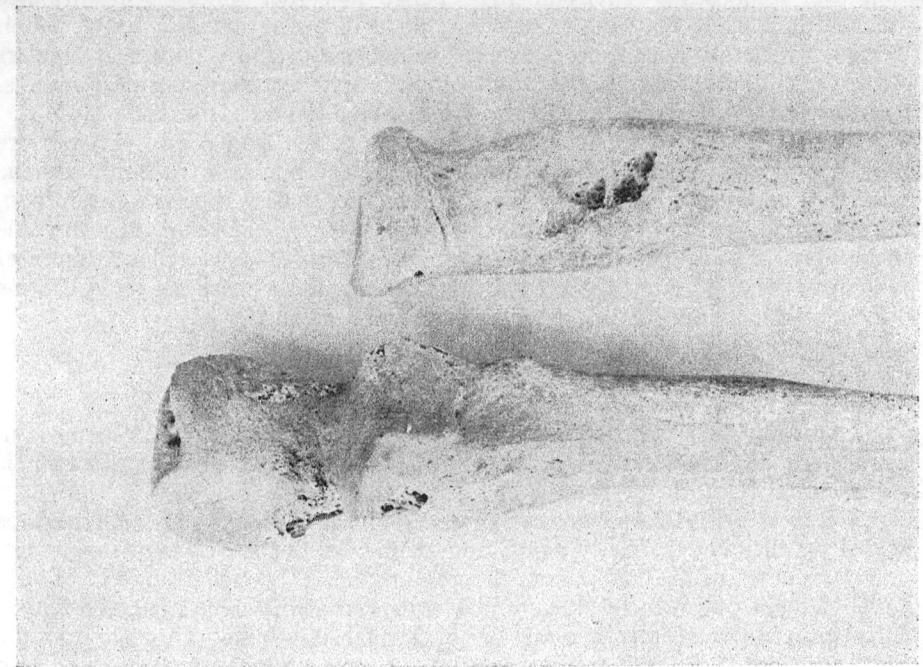

Figure 3. Grave 99. Proximal left radius and ulna.

Both humeri have atypical, roughened insertions in the inferior margin of the bicipital grooves. In the left the elaboration resembles cancellous bone tissue but it appears that no penetration of cortical bone was achieved. The bilateral occurrence of this condition suggests some systemic inflammation if these lesions are a form of osteitis.

F. DENTAL PATHOLOGY

Diseases associated with the human dentition have a history stretching well back into the Paleolithic (despite some popular notions) and the people of Stobi were not immune to dental problems. Dental disease can begin in the soft tissues of the mouth and eventually involve the bony supporting structures of the teeth and the teeth themselves. Conversely, they can begin in the hard tissues (teeth or bone) and eventually involve fleshy tissues. Skeletal studies employ classifications of oral disease much simplified from those of practicing diagnosticians[37] and this study recognizes the following conditions in the Stobi materials.

---

[37] A very useful summary of oral pathology in the living is S. N. Bhaskar, *Synopsis of Oral Pathology* (St. Louis 1969).

1. *Caries.* Dental cavities visible on the tooth surface.

2. *Abscesses.* These can develop from deep caries, extensive dental attrition, peridontal inflammation, or can appear to be idiopathic when no cause can be identified. Naturally, only those abscesses which involved bony tissues are evidenced.

3. *Ante-mortem tooth loss.* A distinction cannot be made between those teeth exfoliated from disease, those accidently knocked out, and those intentionally extracted. A healed-over tooth socket is simply regarded as a tooth lost during life.[38]

4. *Enamel hypoplasia.* These are macroscopic irregularities in enamel calcification as a result of some metabolic insult during formation of the tooth crown in childhood. That is, as the tooth is forming in a youngster's mouth, stresses such as prolonged high fevers or malnutrition may interfere with the development of individual teeth. Thereafter, the teeth will display "rings" of malformed enamel. There is a wide range in the severity of this condition.

The lack of complete and well-preserved dentitions in the collection is annoying. The sample is composed of fragments of 43 adult dentitions, and 5 adult dentitions which are classed as "reasonably complete". Twenty-four of the fragmentary dentitions are merely alveolar fragments[39] from cremations; in these only the tooth sockets (and occasionally a stub of burnt dentine) are preserved (Fig. 4). These cremated specimens have some value in an examination of tooth loss ante-mortem, since healed-over sockets can be deduced from the pattern of remaining sockets. A number of fragments from inhumations have lost a number of teeth post-mortem; field archeologists are familiar with the vicissitudes of burial environments which may completely destroy teeth.

1. *Caries*

There is a total of 11 dental caries in the collection, all in inhumations (as might be expected). All the caries were in the 5 well-preserved dentitions, and 7 of them were associated with alveolar abscesses (Fig. 5). The 4 caries not associated with abscesses were in molars, and only 2 dentitions shared these caries (Graves 17 and 102).[40]

2. *Abscesses*

A total of 22 alveolar abscesses was noted, 7 of which were associated with a carious tooth (these were shared among Graves 17, 102, and 112). Of the remaining 15 abscesses, 10 had the associated tooth retained in the socket, 3 were from 2 cremations (Graves 43 and 48), 1 had lost the tooth post-mortem, and 1 tooth appears to have been exfoliated during life. Each of the 11 dentitions having 1 or more dental lesions has at least 1 abscess.

---

[38] Hypodontia (agenesis of one or more teeth in the living) will be noted *infra* as a complicating factor in assessing ante-mortem tooth loss.

[39] The alveolus is simply the tooth-bearing portions of the jaws.

[40] Tables II and III show the distibution of dental lesions in inhumations and cremations.

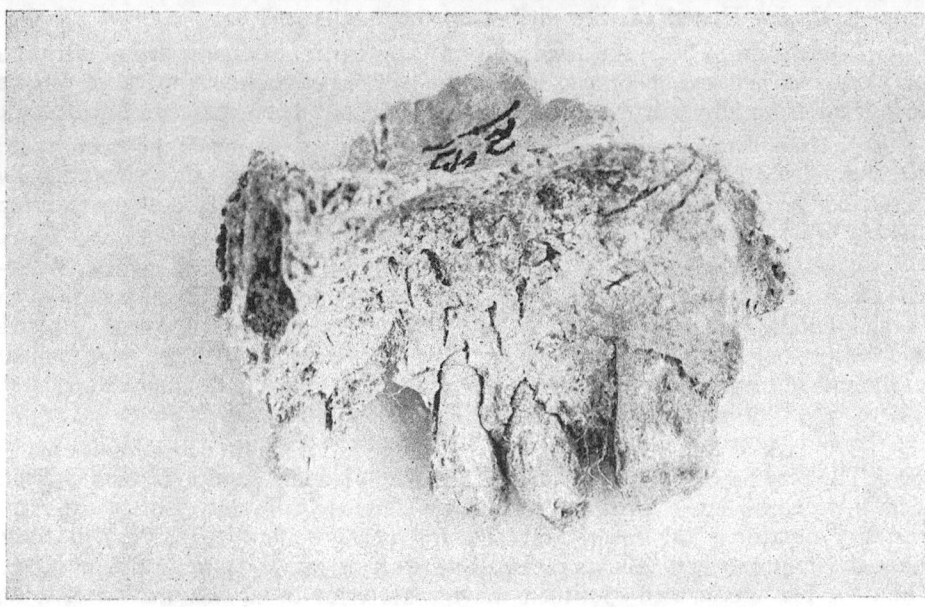

Figure 4. Example of alveolar fragment from a cremation (Grave 245).

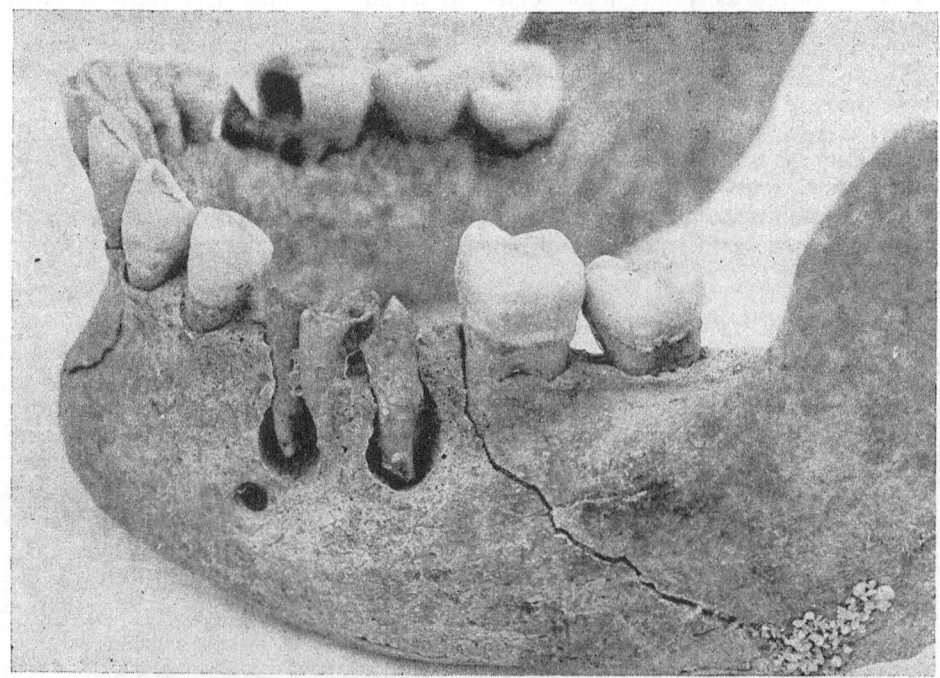

Figure 5. Example of decayed teeth and associated abscesses (Grave 101).

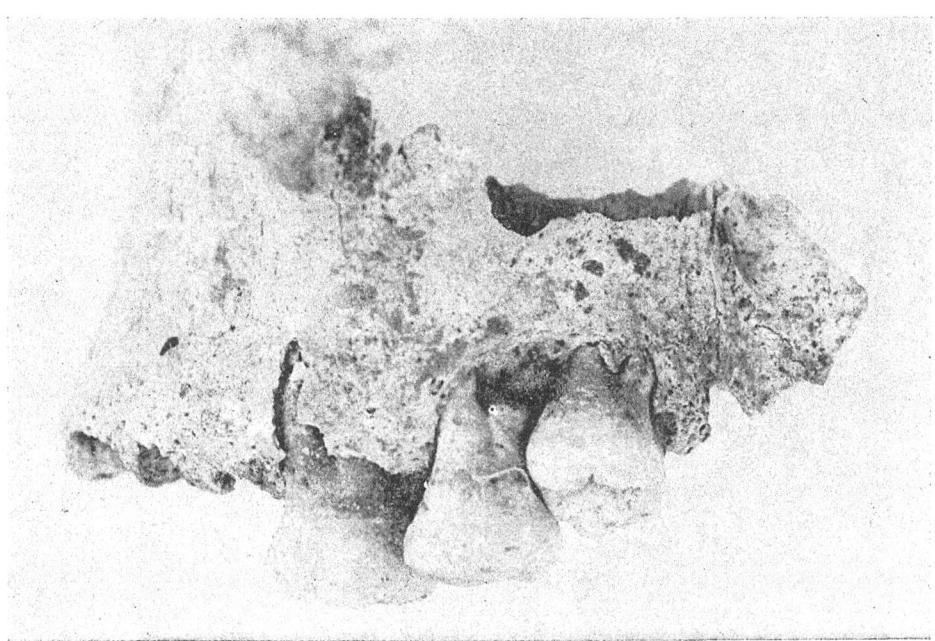

Figure 6. Grave 190. Impacted 3rd molar and abscessed 2nd molar.

One abscess, in Grave 190 (Fig. 6), is the result of an upper left 3rd molar impacted against the 2nd molar. In Grave 17 (Figs. 7, 8), a rotten upper left 2nd premolar has produced a sinus on the buccal side of the maxilla, and what appears to be a radicular cyst in the left maxillary sinus.[41]

TABLE II
Distribution of Dental Caries and Abscesses in Inhumations

	I1	I2	C	PM1	PM2	M1*	M2	M3
Number of Teeth Present	23	25	27	28	31	35	38	32
Caries Observed	0	0	0	0	0	0	3** (8%)	1 (3%)
Caries-Abscesses Observed	0	0	0	0	4 (13%)	2 (6%)	0	2 (6%)
Abscesses Observed	0	0	1 (4%)	2 (7%)	1 (3%)	1 (3%)	4 (4%)	2 (6%)

* A single observation of an abscess with no associated carie, between an M1 and an M2, is not listed on this table.

** Figures in parentheses are the percentage of lesioned teeth in that particular kind of tooth.

---

[41] V. Alexandersen, "The Pathology of the Jaws and the Temporomandibular Joint," in Brothwell and Sandison, op. cit. (in note 7) 551—595, illustrates a very similar example in Fig. 11. He classifies this kind of a cyst, along with two different varieties of abscesses, as "peripical osteitis" (bone infection at the tip of a tooth root) p. 577.

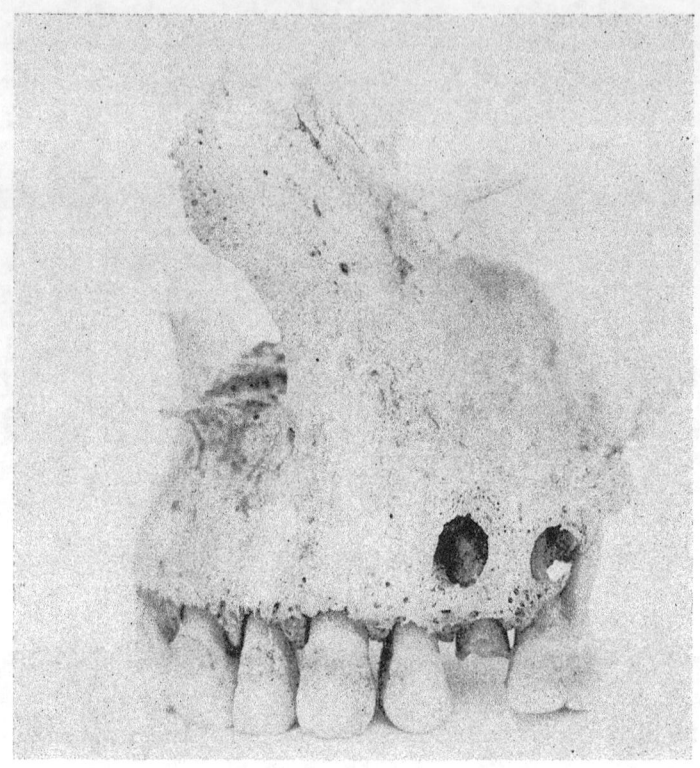

Figure 7. Grave 17. Maxillary abscesses, lateral view.

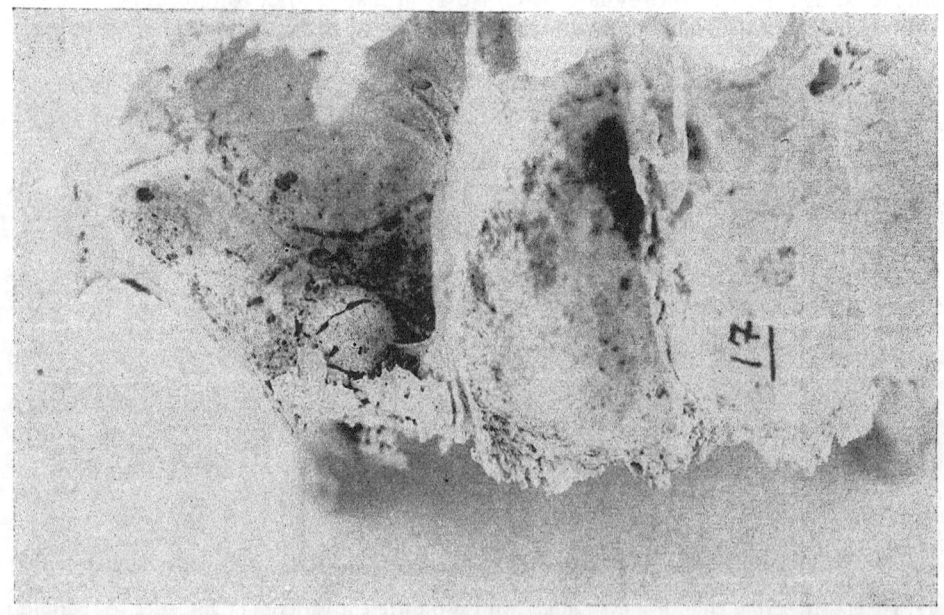

Figure 8. Grave 17. "Radicular cyst" on interior of maxilla. Associated with abcessed 2nd premolar.

3. Ante-mortem tooth loss

Ante-mortem tooth loss was evaluated by examining the patterns of tooth sockets present. The presence of the tooth, or sharp edges of the socket if the tooth was missing, indicated that the associated tooth was present at the time of death. Since there is an uncertain probability of 3rd molar agenesis,[42] in only one instance was there reason to believe that ante mortem tooth loss was so widespread in a single dentition that the loss of a 3rd molar was suspected. Otherwise, "missing" sockets for 3rd molars were not counted. Consequently it is likely that 3rd molars are under-represented as regards pre-mortem loss in Table III.[43]

TABLE III

Ante-mortem Tooth Loss in Cremations and Inhumations

Cremations*	I1	I2	C	PM1	PM2	M1	M2	M3
Number of Sockets or Teeth Present	62	62	61	50	45	39	31	15
Teeth Lost Ante-Mortem	1	2	1	2	3	5	3	1
Persentage of that type of Tooth Lost Ante-Mortem	2%	3%	2%	4%	7%	13%	10%	7%
*Inhumations***								
Number of Sockets or Teeth Present	59	58	54	54	51	50	48	50
Teeth Lost Ante-Mortem	0	0	0	0	2	7	8	3
Percentage of that Type of Tooth Lost Ante-Mortem	0%	0%	0%	0%	4%	14%	17%	6%

* Number of *dentitions* with — tooth lost ante-mortem: 7
** Number of *dentitions* with — 1 tooth lost ante-mortem: 9

If the loss of a tooth before death is counted as a lesion along with caries and abscesses, 13 (66%) of 24 inhumation dentitions are lesioned, and 8 (33%) of 24 cremation dentitions are lesioned.

---

[42] This is the naturally occurring instance of a lack of one or more "wisdom" teeth.
[43] H. Brabant, "Palaeostomology," in Brothwell and Sandison, op. cit. (in note 7) 538—550, notes that 3rd molar agenesis may vary between 10% and 26% depending on the group under consideration. The other teeth most likely to be congenitially absent — the upper lateral incisors and premolars — are absent in 1% or less of his cases. The probability of agenesis of teeth other than the 3rd molar is so small that it was ignored in the present study.

4. Enamel hypoplasia

Enamel hypoplasia, irregularities in the formation of dental enamel, is thought to be one of the results of systemic disease[44] or some other metabolic insult during childhood. Such hypoplastic defects will be retained for life, but once tooth calcification is fully accomplished no hypoplastic lines can be incurred.

The only observations of enamel hypoplasia were on inhumations. Five adults were noted with hypoplasia,[45] but not one of the 11 sub-adult dentitions were recorded as being defective.

SUMMARY

There are few quantitative surveys of the pathology of sizeable samples from Roman cemeteries in the Balkans. J. L. Angel's[46] sample of Roman skeletons is too small to present an adequate picture of the health configuration of the population from which they were drawn.

This author[47] reports on a collection of 164 individuals from a 4th through 6th centuries A.C. cemetery in Ancient Corinth. The skeletons were very poorly preserved, and 153 come from tombs with multiple interments in varying degrees of articulation and completeness. The incidence of observation is not given,[48] but only one fracture, one inflamed tibia, two skull vaults with small lesions, and occasional instances of arthritic lipping were noted. Seven adults possessed abnormally thickened cranial vaults.[49] There were 48 fragmentary adult dentitions in the Corinth series, and only 1 carious tooth and 3 alveolar abscesses were observed.

These comparisons are specious in some ways, since we are assuming equivalency in several variables of which we cannot be certain. The Stobi sample has 4 graves of the 2nd century B.C. and spans the first 350 years of our era; the Corinth sample is later. Both collections are from urban sites with likely similar economies, but the graves surely possess social distinctions that our archeology cannot as yet detect.

At Stobi there were 39 adult inhumations with lower legs preserved and only 2 (4.5%) displayed fractures. These were the only fractures observed in the series. Complete spinal columns were so infrequent that no quantitative statement can be made concerning the incidence of inadequately fused neural arches or of osteoarthritis. A dozen or so sacra were preserved, and one had an open sacral canal.

---

[44] C. Wells, "A New Approach to Palaeopathology: Harris Lines," in Brothwell and Sandison, op. cit. (in note 7) 390—404.
[45] These were from Graves 17, 35, 99, 112, and 113a. Of the 24 adult inhumation dentitions, 21% were affected. None of the 11 fragmentary sub-adult dentitions possessed macroscopic hypoplastic defects.
[46] "Skeletal Material from Attica," *Hesperia* 14 (1945) 279—363.
[47] "The Skeletons of Lerna Hollow," *Hesperia* 42 (1973) 340—351.
[48] All were inhumations.
[49] Five possible cases were noted. There were 110 adults in the entire sample.

The individual with an abnormally thickened cranial vault and pelvis bones was the only one so afflicted of 70 inhumations. Some form of anemia may be involved, but not necessarily one of the varieties associated with population-level responses to endemic malaria.[50]

Five percent of the teeth in the Stobi series were carious, and two-thirds of the dental pathology was associated with the molar teeth. The greater surface area and the presence of pockets in the enamel of the chewing surfaces of back teeth make them more susceptible to decay than the other teeth. A similar pattern of the contribution of the molars to pathology is reflected in pre-mortem tooth loss.[51]

One has the impression that the sample from Stobi reflects a reasonably healthy group. There are at least 70 inhumations, and only 2 cases of trauma, 2 cases of bone inflammation, 1 hematologic disorder, and 3 relatively minor developmental anomalies were noted. The incidence of 8 adults with lipped vertebrae suggests that spinal pathology was not widespread.

It must be borne in mind that many of the deaths in the sample did not result from natural causes or old age. Certainly the immature ones and the young adults died from trauma, disease, or physiological mishap that left no discernible trace on the skeletons. There are only three instances in the Stobi series where the cause of death *might* be *reflected* in the bones: the two cases of bone inflammation and the presumed hematologic disorder. Some of the more massive alveolar abscesses could have served as debilitating infections which lowered bodily resistance to other ailments.

In the final analysis, this survey is like many other studies in paleopathology in that it can *suggest* the cause of death in only a small percentage of the individuals present. The skeletal evidence suggests that the group was relatively healthy. Future studies of mortality configurations should provide some insight into the demographic status of this group.

---

[50] In a few parts of the world where malaria is endemic, some populations have genetically endowed resistance to the disease. Under certain genetic combinations, however, the resistance to malaria accompanied by anemia (in one of several severities) may be fatal in childhood.

[51] See Table III.

ПАТОЛОГИЈА НА ОСТАТОЦИТЕ ОД ЧОВЕК ВО СТОБИ

АЛ. Б. ВЕЗАЛОВСКИ

Во периодот од 1970—1973 год. 243 гробови беа пронајдени на 7 сектори во Стоби, од кои 4 датираат од II век п.н.е, а останатите од првите четири века на нашата ера (Т. I). Од овие гробови 125 остатоци од најмалку 141 индивидуа (од кои 68 или 54% се кремирани). Во овој труд се прикажува колкава е корист од овие остатоци во проучувањето на здравјето на некогашните жители во Стоби.

Палеопатологијата претставува наука за болестите кои постоеле во поранешните времиња. Праучувањата се вршат директно преку испитување на коските или другите органски остатоци, индиректно од забелешките во античките извори и од презентираните деформации или болести во уметничките претстави (види забелешки 2, 3, 9, 11). Постојат две многу важни размислувања во палеопатологијата:

1. Различни болести можат да причинат сосема слични повреди на коските;

2. Многу процеси на болести или трауми не оставиле знак на коските за некаква повреда или причина за смртта, туку тие дејствувале само на меките оштетени делови на телото.

Сепак палеопатологијата може да проучи само дел од спектарот на човечките страданија. Ова особено се потврдува кога постојат фрагменти од изгорени коски останати после кремацијата.

Два костура (гробови 3 и 17) имале многу слично залечени фрактури, долниот дел од ногата тибијата и фибулата биле сраснати. Три индивидуи (гробови 20, 141, 160Б) имале помали вродени аномалии на грбнекот. Артритисот не бил многу раширен. Еден гроб на еден возрасен (гроб 140) мора да имал некаква болест во крвата која предизвикала проширување на просторот за сржта во коските на черепот и карлицата. Во гробот 112 костурот имаше малку нагорена тибија.

Одредувањето на денталната патологија се базира врз 5 прилично комплетно сочувани вилици со заби од возрасни и 43 фрагментирани (од кои 24 беа од кремирање).

Овие пет комплети на вилици ги имале сите 11 случаи на кариас од целокупно проучуваниот материјал а исто така и 7 од 22-та случаи на гангрена.

Се добива впечаток дека проучуваниот материјал од Стоби зборува за релативно здрава човечка група: во 70 погребувања со инхумација се повторуваат два случаа на траума, еден сигурен случај од нагорување на коски, еден од болест во крвта и 3 со помали вродени деформации. Сепак, поголем број на смртни случаи од целата група не можеле да бидат резултат на природни причини или старост: децата и младите морале да умираат од траума, болест или некое физиолошко пореметување, кои не оставиле видливи трагови на коските (некои од големите забни гангрени веројатно го ослабнувале организмот и можеби се симптоми за посериозни заболувања).

Обично, палеопатологијата може само да је претпостави причината за смртта во помал број на случаи, но затоа пак демографските проучувања даваат увид во утврдувањето на морталитетот кај населението.

WALL DECORATION AT STOBI

by

JAMES WISEMAN AND DJORDJE GEORGIEVSKI

1. INTRODUCTION

The interior walls of many of the buildings at Stobi were decorated with fresco or molded stucco.[1] Some of these decorative surfaces are of exceptional historical interest, such as the fresco from the Baptistery of the Episcopal Basilica which preserves the earliest portraits yet found in quantity from a Christian structure in Yugoslavia (Fig. 1).[2] Others are of somewhat less historical or specifically aesthetic interest, such as some examples of monochrome fresco secco (painting on dry wall plaster) or even of paint applied to wall surfaces that are basically clay in content.

The frescoes and molded stucco are still being mended and the study of the decorative compositions has only begun, though already a number of aspects of the evolution of stylistic preferences in wall decoration at Stobi have become evident. Future studies will be concerned with the decorative elements, style, composition, representations, and other related considerations.

This article is concerned chiefly with methods of application of a number of those decorative surfaces and with the composition of the clays, mortars, and pigments employed. The study is based both on examination in the field and on a number of chemical analyses performed in laboratories in Skopje and Zagreb.

Wall decorations in 10 buildings will be considered: a structure near the Large Bath that was destroyed in the 1st century A.C.; a building below the House of the Fuller that was destroyed in the late 1st or early 2nd century A.C.; Synagogue I (3rd century A.C.); the elaborate hall below the Central Basilica (early 4th century

---

[1] Wall mosaics and marble revetment have also been found but will not be discussed in this article.

[2] Other portraits from the Baptistery are published in W—MZ (1972) figs. 44—45; W—MZ (1974) figs. 30, 31; Wiseman, *Guide*, fig. 14; Dj. Mano-Zissi, "Stratigraphic Problems and the Urban Development of Stobi," *Studies* I, fig. 110.

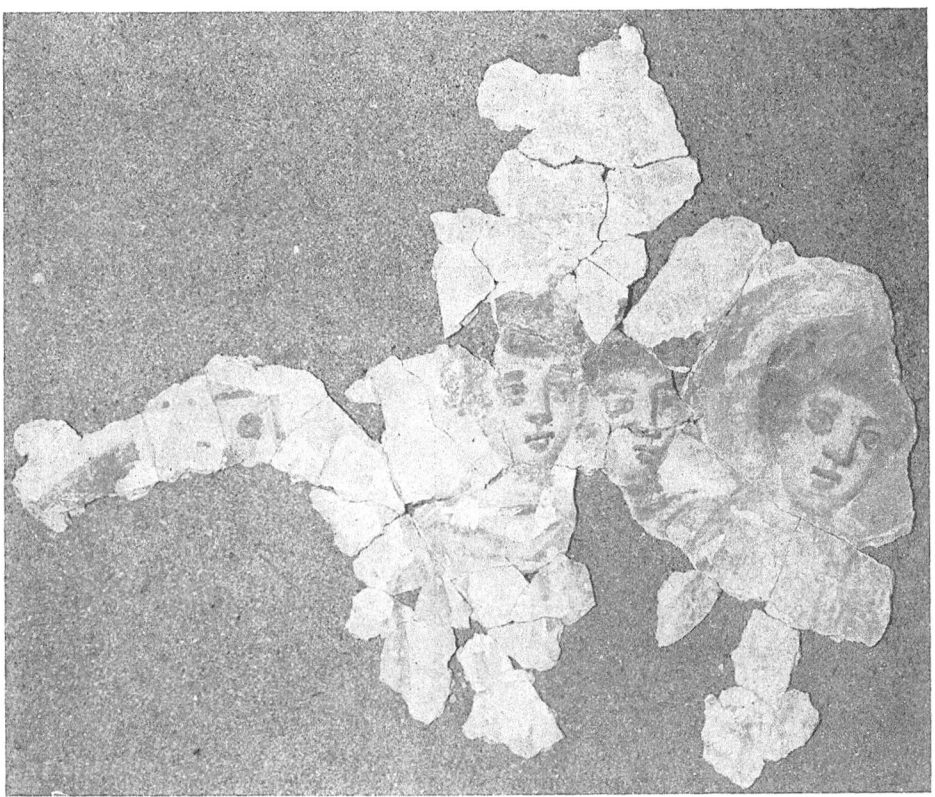

Figure 1. Group of three portaits from the E wall of the Baptistery.

A.C.); the Casa Romana, which may have been built earlier than the 3rd century A.C.; a building whose S wall lies below the S aisle of the Episcopal Basilica (perhaps early or mid-4th century A.C.); a structure near the Episcopal Basilica (at least 4th century A.C.); the Episcopal Basilica (the fresco probably dates to the 5th century A.C.); the Baptistery of the Episcopal Basilica (the fresco probably dates to the 5th century A.C.).[3] From these structures a total of 31 mortar and clay samples were selected for quantitative analysis (Table 1[4]).

---

[3] See the Plan of the Site for the location of the buildings mentioned. The dates of the buildings and their wall decoratons are discussed in greater detail in the appropriate sections.

[4] In the "SAMPLE" column, "Fresco" refers to the mortar layer to which pigment was applied; "Mortar" refers to a mortar layer underlying either stucco (fine mortar) or fresco; "Clay," as will be seen in Tables 2—6, contains some amount of lime. Fresco Storage Trays at Stobi are numbered sequentially by accession and may be sub-divided; they are merely storage units and are kept in the quonset hangar at Stobi. Fresco panels too large for trays are attached to cloth backing and suspended from racks; their storage reference is to the accession number following "Pr" for "Prepared Fresco." A Lot is the descriptive unit of documentation for contextual material and provides references to both inventoried and uninventoried artifacts and specimens.

TABLE 1.
Identification of Clay and Mortar Samples

Sample	Structure	Fresco Storage Tray	Context
1. Mortar 2. Mortar 3. Mortar	Wall LB 7 near Large Bath	231	Lot 938. Fragments found in debris of the 1st century A. C.
4. Fresco	Casa Romana: Room 1	296	Lot 1375. 3rd century A.C. or earlier.
5. Mortar (pilaster) 6. Clay 7. Stucco (panel)	Casa Romana: Room 2	None	No Lot. Samples 5—7 were obtained in 1973 during conservation work on the molded panels and Ionic pilasters of the S wall of Room 2. 3rd century A.C. or earlier.
8. Clay 9. Clay	House of the Fuller Room 26	133	Lot 772. Destruction in the early 2nd century A.C.
10. Clay 11. Stucco 12. Mortar 13. Fresco	Synagogue 1	116	Lot 65. Destruction in 3rd century A.C.
14. Fresco	Hall below nave of Central Basilica	Pr. 3	No Lot. Sample was obtained from a fresco panel that was removed in 1969 from the SW wall (SB Wall 16). 4th century A.C.
15. Clay 16. Fresco	Hall below nave of Central Basilica	7	Lot 815. 4th Century A.C.
17. Clay: Fresco I 18. Fresco I 19. Clay: Fresco II 20. Fresco II	Building below S aisle of the Episcopal Basilica	None Pr. 8	Samples 17—20 were obtained in 1973 during conservation of fresco panels on the S wall of the building. 4th century A.C.
21. Fresco	Building below S aisle of the Episcopal Basilica	223	Lot 957. 4th century A.C.
22. Fresco	Uncertain. Found below latest earthen floor W of Baptistery (EBas South: Room 2).	70	Lot 334. At least 4th century A.C.
23. Mortar 24. Fresco	Episcopal Basilica	43	Lot 323. Destruction in the late 6th century A.C.
25. Fresco 26. Fresco 27. Fresco 28. Fresco 29. Fresco	Baptistery: SE Baptistery: SE Baptistery: N Baptistery: W Baptistery: N	79 79 73 81 65	Lot 365. The Baptistery was destroyed in the late 6th century A.C.
30. Fresco 31. Fresco	Baptistery: W Baptistery: NW	61 60	Lot 364. Lot 365.

The 21 samples that underwent pigment analysis were from only four of those structures: Room 26 of the House of the Fuller, the Casa Romana, Synagogue 1, and the Baptistery of the Episcopal Basilica. The results of the pigment analyses will be considered in Section 6.

The wall surfaces, then, that are discussed in this study range in date over a period of at least five centuries. This long period of time and the number of samples analyzed make possible a consideration of the continuity and variety of mural techniques at Stobi as well as a number of other observations on wall decoration.

2. ANALYSES OF CLAYS AND MORTARS

The quantitative analyses of Samples 22 and 25—31 (Tables 4 and 5) were carried out in 1972 in the chemical laboratory of the Fabrikata za Stakla i Staklena Volna (Glass and Glass Insulation Factory) at Skopje, Macedonia, by Tepi Staniševa of the Conservation Institute of Macedonia.

The clay from the House of the Fuller (Table 3) was examined in two laboratories in 1972. Sample 8 was analyzed by Nevenka Antonov at the Laboratorij Restauratorskog Zavoda Hrvatske in Zagreb and Sample 9 was analyzed by Božana Naumovska, a chemist at the Glass and Glass Insulation Factory in Skopje. Sample 8 proved to be smaller than desirable, according to the report from the laboratory.

Aleksandra Jovanovska, a chemist at the Jugohrom-Jagunovce Factory in Tetovo and wife of Dj. Georgievski, analyzed Samples 1—3, 5—7, 10—21 (Tables 2 and 4) in 1973 and Samples 4, 23, and 24 in 1974.

Although the reports from the several analysts have been partially standardized by the authors, the tables still exhibit some variation in form and content. The variations are more indicative of differences in reporting procedures than in the approach to the analyses performed. A few observations on those procedures and on some of the laboratory methods follow which should prove helpful in understanding Tables 2—5 and in evaluating the discussions in later sections.

The quantity of each of the principal contents of the samples is expressed by a percentage figure. That figure is based on gravimetric procedures except in the cases of magnesium oxide and calcium oxide in Samples 22 and 25—31,[5] which were determined by metric titration. That is, the sample was weighed after each successive removal of a particular content and the weight loss then calculated in relation to the original weight of the sample.

More specifically, the procedure adopted in determining the first two characteristics listed in the tables was as follows. After recording the weight of the sample to be analyzed, moisture (hygroscopic water) was removed by drying the sample at a temperature of $105°C$ in an electric dryer. The sample was then weighed again and the loss of weight expressed by a percentage figure. Organic materials and carbon dioxide were eliminated next by glowing the sample at $1000°C$ in the electric oven and the sample weighed again. The new weight loss was also transposed into the percentage of the original weight.

---

[5] Murexide and Erikron T were used as indicators.

The insoluble residue is the amount of sand and clay remaining after the sample was twice dissolved in 50% diluted hydrochloric acid and dried at a temperature of 1000°C for an hour each time, and finally, after filtration, dried again at the same high temperature. A. Iovanovska reports that laboratory conditions were not ideal in 1973 and that the percentage figures given for the insoluble residue are not entirely reliable for the samples analyzed during that year. The chief problem was inadequate filtration equipment. The results most adversely affected were those reported for Samples 1, 6, 7, and 12. The overall percentage figures, however, that are given in the tables below the "Total" line are based on the analysis of other portions of the samples and those figures, even for the four samples cited above, are reliable.

3. THE EARLY ROMAN PERIOD

A number of fragments of fresco were found in 1973 alongside the W (interior) face of a wall belonging to a structure of undetermined function near the SE corner of the Large Bath (Plan of Site, No. 8). The fragments were in a deposit of mixed debris and earth representing a destruction and partial filling-in during the 1st century A.C.[6] The wall, designated LB Wall 7, lies above part of a colonnade (perhaps a peristyle) which was in ruins by sometime in the 1st century A.C., perhaps as early as the reign of Augustus.[7] The fresco, therefore, is securely dated to sometime within the 1st century A.C.

The wall itself has a substructure of re-used blocks while the curtain of the wall was of adobe brick or, more likely, terre pisé, since there is no trace of formed bricks and we should have to suppose their complete deterioration. Such a wall provides poor protection for a fresco since it is easy for moisture to penetrate from the exterior and damage the fresco. In order to offset at least partially the porosity of the wall and to provide a firmer surface for the mortar, stucco fragments ca. 0.025—0.045 m. thick were set into the wall face (Fig. 2). The stucco fragments had originally coated the columns of the colonnade(s) over which the wall was built. One column was found *in situ* and a second fallen to the side: both were still partially covered with the same type of stucco.

The wall was then covered with a very sandy clay-lime mortar containing straw as an additive to serve as a levelling layer 10—12 mm. thick (Table 2, Sample 1). A second layer of mortar (7—8 mm. thick) with a high lime content and crushed brick for added strength was then applied. The third and final layer of mortar, only slightly higher in lime content but more refined and without inclusions, is 4—5 mm. thick (Sample 3). Pigments were applied to this third coating of plaster after it dried (fresco secco).

---

[6] Lot 938, which represents the material found N of a later intrusive wall, and Lot 940, which was S of the same late wall. A lamp (L-73-4), probably imported from the Ephesus region, was found with the deposit of Lot 940. Richard H. Howland dates the lamp type to the late 2nd and early 1st century B.C. but notes its later appearance (second half of 1st century B.C.) elesewhere: *The Athenian Agora* IV: *Greek Lamps and their Survivals* (Princeton 1958) Type 49A, pp. 166—169.

[7] Lot 939 represents the material found *within* the terre pisé and provides the *terminus post quem* for Wall 7. The ceramics indicate a date near the turn of the era, i.e., late 1st century B.C. or early 1st century A.C.

Figure 2. Line of stucco fragments used to face the terre pisé construction of LB Wall 7. View from the S. The later wall in the foreground cuts through the N—S line of LB Wall 7.

TABLE 2.
Quantitative Analyses of Samples from Early Roman Structures (1st—3rd Centuries A. C.)

Characteristics	Sample Number										
	1	2	3	4	5	6	7	10	11	12	13
Hygroscopic water	0.65	0.30	0.55	—	0.33	1.37	0.42	0.65	0.45	0.33	0.86
Loss at 1000°C	14.90	41.10	41.70	21.47	42.63	7.48	16.85	13.51	24.95	10.55	17.41
Insoluble Residue	55.56	5.30	3.80	48.85	0.53	89.90	34.63	67.50	30.54	70.74	50.68
$R_2O_3 (Al_2O_3 + Fe_2O_3)$	2.21	1.09	1.04	1.51	1.21	0.62	2.35	4.59	2.33	2.16	8.50
CaO	17.37	52.20	53.06	27.56	53.52	9.84	19.55	12.50	38.05	11.40	18.98
MgO	0.96	0.31	0.40	0.52	0.55	0.17	0.66	2.08	0.95	0.67	2.91
TOTAL	91.65	100.30	100.55	99.92	98.77	109.38	74.46	100.83	97.27	95.85	99.34
Lime	43.02	94.70	96.20	51.14	99.47	10.10	65.37	32.50	69.46	29.26	49.32
Sand	50.74	3.82	3.20	36.16	—	67.34	27.20	48.43	13.24	55.47	38.99
Clay	4.82	—	0.60	12.70	0.55	22.56	7.13	19.07	17.30	15.27	11.69
Other Additions	Straw	Brick	—	Straw	Straw	Straw	Straw	Straw	Straw	—	Brick

The use of a mixed clay and lime mortar layer to level a wall surface before the application of lime mortar for fresco work appears to have been customary during the Early Roman period at Stobi and continued as a tradition, at least in some structures, into the 5th and 6th centuries. Another instance of its early use, which may also serve as an example of the negligence with which some wall surfaces were prepared, was found in Room 26 of the House of the Fuller (Plan of Site, No. 15). Room 26, excavated in 1972, was part of a private house that was destroyed by fire in the 2nd century A.C.[8] In this room clay was used not only to provide a levelling layer on an earthen wall but also as the field on which part of the decorative composition was painted. The most likely explanation is that when the plaster layer was applied, which was intended to receive the painted designs,[9] the decorator carelessly did not cover the highest upper part of the wall and then allowed the painted designs to extend onto the clay. Some patches of painted plaster were found still adhering to the lower part of the wall where the design imitated a dado of brecciated marble.

Table 3 lists the characteristics of Samples 8 and 9 from the painted clay. Lime was also present in the clay, as indicated by the amount of aluminum and iron hydroxides (Al_2O_3, Fe_2O_3), calcium oxide (CaO), and magnesium oxide (MgO).

A wider range of wall decoration is found in the Casa Romana, a large structure of still undetermined function that appears to have been abandoned before the end of the 3rd century A.C. Since the floor of the structure lies below the water table it has not been possible to dig tests for construction deposits.[10]

---

[8] W—MZ (1973) 397 and note 19 where coin 72-87 was too confidently dated as "Flavian." This coin is illegible though the profile of a head can be made out on the obverse; M. H. Crawford suggests that it could belong to the 2nd or 3rd century. Two other coins found in the same context are illegible pre-Augustan issues: 72-78 and 72-113. The ceramic material has been provisionally dated to the late 1st, early 2nd century A.C. A fill immediately above this deposit, Lot 771, had no coins but did contain somewhat more pottery sherds (120 as compared to 74). The date indicated by the ceramics is 2nd century. The deposit of Lot 771 was overlain by a deposit (Lot 770) whose date in the 3rd century is based both on ceramics and two coins, 72-57 and 72-85.

[9] Flowers, abstract quadrupeds (probably horses), and a dado imitating marble encrustation.

[10] See Plan of Site, near No. 26. The excavations in the Casa Romana and its date have been discussed in W—MZ (1972) 412; W—MZ (1973) 394—397; W—MZ (1974) 126—128. The

TABLE 3.

Quantitative Analyses of Clay and Lime Mortar from Room 26 of the House of the Fuller, Early 2nd Century A.C.

Characteristics	Sample Number	
	8	9
Hygroscopic Water	1.33	2.50
Loss at 1000°C	9.20	8.00
R_2O_3 ($Al_2O_3 + Fe_2O_3$)	13.52	19.72
Al_2O_3	9.18	16.70
Fe_2O_3	4.34	3.02
CaO	12.00	8.89
MgO	2.31	3.16
SiO_2	56.70	57.40
K_2O	1.81	Not reported
Na_2O	3.09	Not reported
TOTAL	99.96	99.67

The building was discovered in fall, 1970, when test trenches were dug near the Crna River preparatory to construction of a museum. The obvious importance of the structure called for more extensive exploration and necessitated a change of locale for the museum, which now occupies part of the former railway depot. The great depth of fill (nearly 8 m. in some areas), a rise in the water table since antiquity, and the presence of modern structures in the immediate vicinity have frustrated our attempts to determine fully the form, function, and history of the building. A number of features of the building, however, have become clear and will be discussed in detail in a later publication. The plan published here as Figure 3 was drawn at the end of the 1974 campaign and reveals a building of several large rooms, all of which display highly decorative wall surfaces.

Room 1 is a corridor whose walls, at least on the E and S, were originally covered with a brightly painted fresco. The upper register has red panels framed with thin lines of yellow paint, then larger bands of yellow and green. These are separated by carefully painted Ionic columns (Fig. 4). The lower register is only partially exposed and in some areas has been interrupted by a later application of a coarse gray plaster. What is visible is only a red-painted surface. There may, however, have been figures either in some of the upper panels or lower register since some figured fragments were found in the adjacent Room 2.[11]

Sample 4 (Table 2) is from the fresco in Room 1 and was analyzed in 1974. The plaster to which the paint was applied was partially dry at the time and was immediately polished, probably with a metal spatula. There may have been a second polishing with wax after the paint was dry. The mortar contained a relatively high proportion (nearly half) of sand and clay. Straw is present only in traces.

---

stone-paved street between the E outer wall of the building and the City Wall was covered to a depth of over a meter with refuse and earth by sometime in the 2nd half of the 3rd century A.C. The date is indicated both by the ceramic material (Lots 1405, 1407—1410) and a coin tentatively identified (Wiseman) as an issue of the Emperor Vibius Trebonianus Gallus, 251—253 A.C. (Coin 74-444).

[11] W—MZ (1973) pl. 66, fig. 8.

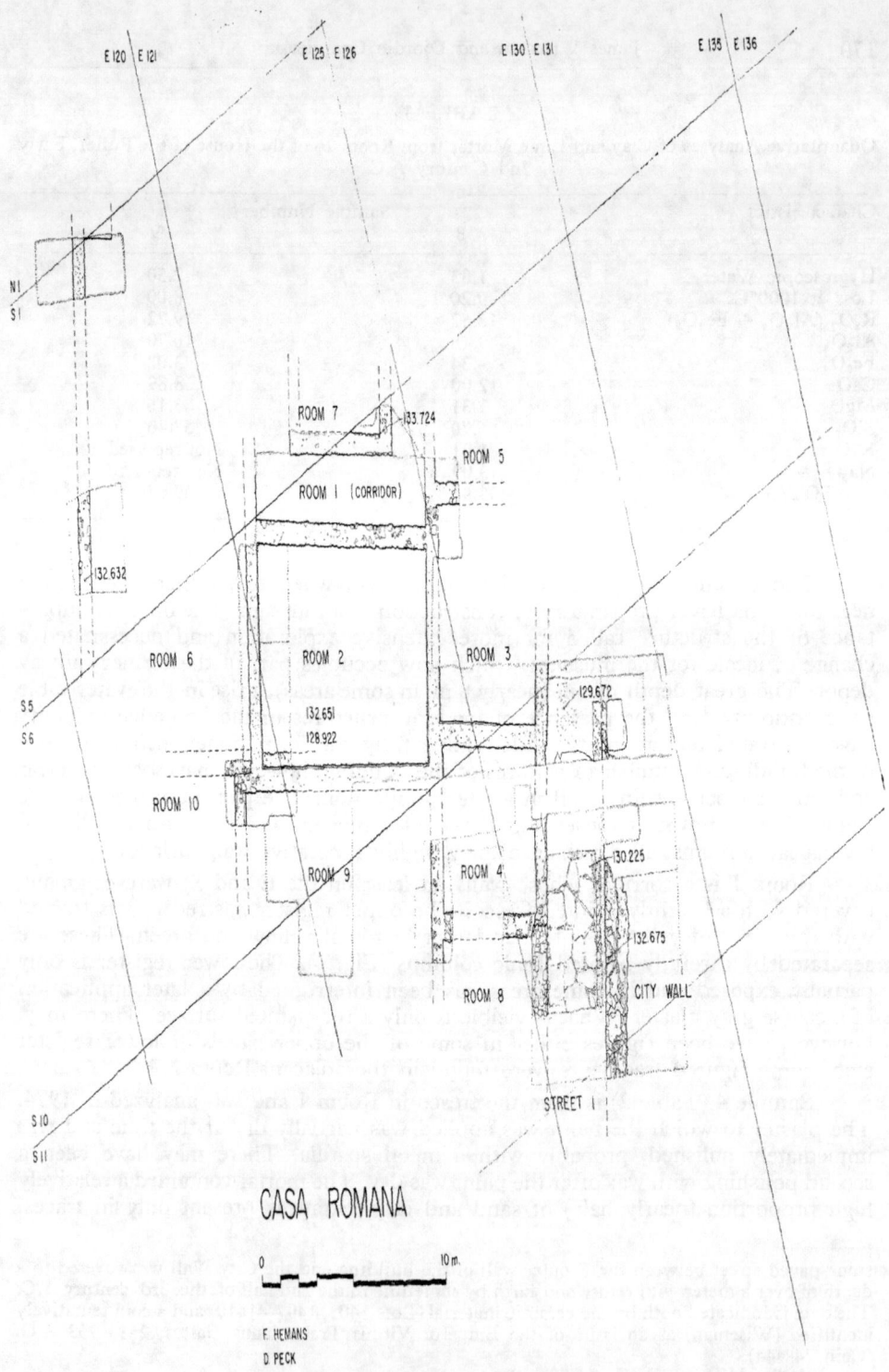

Figure 3. Plan of the Casa Romana. Drawing by F. Hemans and D. Peck.

Figure 4. Fresco on the S wall of Room 1 of the Casa Romana.

The upper register of the walls in Room 2 is comprised of imitation marble decoration in molded stucco. The S wall (Fig. 5) is illustrative. There are a total of 5 vertical panels (including one of double size) separated by Ionic pilasters and there are pilasters in the corners as well. The central surface of each zone is emphasized by a profiled rectangular frame. A profiled string course of molded stucco, 0.20 m. high, beginning ca. 2 m. above the floor level, separates the imitation marble from the lower register which, where preserved and visible, is red-painted plaster. A later gray plaster, as in Room 1, interrupts and partially covers the surface just described.

Figure 5. Molded stucco on the S wall of Room 2 of the Casa Romana.

The molded panels and pilasters were removed in 1973 and 1974 in order to preserve them.[12] The wall decoration could be seen to have been applied in

---

[12] Samples 5 and 6—7 were taken from the 3rd pilaster and the 4th panel, respectively, E of the W wall of the room.

The *distacco* technique is one of the most commonly used methods for removing frescoes from walls and is here briefly described. A solution of Indian shellac in alcohol (12 grams of shellac per one liter of alcohol) is first applied to the face of the fresco. Honey is often used instead of alcohol, but was not used in the Casa Romana because it takes longer to dry and there was already a problem with excessive moisture in the wall surfaces there. A glue with a mucilage base is then used to secure a layer of gauze to the face. The glue contains 1 kg. of mucilage dissolved in 1 liter of water to which 0.2 liter each of vinegar and bile is added; the glue should be liquid and warm when applied. After the application of the gauze the same glue is used to attach a layer of strong linen. The glue is then allowed to dry before removing the fresco. The panels are then removed by driving spear-shaped metal bars between the fresco and the wall. The reverse of the fresco is then cleaned and covered with a large quantity of milk which makes the mortar less crumbly before the final application of preservative. When the mortar is dry a layer of linen is stuck to the back by a coating of glue with a casein base. The fresco may then be turned over and the face cleaned of linen, gauze, and mucilage with warm water.

three layers: 1) a dark, ocher clay with straw temper 20—25 mm. thick laid directly on the wall (Sample 6); 2) a layer of mortar 5 mm. thick composed of lime and sand; 3) a layer of finer mortar and sand (stucco) which was formed into the vertical panels already described (Sample 7). As a final step the surfaces of the stucco were planed with a coating of slaked lime. All the surfaces may later have been coated with wax to provide a gloss, but tests for resin have not yet been performed to provide confirmation for this application either in Room 2 or Room 1. The pilasters were made of nearly pure lime for easier modelling (Sample 5).

Figure 6. Earlier molded stucco on the S wall of Room 2 of the Casa Romana.

Giornate, that is, the areas plastered at one time, in some cases "a day," are indicated by overlapping seams in the mortar bedding. The *giornate* observed during the removal of the stucco indicate that the wall was covered proceeding from the lower to the upper surfaces.

The use of the clay layer, which contains only a small amount of lime, to provide an even surface for the mortar beds is similar to the practice already seen in the other wall surfaces discussed. The major difference here is in the case of walls made of roughly cut stones and mortar instead of earth and clay.

A still earlier surface of rectangular, stuccoed panels was discovered on the S wall when the stucco there was removed in 1974 (Fig. 6). This surface too has been removed for preservation, but the analysis of the mortar has not yet been performed.

Both fresco and molded stucco imitating carved marble may be associated with the Synagogue of Polycharmus (Synagogue 1). The fragments were found together below the mosaic floor of the hall below the nave of the Central Basilica and include numerous pieces bearing parts of the repeated legend, Πολύχαρμος ὁ πατὴρ εὐχὴν.[13] The fragments were found in mixed debris of the 3rd century and probably belong to a wall built in the same century.[14]

The Polycharmus dedications were painted on dry plaster (fresco secco) with a high sand content and brick inclusions (Sample 13). The painted layer had been applied to a mixed mortar and sandy clay bed (Sample 12). It is not clear whether or not yet another clay layer had been used to even the wall surface to which the layers of the fresco were applied. The molded stucco, with a higher lime content than the Polycharmus fresco, was applied over a bedding of similar composition (Sample 10).

4. THE LATE ROMAN PERIOD

The hall below the Central Basilica was constructed in the early 4th century A.C. and some technical aspects of the mosaic are discussed elsewhere in this volume.[15] During the excavation of this hall in 1969 by members of the Conservation Institute of Macedonia, Djordje Georgievski removed a panel of fresco from a wall facing E on the S side of the hall.[16] This wall of stone and earth mortar forms part of the Southwest Room that opened N into the hall itself. Sample 14 (Table 4) was taken from the painted plaster (fresco secco) of that panel.

TABLE 4.
Quantitative Analyses of Samples from the Late Roman Period

Characteristics	Sample Number								
	14	15	16	17	18	19	20	21	22
Hygroscopic water	0.48	1.36	0.42	1.48	1.05	1.13	0.66	1.95	1.66
Loss at 1000°C	29.89	12.23	32.31	13.90	18.25	15.53	46.00	38.35	38.20
Insoluble residue	29.20	66.78	22.53	59.99	51.99	64.57	1.90	15.81	13.40
R_2O_3	2.87	7.50	1.88	6.12	3.07	6.70	0.48	2.58	2.28
CaO	34.83	10.35	37.25	14.23	24.06	10.28	49.44	41.70	35.69
MgO	1.42	2.68	2.00	0.65	0.86	0.72	0.85	1.56	7.59
TOTAL	98.69	100.90	96.39	96.37	99.28	98.93	99.33	101.95	98.82
Lime	70.80	33.22	77.47	40.01	48.01	35.43	98.10	78.64	60.38
Sand	25.21	50.43	21.29	46.12	36.68	48.13	0.52	11.93	
Clay	3.99	16.35	1.24	13.87	15.31	16.44	1.38		
Other additions	Straw Brick	Straw	Straw	Straw	Straw	Straw	—	Straw Brick	Straw

---

[13] W—MZ (1971) 409—410; W—MZ (1972) 410.
[14] For the date of Synagogue 1 see the references in note 11 and Martin Hengel, "Die Synagogeninschrift von Stobi," *ZNTW* 57 (1966) 145—183.
[15] The Central Basilica and the "hall below the nave of the Central Basilica" have been referred to in earlier reports as the Synagogue Basilica and Synagogue 2, respectively: W—MZ (1971) 406—411; W—MZ (1972) 408—410. See also the article by Ruth Kolarik and Momčilo Petrovski in this volume.
[16] The wall has since been designated SB Wall 16.

For comparison we may examine Sample 16 which was found during the 1970 excavations by the current Stobi Project in debris near the S wall (SB Wall 8) of the hall. The similarity of geometric motives, the use of the fresco secco technique, and the archaeological context had already convinced us of the high probability that the two frescoes were from the same structure. Their close similarity in content (see Table 4) under the circumstances leaves little room for doubt that they belong to the same building and time period.

The clay-lime mortar backing of Sample 16 was also analyzed and is listed in Table 4 as Sample 15. Lime is present in approximately the same quantity as we have observed it in other "clay" levelling layers of the Early Roman period (cf. Samples 10 and 12, and Sample 1 to a lesser degree; but Sample 1 had only 10.10% lime content).

Figure 7. Roof tile fragments along the face of the terre pisé superstructure of SB Wall 8. The S stylobate of the Central Basilica is visible in the background.

An additional sector of SB Wall 8 was cleared in 1974; this is the wall that the fresco represented by Samples 15 and 16 must have decorated. The socle of the wall was made of stone and the upper curtain was terre pisé. In the newly excavated sector it could be seen that baked terracotta roof tiles had been set into the inner face of the terre pisé (Fig. 7) in the same manner that stucco fragments had been re-used in the 1st century structure near the Large Bath.[17] Part of the interior face of the N wall of the hall was also cleared in 1974. In the latter excavations not only were similar fresco fragments found in large quantity alongside the wall, but a few patches were preserved in their place on the wall (both on the terre pisé and on the stone socle).

---

[17] See above in Section 3.

Another structure that went out of use towards the end of the 4th century or very early in the 5th century A.C. was discovered in 1973.[18] A portion of the S wall of the building was excavated below the S aisle of the Episcopal Basilica and was found to have two layers of fresco on its interior face. The later layer (Fresco II, Fig. 8) was in poor condition and was removed for preservation by the *strappo* technique.[19] The earlier fresco (Fresco I), though it shows signs of damage, is in better condition and has been left on the wall. The later fresco is very similar in design to Fresco I: there are tapestry designs and imitation marble encrustation between Ionic pilasters. The later representations are somewhat simplified versions of the earlier work and are rendered in fresco secco. Fresco I is true fresco and is illustrated in W-MZ (1974) Figure 30.

During the removal of Fresco II and preservation of the earlier fresco *in situ* samples for analysis were taken from all layers and, since holes in Fresco I exposed the wall behind, observations could be made on the manner of application of both frescoes. The characteristics of the samples (17—20) are reported in Table 4.

The wall on which the frescoes had been applied is made of a stone and cement socle rising 1.61 m. above the painted mortar floor of the building. Adobe brick in earth mortar was used for the upper curtain of the wall; the fresco was found preserved on both the stone and brick zones of the wall. A sandy clay, with a lime content similar to those already noted, was applied to the wall as a levelling layer 25—35 mm. thick. The overlapping seams of *giornate* show that the bedding was layed from the upper surfaces downward. The plaster on which the designs were painted was 5—6 mm. thick and contained relatively little more lime (8%) than the bedding.

The bedding for Fresco II (Sample 19) was a layer of clay and lime, 20—25 mm. thick, applied over the entire surface of Fresco I. The final layer (Sample 20) was thin, 4—5 mm. as Fresco I had been, but the composition was remarkably different. The lime content is over 98% and no inclusions were detected, whereas straw was found in Samples 17—19. Only Samples 2 and 3 from the structure near the Large Bath and Sample 5, the pilaster from the Casa Romana, exhibit a comparable quantity of lime. Two of those samples date to the 1st century and the third (from the Casa Romana) could be as early; the latter, as demonstrated above, is certainly earlier than the late 3rd century.

The ceiling of the structure may also have been covered with fresco secco. Several fragments of painted plaster were found that bear distinct impressions of reeds on the back in the debris and dump fill alongside the interior face of the wall. Sample 21, also with a relatively high lime content, was taken from one o.

---

[18] The building below the Episcopal Basilica is discussed in W—MZ (1974) 141—144. There is as yet no firm evidence for its date of construction.

[19] The *strappo* technique was employed because it was apparent that the fresco to be removed overlay yet another fresco which must also be preserved. The use of layers of gauze and linen applied with warm glue is the same as in the *distacco* technique (see note 12), and the glue differs only in that alcohol instead of honey is regular in this technique rather than exceptional. The panel to be removed is cut only slightly with a knife and a spatula is then employed at the edges to separate the painted surface and 1—2 mm. of mortar. The fresco surface is then carefully pulled from its bed, leaving part of its mortar on the face of the earlier fresco which may then be cleaned. The final steps in cleaning and preservation are identical with those described for the *distacco* technique.

Figure 8. Fresco II below the S aisle of the Episcopal Basilica. Water color by B. Damjanovski and M. Petrovski.

those fragments (Fig. 9).[20] Reeds were not used in the wall fresco, at least in the areas so far examined, and would have been useful in providing better adhesion for plaster applied to a ceiling.

Figure 9. Reed impressions on the back of fresco applied to the ceiling of the building below the S aisle of the Episcopal Basilica.

It should be noted that fragments of molded stucco panels with reed impressions on the back have also been found in Room 1 of the Casa Romana where we may be confident that reeds were *not* used to help bed the wall frescoes (Fig. 10). The shape of the impressions on the back of the fragment shown in Figure 10 suggests that it filled an obtuse angle made by the juncture of the ceiling with a wall or other segment of the ceiling.[21]

---

[20] Lot 957. The fragment on the left in fig. 9 is in Fresco Storage Tray 226 and the two fragments on the right in Tray 228.

[21] The fragment was found in 1974 (Lot 1375) and is stored in Fresco Storage Tray 296.

Sample 21 from below the Episcopal Basilica contained both straw and crushed brick, the latter in sufficient quantity to give a reddish tinge to the mortar. The thickening and strengthening of the mortar provided by the brick would have helped

Figure 10. Reed impressions on the back of fresco fragment from a ceiling (probably Room 1) of the Casa Romana.

the adhesion to a ceiling, almost certainly the building near whose wall the fragments were found. The examples with reed impressions from the Casa Romana, however, contain no crushed brick.

Sample 22 is from a group of fresco fragments found in a deposit below the latest earthen floor of Room 2 which lies W of the Baptistery and S of the Episcopal Basilica, whose floor is some 4 m. higher.[22] The type of design could not be determined and there is no definite structure with which the fragments found here can be definitely associated on archaeological grounds, though they are likely to have come from a building near-by. A comparison of the characteristics of Sample 22 with samples taken from other buildings near-by may be made by examining Tables 4 and 5.

Sample 22 bears no resemblance in content or color either to Fresco I or II of the building below the S aisle of the Episcopal Basilica. The difference in lime content should be especially noted. We may, in any case, rule out the earlier

---

[22] Lot 334. There were only 40 sherds in the deposit and no other datable artifacts. The ceramics indicate a date of at least the 4th century A.C.

Fresco I since Sample 22 is fresco secco. Sample 25 from the Episcopal Basilica has some 29% more lime; even the bedding for the Basilica (Sample 24) contains somewhat more lime than Sample 22. Samples from the Baptistery (25—31), however, are not only closely similar in lime content but even in the percentage of calcium oxide, the principal ingredient of lime. A more remarkable similarity is seen in the quantity of magnesium oxide, 7.59% in Sample 22 and ranging from 4.13 to 14.88% in the samples from the Baptistery. Only one other sample tested contained over 3% (Sample 9: the clay and lime mortar from the House of the Fuller) and 13 of the samples contained less than 1%.

These comparisons suggest that the fresco-makers who prepared the figured wall decoration of the Baptistery used the same basic formula as those who created the fresco to which Sample 22 belonged. There is no possibility that Sample 22 is from the Baptistery itself, because the Baptistery frescoes are entirely true fresco.

5. THE EARLY CHRISTIAN PERIOD

Table 5 records the characteristics of samples from the Episcopal Basilica (23—24) and the Baptistery (25—31). Since some of the more remarkable features of these samples were discussed in the previous section, it is necessary here only to emphasize the considerable difference between the contents of the two frescoes: the Basilica fresco is higher in lime content, but much lower in the amount of magnesium oxide; a circumstance that probably is the result, at least in part, of the utilization of stone from a different quarry.

TABLE 5.
Quantitative Analyses of Samples from the Episcopal Basilica and Baptistery

Characteristics	Sample Number								
	23	24	25	26	27	28	29	30	31
Hygroscopic water	0.10	0.15	1.66	2.66	2.00	1.75	1.66	1.66	2.66
Loss at 1000°C	28.12	40.60	39.55	40.47	38.80	40.90	39.60	39.15	40.43
Insoluble residue	35.11	8.79	12.06	12.72	11.49	8.58	12.60	12.60	11.69
R_2O_3	1.86	1.36	2.02	2.20	2.93	1.60	2.52	2.13	1.65
CaO	32.08	47.15	32.13	30.58	34.68	42.47	36.03	30.69	27.46
MgO	2.28	1.60	11.43	12.63	8.15	4.13	7.97	11.90	14.88
TOTAL	99.45	99.59	98.85	101.26	98.05	99.43	100.38	98.13	98.77
Lime	64.90	89.35	61.20	61.20	60.45	63.70	61.70	59.93	59.55
Sand	24.90	6.24							
Clay	10.20	2.55							
Other Additions	Straw	Straw	Straw Hemp	Straw	Straw Hemp	Straw	Straw	Straw	Straw

The significance of these differences is difficult to assess at this stage, especially since a qualification in the identity of Samples 23—24 must now be entered. The fragments were found in destruction debris filling the staircase that leads from the narthex of the Basilica to the rooms along the lower S side and eventually to the Baptistery. Among the fragments were several pieces from human figures, including at least one in the attitude of prayer. Both the archaeological evidence and the subject matter of fresco fragments indicate that the fragments came from a fresco adorning either the S wall of the narthex, or perhaps a wall near the SW corner of the S aisle, or from some 2nd story room on either side of the stairway.

In any case, it cannot be doubted that Samples 23—24 are associated with the Basilica, but the fresco need not belong (archaeologically) to the same time period as the narthex fragments found in the 1920s which show a clear stylistic similarity with the Baptistery fresco. The distinctive sideways glance of some figures from both frescoes, the variety of sizes of figures to indicate spatial arrangements, the wide range of portaiture, and a generalized overall "impression" of closeness of style have led to speculation that the same group of artists created both frescoes.[23]

But stylistic comparisons may not always be the best indicator of works by the same artists or groups of artists, just as such comparisons are often misleading in determining the date of a work of art. A change in style may be prompted by ephemeral events, such as a visit by an artist to an area where there is a different style preferred, or perhaps the arrival of an artifact of different style in the artist's own locale. But the technique of manufacture, which is, after all, the fundamental element of any craft, is a capability acquired through instruction and by apprenticeship. It is thus far less subject to change than style which, though controlled to some extent by the conservatism of the culture in which it is created, is also stimulated to change as a reaction *against* the tradition within the culture, or it may be reformed by some external influence.

All this suggests that the makers of the fresco in the narthex used a different quarry and followed a different tradition of manufacture than the artists at work in the Baptistery, despite the similarity of style. It *suggests* only, for only a single fragment from the Basilica was analyzed and that one is not necessarily from the narthex.

Another significant difference in the fragments found in the debris over the stairway and the Baptistery fresco is that the latter was entirely true fresco and the former was not. More precisely, the pieces from the Basilica (or Basilica adjunct) show that the fresco-makers were not troubled when the plaster dried before they applied their pigments, even though they clearly intended to work in true fresco. The result is that the same figured work was rendered partly in true fresco, partly in fresco secco.

There may also be some difference in time between the narthex and Baptistery frescoes. We can be confident that the Episcopal Basilica was built sometime not long after 393 but we have as yet (August 1974) no evidence that would allow a statement of similar confidence in the date of the Baptistery.[24] Architecturally

---

[23] On the narthex mosaics see especially Dj. Mano-Zissi, "Freske u Stobima," *Starinar* 8—9 (1933—1934) 244—48; Kitzinger, *Survey*, pp. 108—110; J. Maksimović, "Contribution a l'étude des fresques de Stobi," *CahA* 10 (1959) 207—216. See also Wiseman, *Guide*, p. 64.

[24] The ceramic material from three trenches dug into deposits laid at the time of construction indicates a date of the late 4th century or early 5th century A.C. The numismatic material provides additional evidence for the time range. The latest fully identifiable coin among the numerous coins found below the level of the first mosaic laid in the S aisle of the Episcopal Basilica is an issue of Theodosius I (Coin No. 74-396) minted in Cyzicus in 393—95 A.C. The reverse is *Gloria Romanorum* Type 18. Two coins (Nos. 74-428 and 429) found in 1974 in similar context, however, may be later. Michael H. Crawford, the Stobi staff numismatist, lists the former

and functionally they are associated. The Baptistery N wall is built against the heavy retaining wall that supports the terrace on which the Basilica was raised, so we can be sure that at least the foundations of the Basilica preceded the construction of the Baptistery. But the frescoes of the Baptistery may belong to a later phase of the structure, after the original dome had been replaced by another roof.[25] The narthex frescoes, too, may belong to one of the later phases of the Basilica.

Finally, we note that the Baptistery frescoes, like most of the frescoes examined, were bedded on a layer of clay where the walls are vertical, but were applied directly to the stone and mortar in the conches.

6. PIGMENTS

Twenty-one pigment samples from six fresco fragments found within four structures were selected for laboratory analyses in 1972. The range of time represented (2nd century A.C. to the 5th or 6th century A.C.) is only somewhat less than that covered by the mortar analyses and the spectrum of colors chosen is broadly representative. The chief purpose of the analyses was to determine the basic components of the pigments, from which we might discover whether or not all the colors could have been made from local materials. Table 6 lists the sample numbers and origin, context, the general color designation, and the laboratory identification. The dates of the structures in Table 6 have already been discussed in previous sections. The following commentary is derived from the report of Nevenka Antonov, engineer-chemist in the chemical laboratory of the Restauratorski Zavod Hrvatske in Zagreb, who performed the analyses.

The pigment samples were prepared and examined in the laboratory as follows. The colored layers were first scraped from the fresco fragments and stored in small gelatin capsules. The samples were then systematically examined visually and by microscope under low magnification. Chemical and physico-chemical tests included: solubility in diluted hydrochloric acid, 4N sodium hydroxide, and concentrated nitric acid; effects of heat and flame tests; specific microchemical drop tests with appropriate reagents on microscopic slides; mounting the particles of the pigments in Canada balsam and noting their color, appearance, size, shape, opacity, transparency, crystallinity, and other characteristics.

Black pigments. Samples 8, 16: charcoal black.

The pigments were made of coarse black and brown particles of irregular shape. They were insoluble in acids and burnt almost completely in open air leaving only a minute inorganic residue.

---

as a 5th century issue with illegible obverse, cross in wreath on reverse; the latter he lists as 5th century illegible.

The deposit (Lot 796) between the mosaic of the original construction period and a later, slightly higher mosaic also contained several coins, the latest of which is an issue of Honorius (Coin No. 72-465) with a reverse of *Gloria Romanorum* Type 22. The indicated date is 408-423 A.C. This coin, however, provides only a *terminus post quem* for the later mosaic.

[25] On the roofs of the Baptistery see the article by William B. Dinsmoor, Jr. in this volume.

TABLE 6.
Identification of Pigments

Origin of Sample	Context	Color	Laboratory Designation
1. Synagogue 1	Lot 799	red	iron oxide red
2.		white	chalk
3. Synagogue 1	Lot 65	white	chalk
4.		dark red	iron oxide red
5.		light red	iron oxide red+chalk
6.		gray	charcoal black+chalk
7. Baptistery	Lot 365	green	green earth
8.		black	charcoal black
9.		white	chalk
10.		light brown (drapery)	chalk+raw sienna
11.		pink (flesh)	chalk+ochre
12. Baptistery	Lot 365	light brown	chalk+raw sienna
13.		white	chalk
14. Casa Romana: Room 2	Lot 718	white	chalk
15.		gray brown	iron oxide red+charcoal black+smalt (?)
16.		black	charcoal black
17.		green	green earth
18.		red	iron oxide red
19. House of the Fuller: Room 26	Lot 772	dark red	iron oxide red
20.		light red	iron oxide red+chalk
21.		gray	charcoal black+chalk

White pigments. Samples 2, 3, 9, 13, 14: chalk.

The chalk may have been simply lime converted by CO_2 into $CaCO_3$. The small white, pale white, and gray white crystalline particles dissolved in diluted HCl and concentrated HNO_3 with effervescence of CO_2. A colorless solution in HCl produced a brilliant red flame indicating C^{++}. Repeated recrystallization after solution in diluted HCl, heating with diluted H_2SO_4, and evaporating to dryness produced a crystalline form resembling sheaves of needles: $CaSO_4.2H_2O$ (gypsum).

Gray Pigments. Samples 6, 15, 21.

Samples 6 and 21 are mixtures of charcoal black and chalk ($CaCO_3$). The chief difference detected between the two is that the black particles in 21 are fine and those in 6 are coarse.

Examination of particles of Sample 15 mounted in Canada balsam showed a mixture of iron oxide red, charcoal black, and minute, pale blue, glassy fragments. The latter may be smalt.[26]

---

[26] *Webster's Seventh New Collegiate Dictionary* (Chicago 1970) defines smalt as: "a deep blue pigment used esp. as a ceramic color and prepared by fusing together silica, potash, and oxide of cobalt and grinding to powder the resultant glass."

Brown pigments. Samples 10, 12.

Both are chiefly mixtures of chalk and raw sienna (hydrated $Fe_2O_3H_2O$). Sample 10 consisted of many white particles mixed with fewer light brown particles. The white particles dissolve in dilute HCl with an effervescence of CO_2; the flame test for Ca^{++} was positive and the yellow solution yielded a positive result when tested for Fe^{+++}. Sample 12 consisted chiefly of raw sienna. The particles were reddish brown, colorless, and transparent yellow.

Red Pigments. Samples 1, 4, 5, 18—20.

All pigments are either iron oxide red only or mixed with chalk (Samples 5, 20). Samples 4, 18, 19 are transparent. The particles of Sample 1 are of an unusually brilliant red color.

Green pigments. Samples 7, 17: green earth.

The samples consist of coarse, crystalline, blue-green particles, some of which are tinged brown, along with colorless particles. The pigment is partially soluble in diluted HCl producing a pale green solution; it is almost completely soluble in concentrated HCl and concentrated HNO_3. Tests for Fe^{+++} and for Fe^{++} were positive.

Pink pigment. Sample 11.

The pigment is a mixture of many white (chalk) and a few red (iron oxide) particles. Tests for Ca^{++} and Fe^{+++} were positive.

7. SUMMARY AND GENERAL OBSERVATIONS

Murals at Stobi were painted on dry plaster throughout the life of the city under the Empire and work in true fresco is known before the late 4th century. Fresco work is also known from the earlier Hellenistic community,[27] but the one example found was removed to the Archaeological Museum of Skopje and, unfortunately, was destroyed in the earthquake in 1963. Molded stucco also had a long tradition at Stobi with examples of the 3rd century A.C. and earlier (Casa Romana, Synagogue 1), the 4th century (hall below the Central Basilica), and in the 5th—6th centuries (Episcopal Residence).[28]

The use of clay as a levelling layer on stone, terre pisé, and adobe walls has been shown to be a continuing tradition at Stobi from the 1st to the 6th century. The clay invariably contained some amount of lime which must have been an intentional ingredient. The re-use of stucco or terracotta architectural fragments to face terre pisé walls preparatory to a levelling layer is a technique noted also in structures from the 1st and 4th centuries A.C.

---

[27] A fresco depicting a water bird was found in 1955—56 on a wall below the Civil Basilica. The excavators date the destruction of the building in which the fresco was found to the late 2nd or early 1st century B.C.; Mano-Zissi, op. cit. (in note 2) pp. 191—198 and fig. 100.
[28] Dj. Mano-Zissi, "Stukatura u Stobima," *Zbornik* 3 (1962) 101—107.

The composition of the mortars used for the mural shows some variety. The discussions above have demonstrated a number of the reasons for the differences in composition. The chief factors influencing the composition of the mortars are as follows.

1) The final layer to which decoration is applied is invariably finer and of higher (though sometimes only slightly so) lime content than the intermediate layer(s).

2) Mortar intended to be heavily molded is of the highest (nearly pure) lime content.

3) Straw is a common temper in both intermediate and final layers for fresco work and crushed brick is sometimes added to an intermediate layer for additional strength and to provide better insulation.

4) Fragments from a ceiling fresco may be identified by reed impressions on the back. The use of crushed brick in the mortar in sufficient quantity to tinge the mortar pink may also be indicative.

5) Time, tradition, and/or source of lime evidently affected the composition of the Baptistery fresco and the sample (22) from the unidentified structure of the 4th century or later.

All the samples from the Baptistery and Sample 22 were similar in their lime content, which is distinctly different from that of (approximately contemporary) Episcopal Basilica samples and from that of the earlier frescoes found below the S aisle of the Episcopal Basilica. They are also alike in the high percentage of magnesium oxide that was contained in the lime; no other samples from any period showed such a high content. These differences could be the result of a change in tradition over the years, or of the introduction of a new tradition from outside Stobi, or of a different source of lime, or some combination of these. There is also the possibility of random mixture, but that seems somewhat improbable since the compositions generally reflect percentages and contents that are demonstrably related in most instances to form, function, perhaps source of material, methods of lime burning, and preferences in mixtures (tradition).

Additional analyses, especially samples from the Episcopal Basilica and other structures of the 4th to 6th centuries, would be required to be confident of the reason(s) for the differences. Such a new selection of samples is planned for the immediate future. At the moment the probability is that lime or marble from geologic formations previously untapped by natives of Stobi were being intentionally utilized for a mortar of distinctively different composition. The high percentage of MgO suggests a quarry of dolomitic limestone or marble whereas earlier lime evidently came from carbonate limestone. If so, the frescoes produced (the Baptistery and Sample 22) do represent the introduction of a new tradition of fresco-making at Stobi.

The results of the pigment analysis are also informative. All the materials used in the colors tested are readily available locally, with the possible exception of the smalt (?) which was found in only one sample.

The results of the analyses discussed here also provide material for future comparisons, not only at Stobi, but elsewhere. A comparative study of application techniques and the composition of ancient mortars from Macedonia and immediately adjacent regions would provide a body of information for comparisons with creations in more distant locales. Such comparisons might be expected to result in more meaningful discussions of fresco "schools," external influences, and artistic revolutions than the study of style alone can provide.

Finally, the study itself demonstrates that the utility of such analyses as those discussed here resides not merely in providing the answers to some specific questions but also in raising questions and possibilities that might otherwise be left completely out of consideration.

ЅИДНА ДЕКОРАЦИЈА ВО СТОБИ

ЏЕЈМС ВАЈЗМАН и ЃОРЃИ ГЕОРГИЕВСКИ

Ѕидовите во ентериерот на многу згради во Стоби беа декорирани со фрески или моделиран малтер. Во идните проучувања ќе се задржиме на декоративните елементи, стилот, композицијата, претставите, и други сродни размислувања. Во оваа статија главно се проучени методите на примена на неколку декоративни површини и композиции од глина, малтер, и пигменти на површината. Студијата е базирана врз истражувања на теренот и врз неколку хемиски анализи извршени во лабораториите во Скопје и Загреб.

Триесет и еден примерок од малтер и глина беа селектирани од 10 градби за квантитативни анализи, презентирани во табелата број 1. Табелите од 2—5 содржат резиме на овие тестови.

Дваесет и еден примерок од тие испитани пигменти со анализата биле само од четири структури; идентификацијата на табела 6.

Во статијата е докажано дека ѕидните фрески во Стоби биле сликани на сув малтер во текот на целото постоење на градот за време на Империјата, а работата врз висинските фрески е позната пред доцниот IV век. Работата врз фреските е исто така позната од најраното Хеленистичко општество, но единствениот пронајден примерок бил изведен и однесен во Археолошкиот музеј во Скопје, кој беше уништен за време на земјотресот во 1963 година. Моделираниот стуко исто така имал долга традиција во Стоби, со примероци од III век од нашата ера, и порано (Каза Романа, Синагога 1) IV век (сала под централната базилика), и во V—VI век (Епископската резиденција).

Употребата на глината како нивелиран слој на ѕидови од камен, од terre pisé и тули покажа дека тоа претставува продолжување на традицијата во Стоби од I до VI век. Без сомнение глината содржела извесно количество на вар којашто била намерно употребена.

Повторната употреба на фрагменти од стуко или теракота архитектура да направи површини за terre pisé ѕидови, препарирање на нивелираниот слој е техника позната исто така од структурите од I и IV век од нашата ера.

Композицијата од малтер употребена во ѕиден опус е различна. Дискусијата погоре во статијата покажува неколку размислувања за разликата во композицијата. Примарни фактори за влијание на композицијата од малтер се следните.

1. Финалниот слој со кој е декорацијата поставена е постојано ситен и повеќе (меѓутоа, понекогаши само малку така) содржи вар од средниот слој.

2. Малтерот што има намера да биде цврсто моделиран содржи најповеќе вар(скоро чист).

3. Сламата е обично средство за поврзување за двата, средниот и крајниот слој на фреско работата а искршените тули понекогаш се додадени во средните слоеви за додатно зајакнување и да спроведуваат подобра изолација.

4. Фрагментите од фреско од таванот можат да се идентификуваат со отисоците од трска од задната страна. Значајна е употребата на искршена тула во малтерот во одредена количина, за да донесе ружичаста боја на малтерот.

5. Времето, традицијата и (или) изворот на варот делува евидентно на фреско композициите на баптистериумот и на примерокот (22) од непозната структура од IV век или подоцна.

Сите примероци од Баптистериумот и примерокот (22) се слични по својата содржина на вар, која е јасно различна од содржината (приближно истовремени) од примероците од Епископската базилика и од тие од најраните фрески најдени под јужниот брод од Епископската базилика. Тие се исто така слични во високиот процент magnesium oxide кој се наоѓа во варот; останатите примероци од друга епоха немале таква висока содржина. Овие разлики можат да бидат резултат од промена во традицијата надвор од Стоби, или од различни извори на варот, или некоја комбинација од обете. Има можност исто така за случајно мешање, меѓутоа, изгледа донекаде неверојатно, бидејќи композициите во главно даваат одраз во проценти и во содржина, кои покажуваат сродство во повеќе случаи на форма, функција, може би извор на материјалот, методи од печење на варот и претпочитање на мешањето како традиција.

Дополнителните анализи, специјално примероците од Епископската Базилика и другите структури од IV од VI век, би требало да бидеме сигурни од разбирањето(та) за разликите. Таква нова селекција на примероци е планирана за скора иднина. Во моментов можноста е дека вар или мермер од геолошките формации во минатото населението на Стоби не употребувало, подоцна со намера го искористуваат за малтер за особено различни композиции. Повеќе проценти од MgO сугерираат каменолом од доломитески кречњак или мермер, додека, понапред вар се добивал евидентно од карбонтски кречњак. Ако е така, правењето на фрески (Баптистериум и примерок 22) се презентира навлегување во нова традиција на фреско производи во Стоби.

Резултатите од пигментната анализа исто така се информативни. Сите материјали употребени во колор тестовите се наоѓаат во близина со можен исклучок на кобалтно стакло(?) кое е најдено само во еден примерок.

Резултатите од анализата дискутирана овде исто така поднесуваат додатни компарации, не само во Стоби, туку и на друго место.

Компаративната студија со објаснување на техника и компарација од античките малтери во Македонија и нејзината близина поднесува корпус информации за компарација со креациите во далечните места од Стоби. Можеме да се надеваме дека таква компарација може да резултира во многу значајни дискусии за фреско "Школа", со надворешно влијание и уметнички револуции, отколку што студиите на стилот сами можат да помогнат.

На крај, оваа студија сама по себе докажува дека корисноста на таква анализа, како о дискутиранава овде, не е само да придонесува на одговорот за некои специфични прашања, туку исто така да постави прашања и можности кои можат за други случаи да бидат надвор од секакво разгледување.

PLAN OF SITE

1 NORTH BASILICA
2 CIVIL BASILICA
3 LITTLE BATH
4 CENTRAL BASILICA AND SYNAGOGUE
5 HOUSE OF PSALMS
6 VIA AXIA
7 CENTRAL FOUNTAIN
8 LARGE BATH
9 VIA PRINCIPALIS INFERIOR
10 HOUSE OF PERISTERIAS
11 VIA THEODOSIA
12 THEODOSIAN PALACE
13 HOUSE OF PARTHENIUS
14 VIA PRINCIPALIS SUPERIOR
15 HOUSE OF THE FULLER
16 EPISCOPAL RESIDENCE
17 SEMICIRCULAR COURT
18 VIA SACRA
19 EPISCOPAL BASILICA
20 BAPTISTERY
21 PORTA HERACLEA
22 WEST CEMETERY
23 THEATER
24 CASINO
25 INNER CITY WALL
26 EAST CITY WALL, TURKISH BRIDGE, CASA ROMANA
27 MUSEUM
28 CEMETERY BASILICA
29 PALIKURA BASILICA

GPSR Authorized Representative: Easy Access System Europe - Mustamäe tee 50, 10621 Tallinn, Estonia, gpsr.requests@easproject.com

www.ingramcontent.com/pod-product-compliance
Lightning Source LLC
Chambersburg PA
CBHW060512300426
44112CB00017B/2634